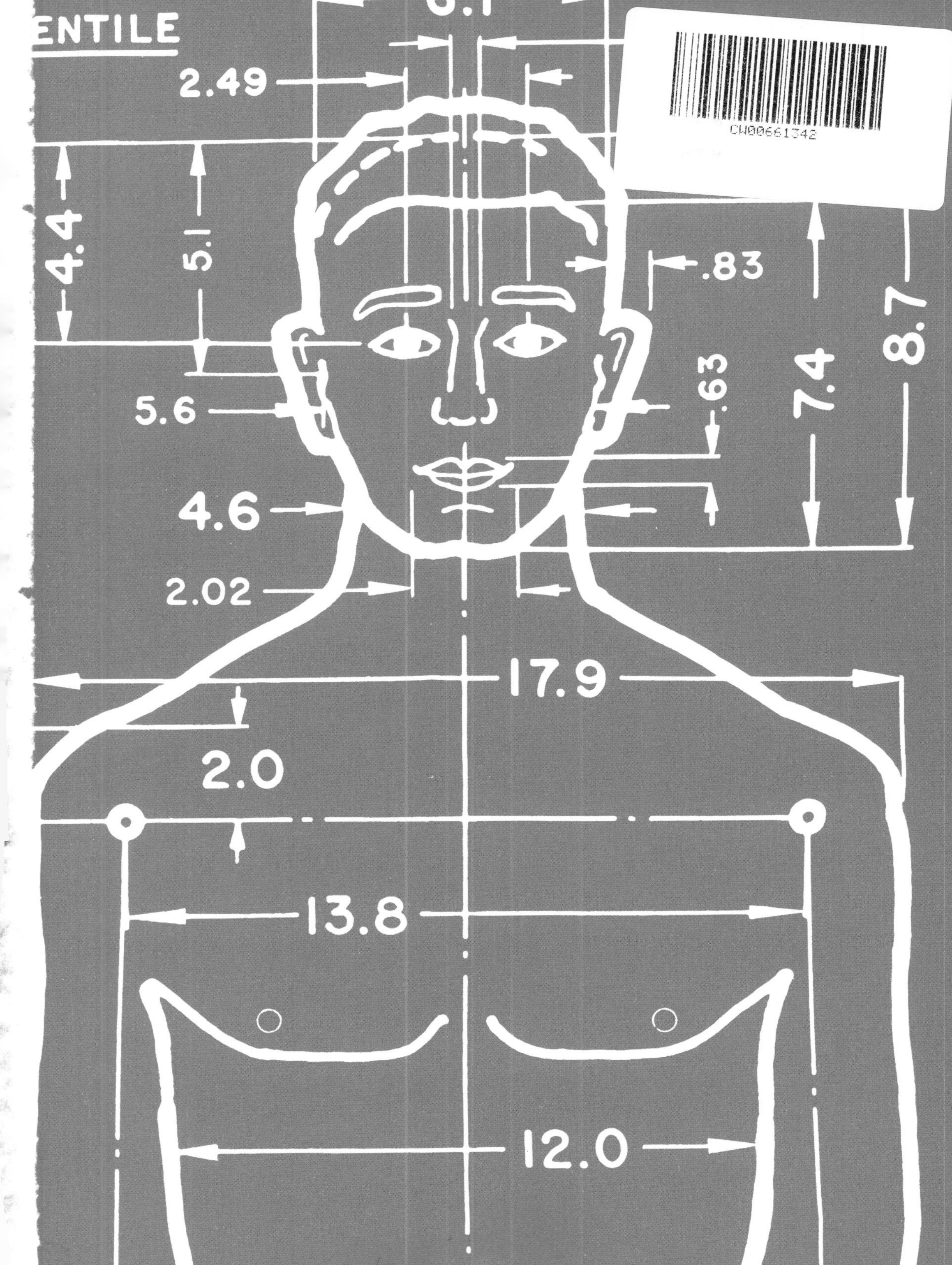
ENTILE
6.1
2.49
.83
4.4
5.1
5.6
.63
7.4
8.7
4.6
2.02
17.9
2.0
13.8
12.0

[illegible]ntage, 1985.
Designed by Mark Sanders (British, b. 1958).
Courtesy of the designer.

beautiful users
designing for people

Ellen Lupton

WITH CONTRIBUTIONS BY
Thomas Carpentier
and Tiffany Lambert

PRINCETON ARCHITECTURAL PRESS
AND
COOPER HEWITT
SMITHSONIAN DESIGN MUSEUM

COOPER HEWITT

Smithsonian Design Museum

Beautiful Users is made possible by major support from the

Additional funding is provided by Amita and Purnendu Chatterjee, the August Heckscher Exhibition Fund, the Ehrenkranz Fund, the Bill Moggridge Memorial Fund, The Richard H. Driehaus Foundation, Deborah Buck, May and Samuel Rudin Family Foundation, Inc., and IDEO.

Published by
Princeton Architectural Press
37 East Seventh Street
New York, New York 10003
Visit our website at www.papress.com.

In association with
Cooper Hewitt, Smithsonian Design Museum
2 East Ninety-First Street
New York, New York 10128
www.cooperhewitt.org

Published on the occasion of the exhibition
Beautiful Users, organized by
Cooper Hewitt, Smithsonian Design Museum
December 2014–Spring 2015

Printed and bound in China
17 16 15 14 4 3 2 1 First edition

Museum Editor: Pamela Horn
Editor: Megan Carey
Designer: Ellen Lupton

Typefaces: Galaxie Polaris and Galaxie Copernicus, designed by Chester Jenkins, 2004–13

Special thanks to: Meredith Baber, Sara Bader, Nicola Bednarek Brower, Janet Behning, Carina Cha, Andrea Chlad, Barbara Darko, Benjamin English, Russell Fernandez, Will Foster, Jan Haux, Mia Johnson, Diane Levinson, Jennifer Lippert, Katharine Myers, Jaime Nelson, Jay Sacher, Rob Shaeffer, Sara Stemen, Marielle Suba, Kaymar Thomas, Paul Wagner, Joseph Weston, and Janet Wong of Princeton Architectural Press
—Kevin C. Lippert, publisher

Library of Congress Cataloging-in-Publication Data
Lupton, Ellen, author.
Beautiful users : designing for people / Ellen Lupton with contributions by Thomas Carpentier and Tiffany Lambert. — First edition.
pages cm
Includes index.
Published on the occasion of the exhibition Beautiful Users, organized by Cooper Hewitt, Smithsonian Design Museum.
ISBN 978-1-61689-291-3 (alk. paper)
1. Design—Human factors—Exhibitions. I. Cooper-Hewitt Museum. II. Title.
NK1520.L865 2014
745.209'040747471—dc23
2014017045

contents

foreword

Cooper Hewitt, Smithsonian Design Museum explores the world of useful things. From textiles and wall coverings to architectural drawings and digital devices, nearly every object housed in our astonishing collections was created with a function—and a user—in mind. In the mid-twentieth century, designers began applying "human factors" (also called ergonomics) to products, services, and interfaces in order to address the needs of human users.

Beautiful Users explores the ethos of "designing for people," a phrase devised by pioneering industrial designer Henry Dreyfuss after World War II. Home to the Dreyfuss Archive, Cooper Hewitt organized the first monographic exhibition of his career in 1997. *Beautiful Users* presents a selection of Dreyfuss's projects within the broader evolution of user-centered design, a field that now encompasses such frameworks as universal design, experience design, interaction design, and open-source design.

Cooper Hewitt seeks to understand the diverse processes involved in planning and making useful things. Design thinking is a methodology that begins with an open-ended exploration of users' needs and continues through an iterative process of ideation, sketching, and modeling. To illuminate the richness of the design process, this book represents drawings and prototypes as well as finished products, including historic and contemporary material from the museum's collections.

Beautiful Users is the first in a series of exhibitions taking place in our first-floor Design Process Galleries. These exhibitions aim to introduce the public to the people and methods that define design as an essential human activity. The galleries offer visitors a range of experiences, from narrative displays about historical and contemporary design to hands-on making, doing, and learning activities. *Beautiful Users* is made possible by major support from the Adobe Foundation. Additional funding is provided by Amita and Purnendu Chatterjee, the August Heckscher Exhibition Fund, the Ehrenkranz Fund, the Bill Moggridge Memorial Fund, the Richard H. Driehaus Foundation, Deborah Buck, May and Samuel Rudin Family Foundation, Inc., and IDEO.

Caroline Baumann, Director
COOPER HEWITT
SMITHSONIAN DESIGN MUSEUM

acknowledgments

Beautiful Users is dedicated to Bill Moggridge (1943–2012), a pioneer of human-centered design. As director of Cooper Hewitt, Smithsonian Design Museum, 2010–12, Moggridge inspired us to reinvent our own design processes. We will always remember this friend and thinker for his warmth, humanity, and inventive intellect.

Cooper Hewitt's new director, Caroline Baumann, has galvanized the museum's staff and board around a reinvigorated, audience-centered vision in our renovated facilities. Cara McCarty, Cooper Hewitt's curatorial director and an early advocate for universal design, has been a guiding light for *Beautiful Users*, supporting the idea from its earliest inception. Dozens of professionals at Cooper Hewitt, including curators, conservators, editors, digital media producers, educators, registrars, development staff, and more, made this book and exhibition possible. Special thanks to Cooper Hewitt staff, including Julie Barnes, Laurie Bohlk, Helynsia Brown, Seb Chan, Michelle Cheng, Kimberly Cisneros, Sarah Coffin, Lucy Commoner, Caitlin Condell, Aaron Straup Cope, Gail Davidson, Deborah Fitzgerald, Sarah Freeman, Vasso Giannopoulos, Jocelyn Groom, Annie Hall, Kimberly Hawkins, Kevin Hervas, Pamela Horn, Halima Johnson, Steve Langehough, Antonia Moser, Kelly Mullaney, Jennifer Northrop, Jessica Nunez, Matthew O'Connor, Caroline Payson, James Reyes, David Rios, Wendy Rogers, Katie Shelly, Larry Silver, Cindy Trope, Micah Walter, Mathew Weaver, and Paula Zamora.

Diller Scofidio + Renfro designed the exhibition; special thanks to Ricardo Scofidio, Andreas Buettner, Imani Day, and Tyler Polich. Eddie Opara's team at Pentagram designed the exhibition graphics; Kimberly Walker offered guidance on the typographic format of this book. Local Projects designed and produced innovative digital experiences for our visitors. We are grateful to our colleagues at Princeton Architectural Press for their careful attention to the craft of publishing; special thanks to Megan Carey, Paul Wagner, and Kevin Lippert. Tiffany Lambert, a rising voice in design studies, contributed vital content and endless managerial energy to this project.

My mother, Mary Jane Lupton, is the most beautiful user I know. By refusing to hide who she is, she taught me that disability is just a difference.

Ellen Lupton, Senior Curator of Contemporary Design
COOPER HEWITT
SMITHSONIAN DESIGN MUSEUM

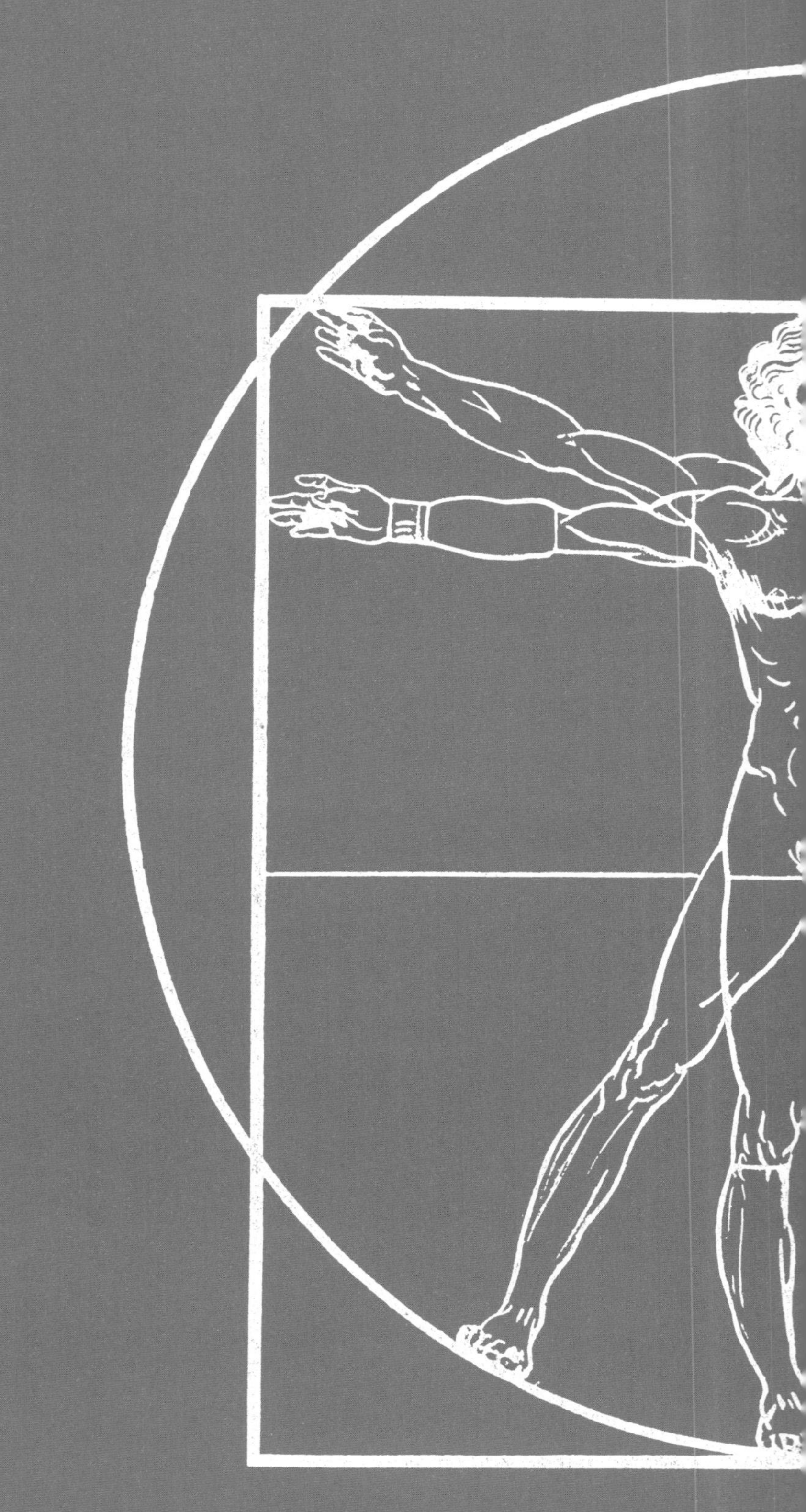

measuring man

Leonardo da Vinci's famous image of an ideal male body canonized the concept of man as the measure of the built world.

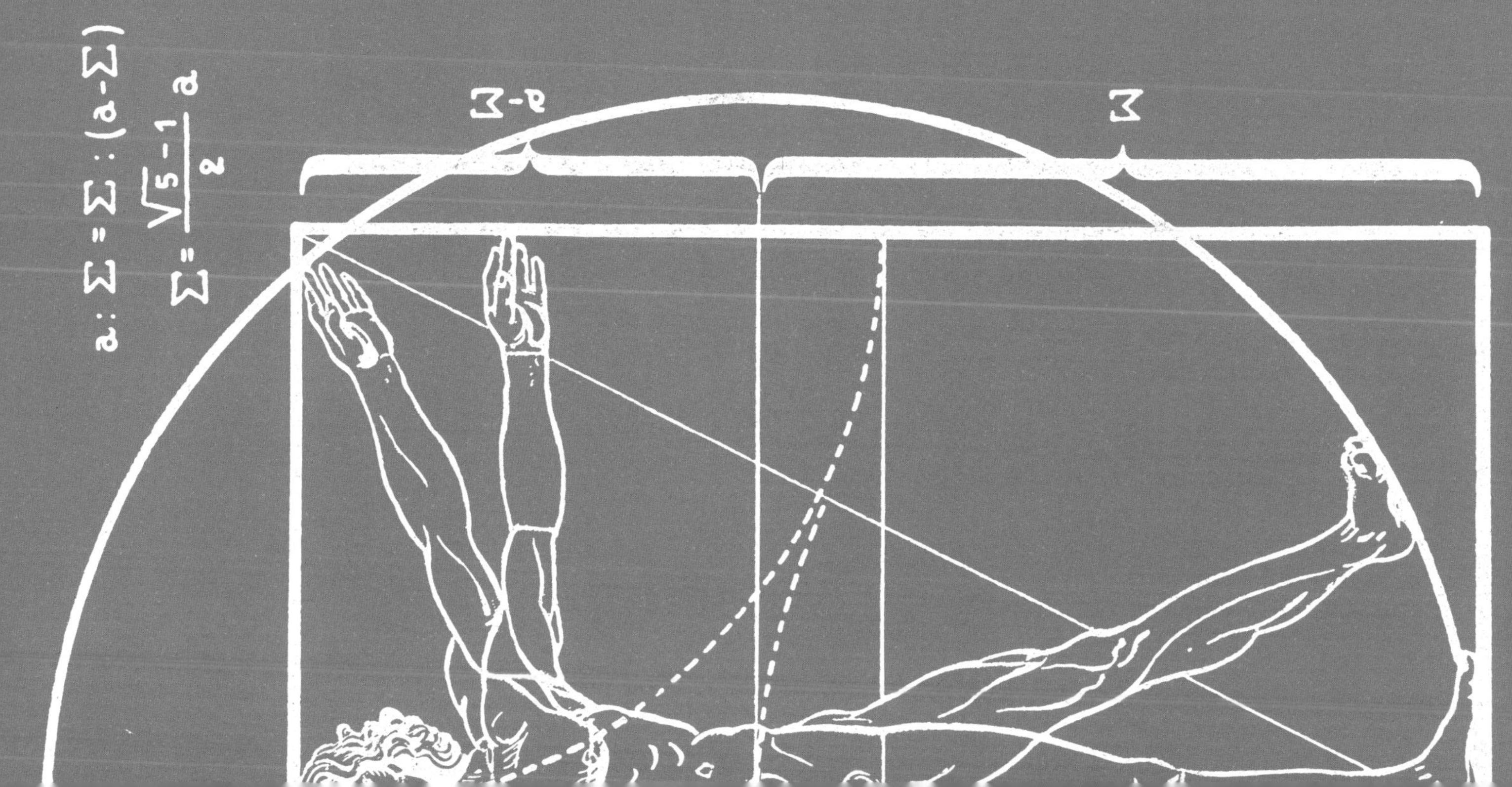

DER MENSCH
DAS MASS ALLER DINGE

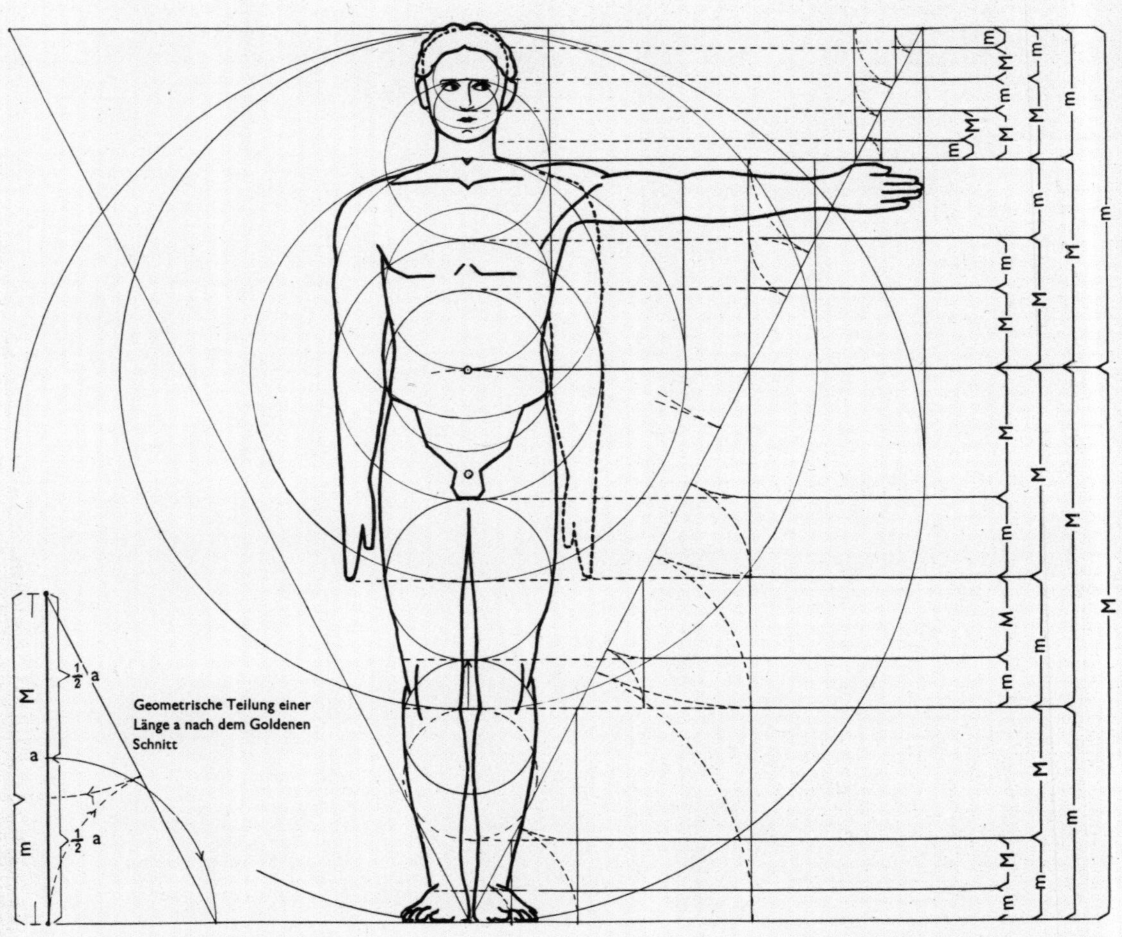

Maßverhältnisse des Menschen,
aufgebaut in Anlehnung an die Ermittlungen von A. Zeising

OHNE WASSERLEITUNG

SPÜLEN

ANORDNUNG

Spüleinrichtung nur zum Geschirrspülen und Waschen von Lebensmitteln benutzen! Licht von oben links ↪ (12) oder von vorn oben ↪ S. 56 (9). Abstellplatz für gewaschenes und schmutziges Geschirr stets links von der Spüle. Letzteres auf Küchentisch ↪ (12) oder Rolltisch ↪ (13), rechte Ablage unbequem (nur für sperriges Geschirr brauchbar), weil die linke Hand, die das Geschirr hält, über die rechte, die die Bürste führt, übergreifen müßte.

Schüssel Ø 35
Höhe 15

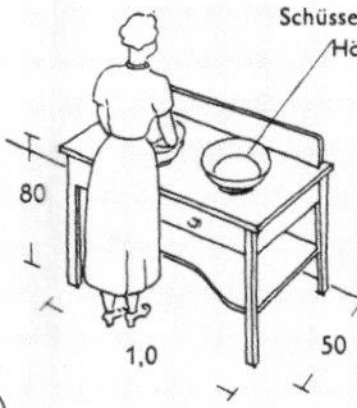

(1) Küchentisch

(2) Küchentisch mit Klappen

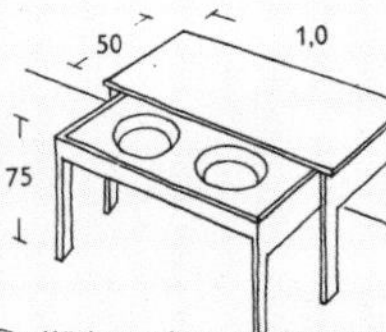

(3) Küchentisch zum Arbeiten im Sitzen, herausschiebbar

MIT WASSERLEITUNG

h = Spültischhöhe für Arbeiten im Stehen 95 cm, für Arbeiten im Sitzen 75 cm, mit nach hinten abgeschrägtem Becken ↪ (7), (12) und (16)

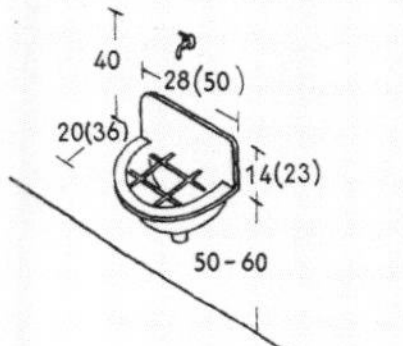

mit geschlossenen Klappen als Tisch verwendbar

1 Becken 43 × 43 × 22

(4) Ausgußbecken

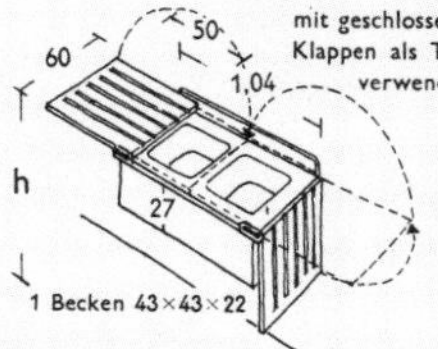

(5) Doppelspülbecken mit Klapplatten

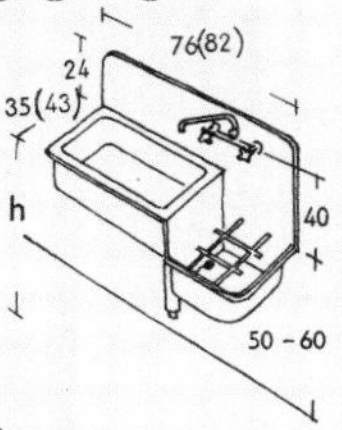

(6) Spülausguß

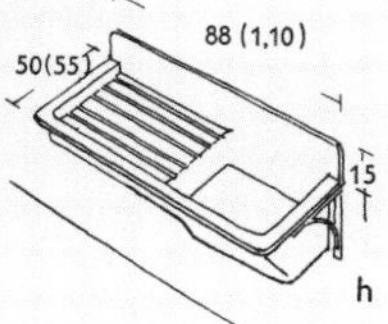

(7) Spülbecken mit Abtropfplatte

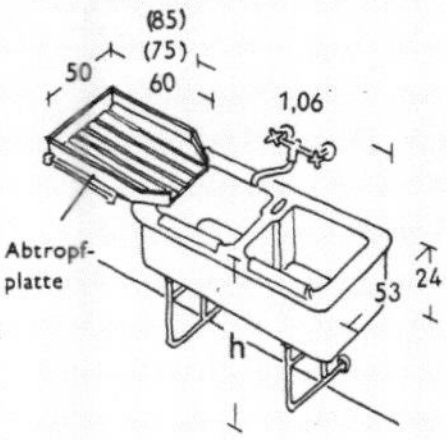

Abtropfplatte

(8) Doppelspülbecken aus Feuerton

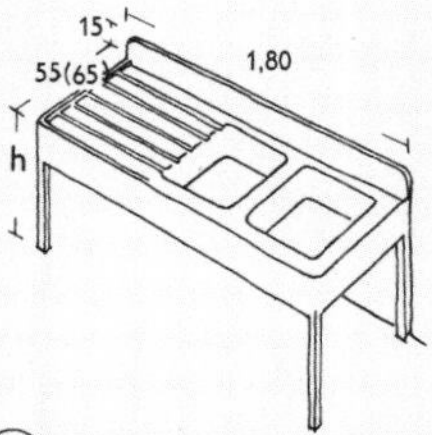

(9) Doppelspültisch mit Abtropfplatte

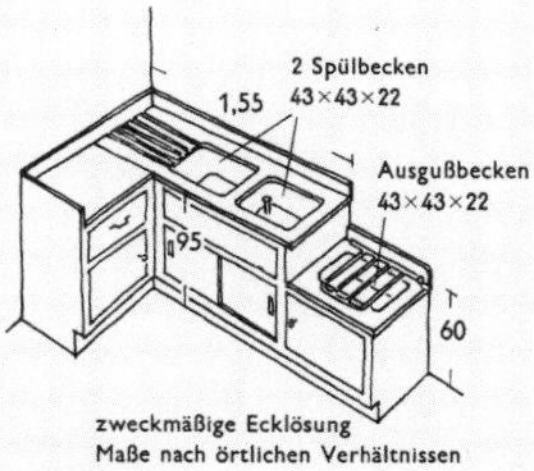

2 Spülbecken 43 × 43 × 22

Ausgußbecken 43 × 43 × 22

zweckmäßige Ecklösung Maße nach örtlichen Verhältnissen

(10) Eckspüle

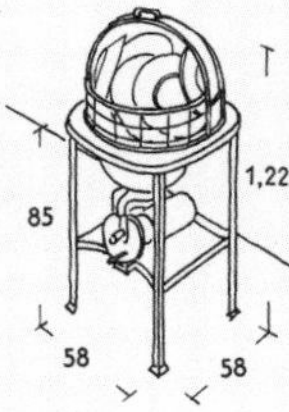

(11) Spülmaschine

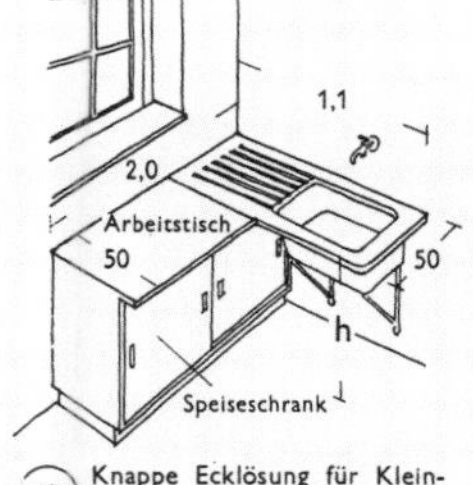

(12) Knappe Ecklösung für Kleinwohnungen

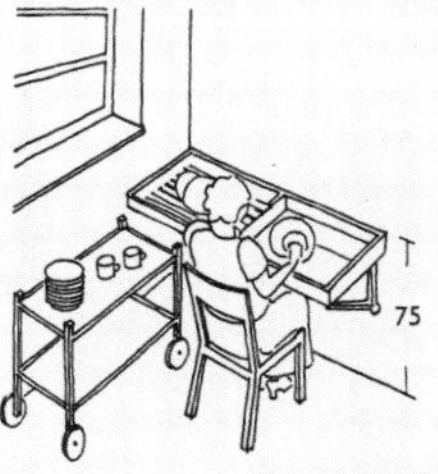

(13) Anordnung für Geschirrwagen

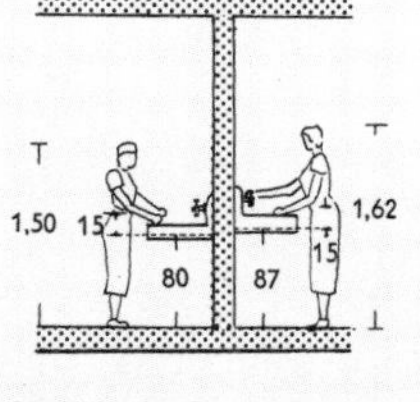

(14) Die Höhe der Geräte, vor allem der **Spültische**, ist der Größe der daran Arbeitenden anzupassen

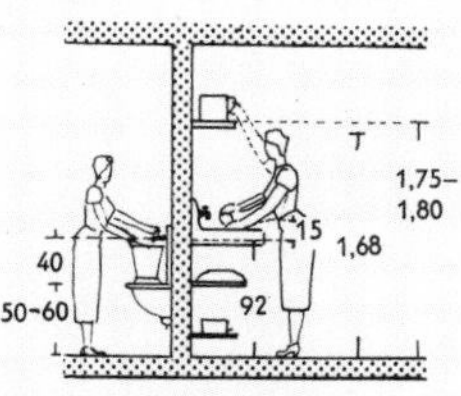

(15) Übliche Höhe für Ausgüsse und höchste Höhe für Spültische mit höherer brauchbarer Bordlage für seltener gebrauchtes Geschirr

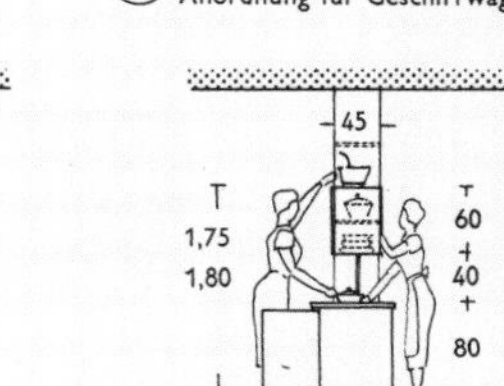

(16) Normalhöhe für Spültische, an denen sitzend gearbeitet wird. Bei der Lichtanlage Schattenbildung von Mensch und Gerät berücksichtigen!

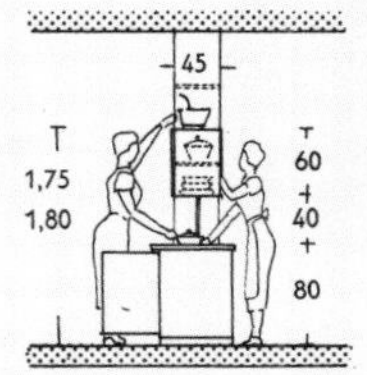

(17) Durchgabe zwischen Küche, Spüle oder Anrichte zum Speisezimmer. Mit darüberliegenden Geschirrfächern, nach beiden Seiten zu öffnen

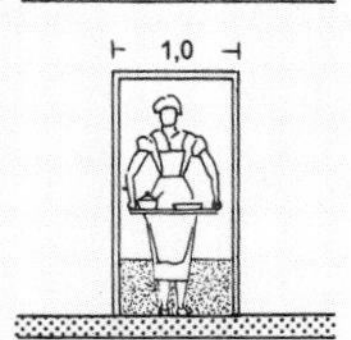

(18) Zwischen Anrichte usw. und Speisezimmer am besten Pendeltür von ≧1,0 m Breite

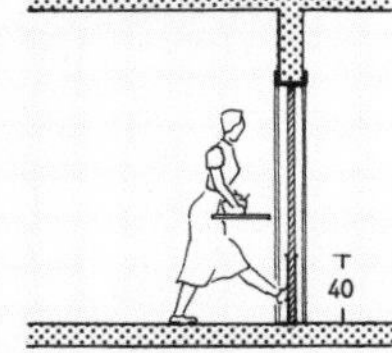

(19) Pendeltüren bis 40 cm Höhe mit Metall beschlagen, da Tür oft mit Fuß aufgestoßen wird

Bauentwurfslehre (Architects' Data), **1938.** Designed by Ernst Neufert (German, 1900–86). Published by Bauwelt-Verlag (Germany); first published in 1936. Offset lithograph.

Bauhaus architect Ernst Neufert sought to standardize human tools and habitats in relation to an ideal human form.

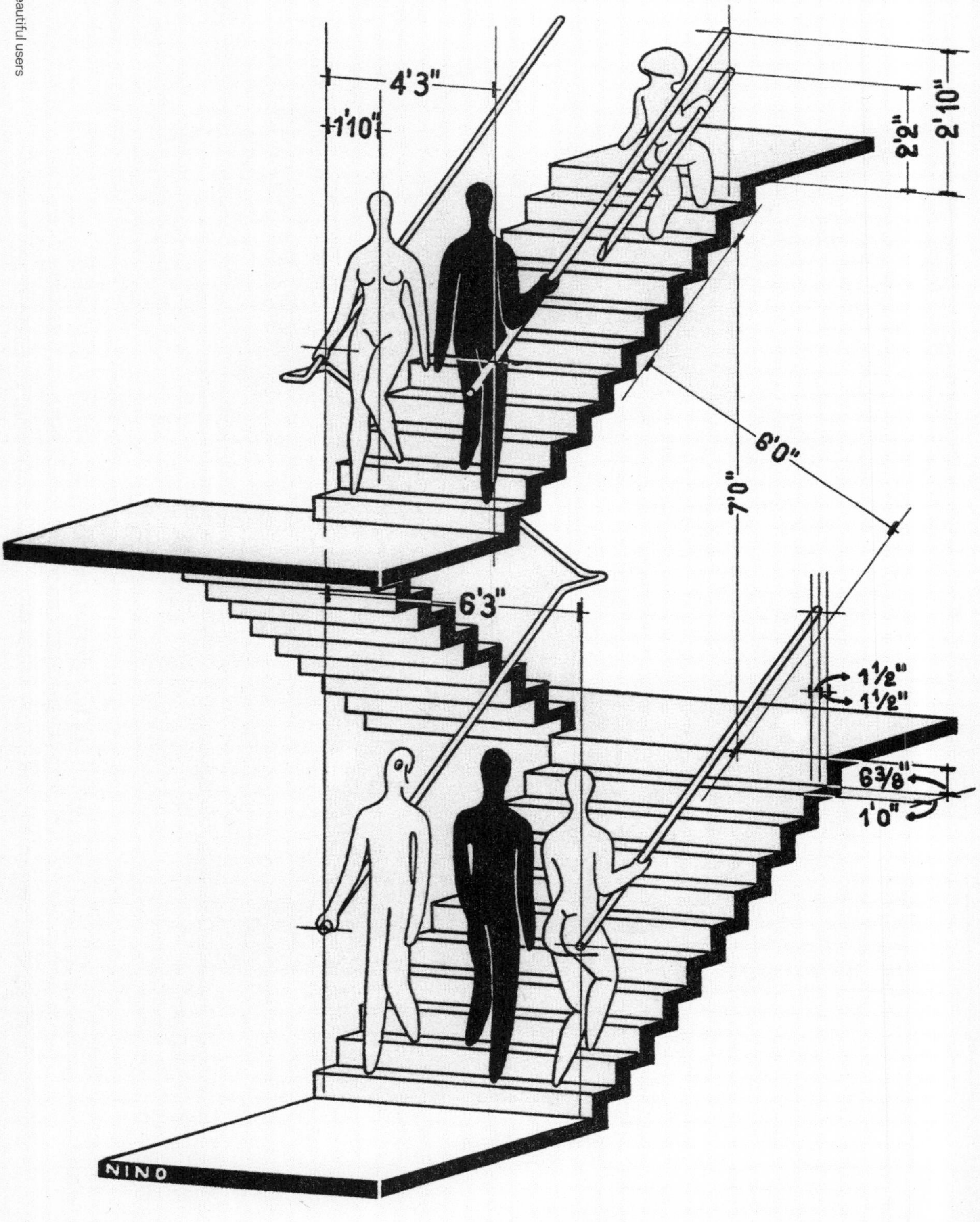

4'3"
1'10"
2'10"
2'2"
6'0"
7'0"
6'3"
1 1/2"
1 1/2"
6 3/8"
1'0"
NINO

Francis de N. Schroeder and Nino Repetto created measured diagrams for interior designers that depict people interacting with one another in social spaces.

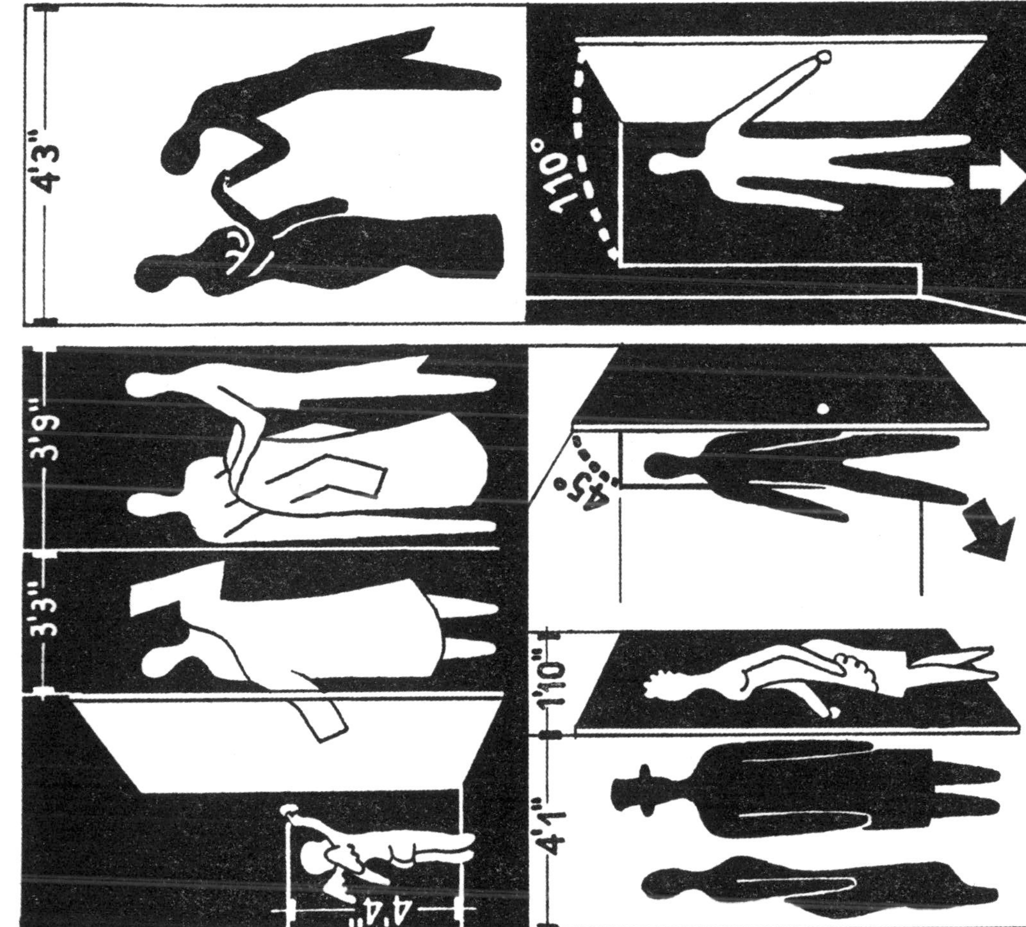

***Anatomy for Interior Designers*, 1948.** Authored by Francis de N. Schroeder. Illustrations by Nino Repetto. Published by Whitney Library of Design (USA). Offset lithograph.

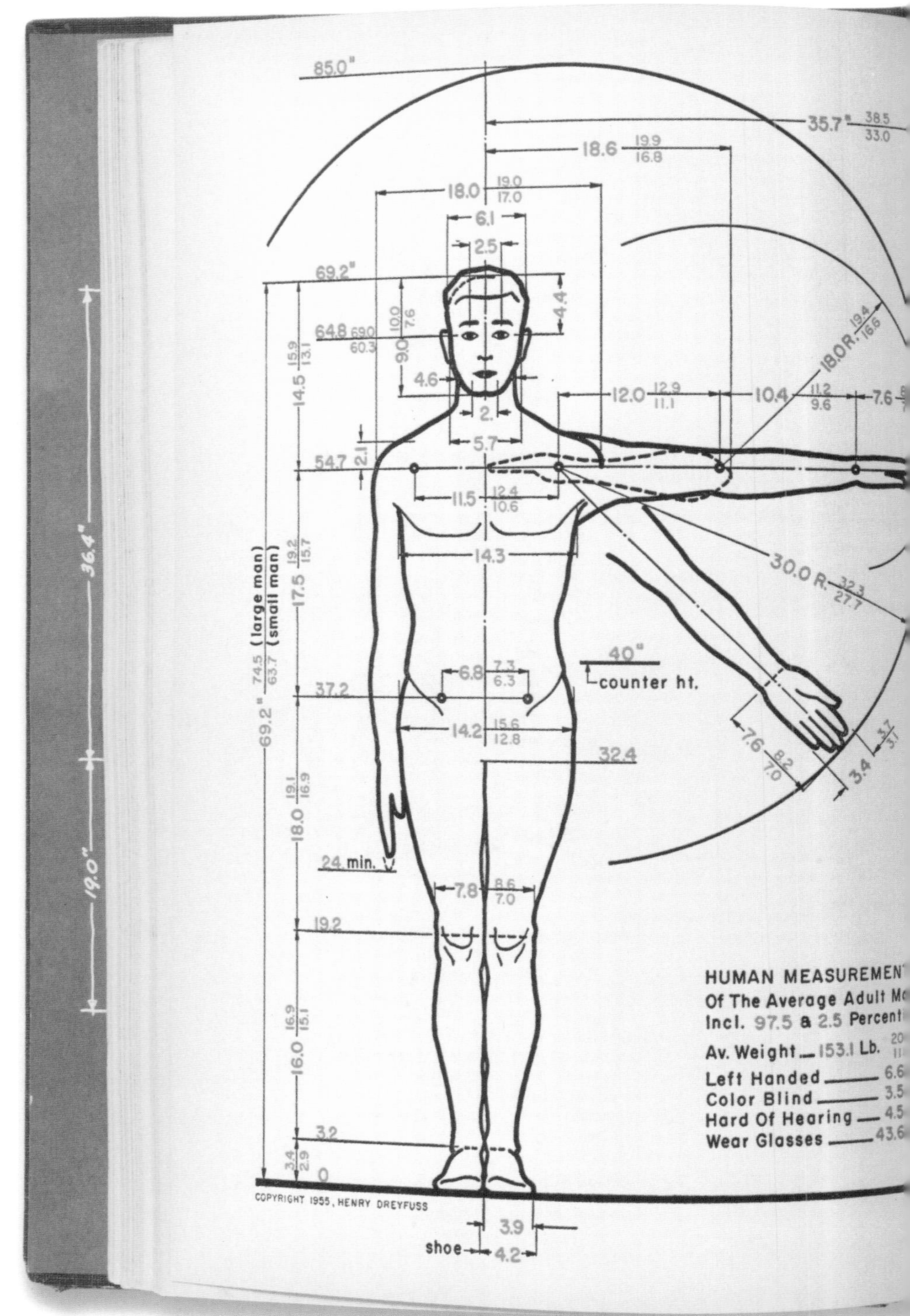
HUMAN MEASUREMEN
Of The Average Adult M
Incl. 97.5 & 2.5 Percent
Av. Weight — 153.1 Lb.
Left Handed — 6.6
Color Blind — 3.5
Hard Of Hearing — 4.5
Wear Glasses — 43.6
69.2" 74.5 (large man) 63.7 (small man)
40" counter ht.
24 min.
shoe 4.2
3.9
COPYRIGHT 1955, HENRY DREYFUSS
85.0"
35.7" 38.5 33.0
18.6 19.9 16.8
18.0 19.0 17.0
30.0 R. 32.3 27.7
18.0 R. 19.4 16.6
36.4"
19.0"

Designing for People, 1955. Authored by Henry Dreyfuss (American, 1904–72). Drawn by Alvin R. Tilley (American, 1914–93), Henry Dreyfuss & Associates (USA). Published by Whitney Library of Design (USA). Offset lithograph. Collection Cooper Hewitt, Smithsonian Design Museum, Henry Dreyfuss Archive, gift of Henry Dreyfuss, 1954–68. Photography: Matt Flynn.

Henry Dreyfuss and Alvin R. Tilley depicted "Joe" and "Josephine" as typical American users of products and spaces.

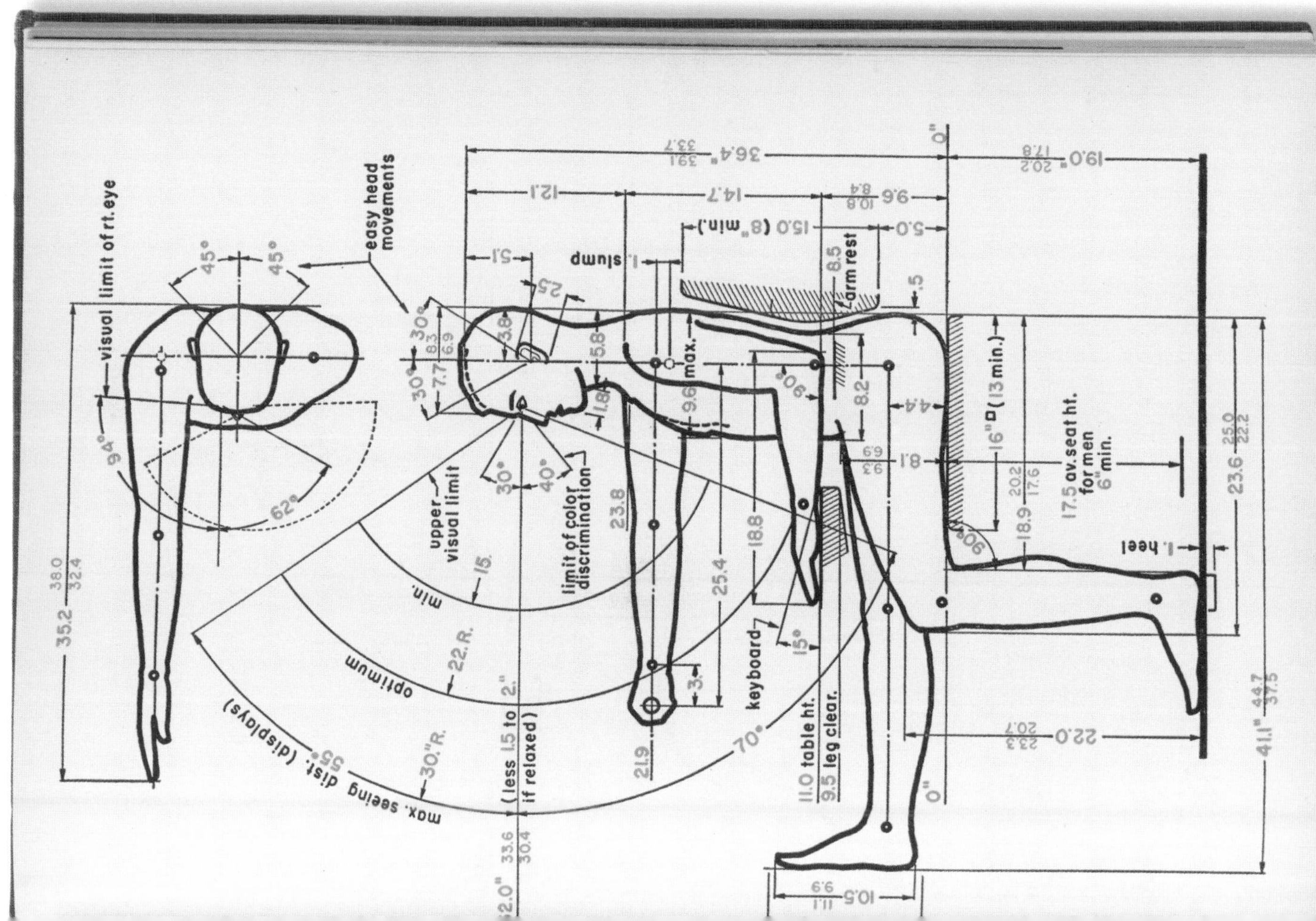

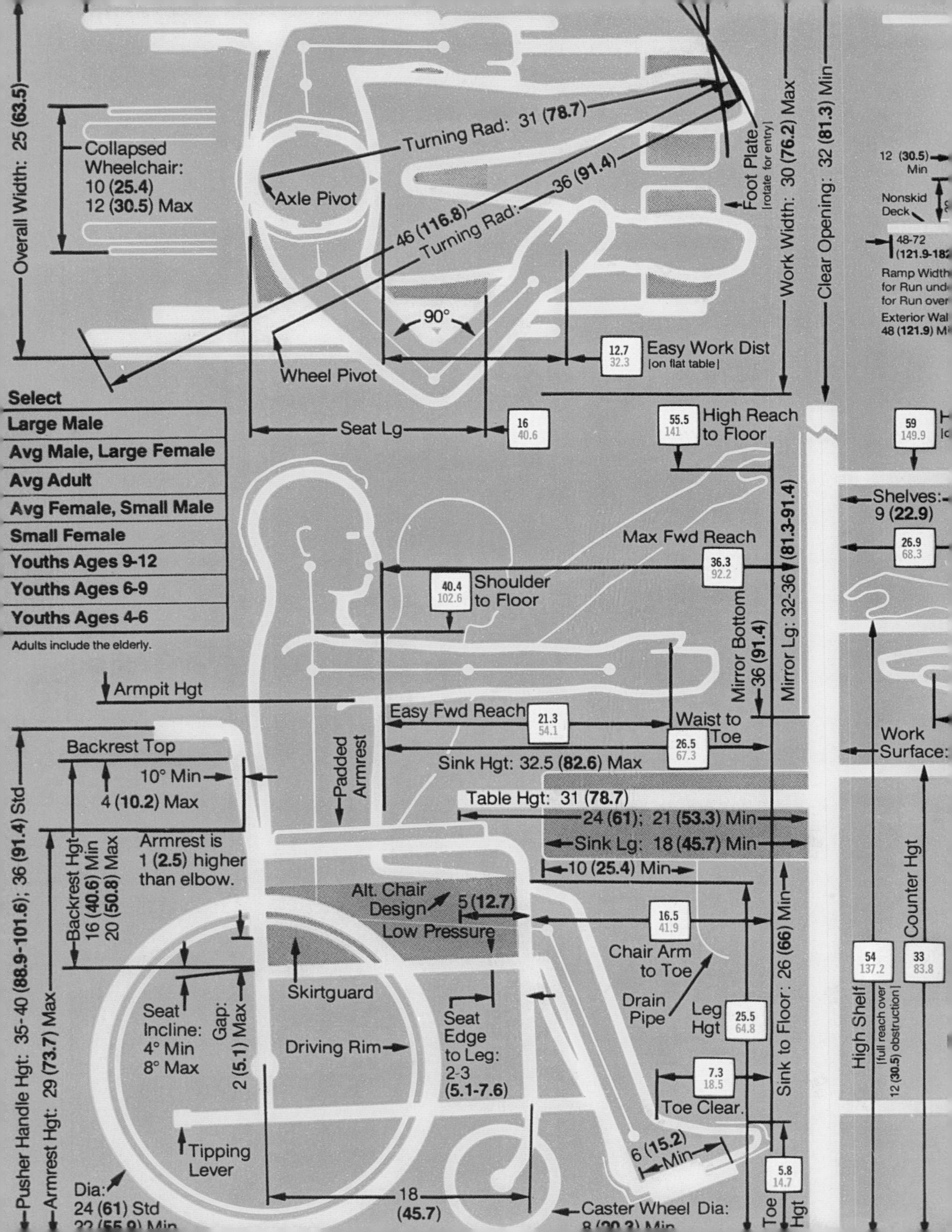

Overall Width: 25 (63.5)
Collapsed Wheelchair:
10 (25.4)
12 (30.5) Max
Axle Pivot
Turning Rad: 31 (78.7)
36 (91.4)
Turning Rad:
46 (116.8)
Wheel Pivot
90°
Foot Plate
[rotate for entry]
Work Width: 30 (76.2) Max
Clear Opening: 32 (81.3) Min
12 (30.5) Min
Nonskid Deck
48-72
(121.9-182
Ramp Width
for Run unde
for Run over
Exterior Wal
48 (121.9) M
12.7
32.3
Easy Work Dist
[on flat table]
Seat Lg
16
40.6
Select
Large Male
Avg Male, Large Female
Avg Adult
Avg Female, Small Male
Small Female
Youths Ages 9-12
Youths Ages 6-9
Youths Ages 4-6
Adults include the elderly.
55.5
141
High Reach to Floor
59
149.9
Shelves:
9 (22.9)
26.9
68.3
Max Fwd Reach
36.3
92.2
Mirror Lg: 32-36 (81.3-91.4)
40.4
102.6
Shoulder to Floor
Mirror Bottom 36 (91.4)
Armpit Hgt
Easy Fwd Reach
21.3
54.1
Waist to Toe
26.5
67.3
Sink Hgt: 32.5 (82.6) Max
Work Surface:
Backrest Top
10° Min
4 (10.2) Max
Padded Armrest
Table Hgt: 31 (78.7)
24 (61); 21 (53.3) Min
Sink Lg: 18 (45.7) Min
10 (25.4) Min
Pusher Handle Hgt: 35-40 (88.9-101.6); 36 (91.4) Std
Armrest Hgt: 29 (73.7) Max
Backrest Hgt
16 (40.6) Min
20 (50.8) Max
Armrest is
1 (2.5) higher
than elbow.
Alt. Chair Design
5 (12.7)
Low Pressure
16.5
41.9
Chair Arm to Toe
Counter Hgt
Skirtguard
Seat Incline:
4° Min
8° Max
Gap:
2 (5.1) Max
Driving Rim
Seat Edge to Leg:
2-3
(5.1-7.6)
Drain Pipe
Leg Hgt
25.5
64.8
Sink to Floor: 26 (66) Min
High Shelf
[full reach over 12 (30.5) obstruction]
54
137.2
33
83.8
7.3
18.5
Toe Clear.
Tipping Lever
6 (15.2) Min
Dia:
24 (61) Std
22 (55.9) Min
18
(45.7)
Caster Wheel Dia:
8 (20.3) Min
Toe Hgt
5.8
14.7

***Humanscale* Body Measurements Selector, 1974.** Authored by Niels Diffrient (American, 1928–2013), Alvin R. Tilley (American, 1914–93), and Joan C. Bardagjy, Henry Dreyfuss & Associates (USA). Graphic design by Valerie Pettis (American, b. 1946). Published by MIT Press (USA). Offset lithograph on plastic with rotary wheel. Photography: Matt Flynn.

Niels Diffrient's *Humanscale* calculates human form and motion on a continuum of physical dimensions.

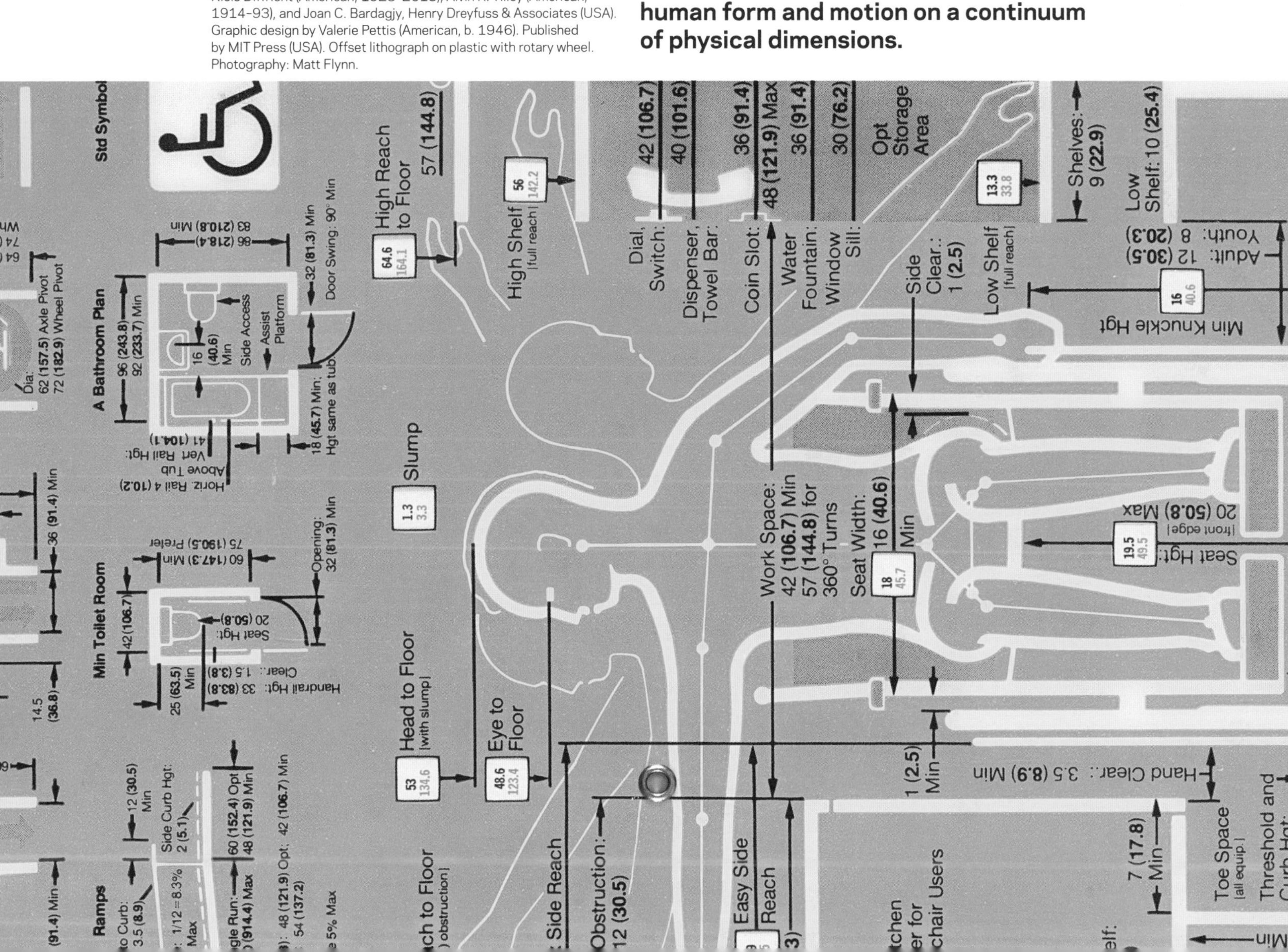

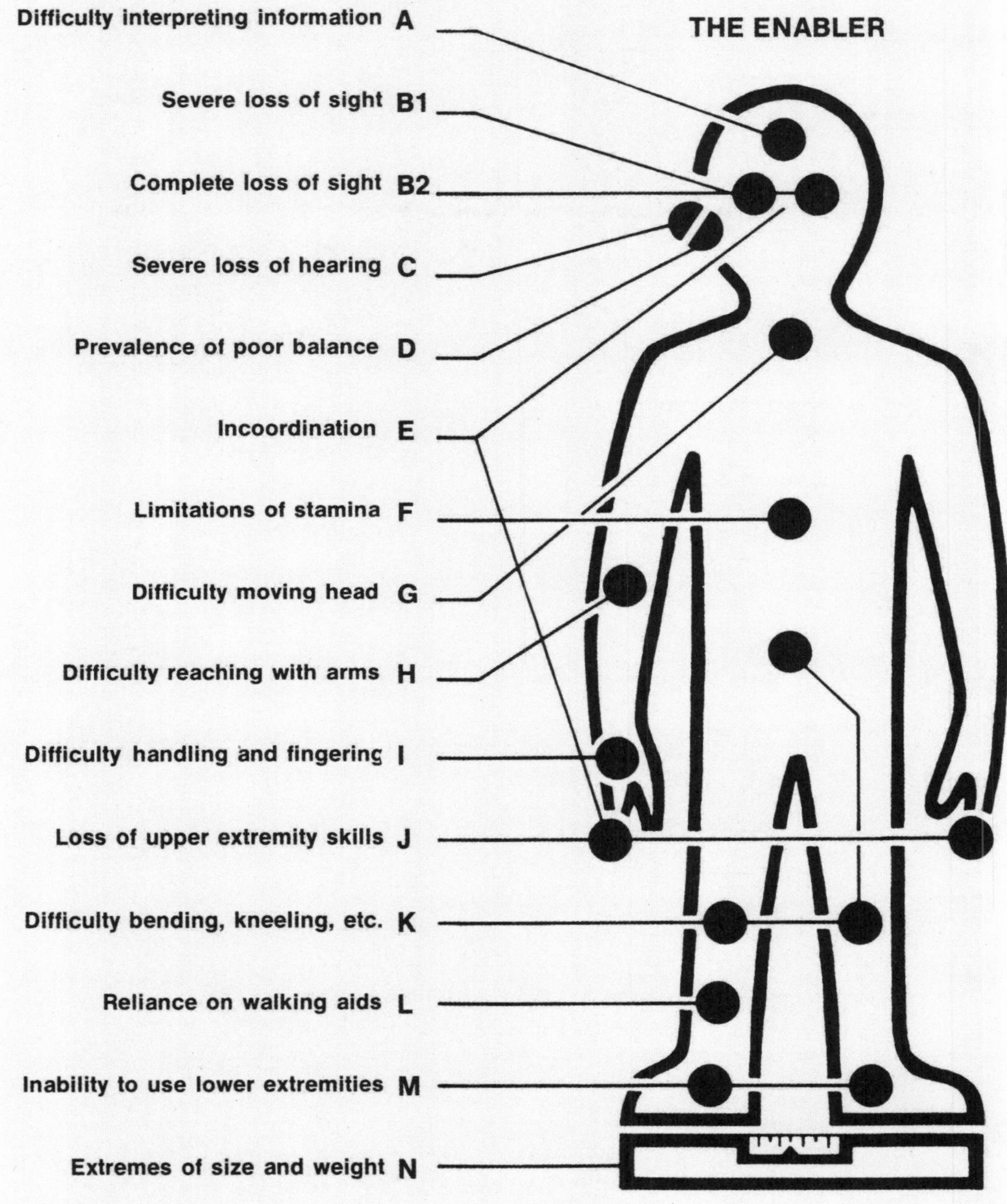
THE ENABLER
Difficulty interpreting information A
Severe loss of sight B1
Complete loss of sight B2
Severe loss of hearing C
Prevalence of poor balance D
Incoordination E
Limitations of stamina F
Difficulty moving head G
Difficulty reaching with arms H
Difficulty handling and fingering I
Loss of upper extremity skills J
Difficulty bending, kneeling, etc. K
Reliance on walking aids L
Inability to use lower extremities M
Extremes of size and weight N

The Enabler, 1977. Designed by Rolf Faste (American, 1943–2003). Published in "New System Propels Design for the Handicapped," *Industrial Design Magazine*, July 1977, 51. Courtesy of Rolf A. Faste Foundation for Design Creativity.

Rolf Faste's diagram "The Enabler" pinpoints potential areas of disability as prompts for design innovation.

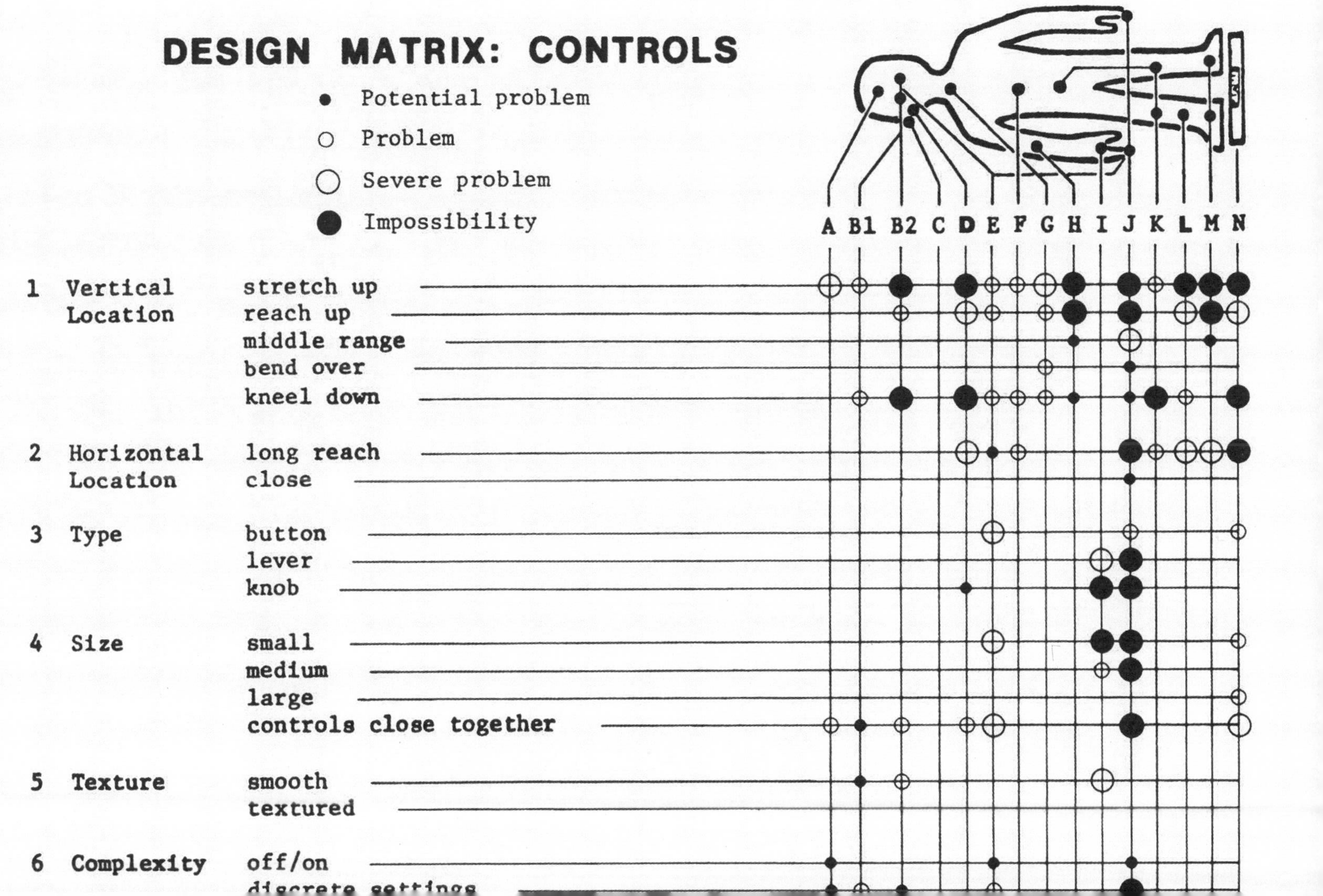

DESIGN MATRIX: CONTROLS

- • Potential problem
- ○ Problem
- ◯ Severe problem
- ● Impossibility

			A	B1	B2	C	D	E	F	G	H	I	J	K	L	M	N
1	Vertical Location	stretch up	◯	○	●		●	○	○	◯	●		●	○	●	●	●
		reach up			○		◯	○		○	●		●		◯	●	◯
		middle range									•		◯			•	
		bend over								○			•				
		kneel down		○	●		●	○	○	○	•		•	●	○		●
2	Horizontal Location	long reach					◯	•	○				●	○	◯	◯	●
		close											•				
3	Type	button						◯					○				○
		lever										◯	●				
		knob					•					●	●				
4	Size	small						◯				●	●				○
		medium										○	●				
		large															○
		controls close together	○	•	○		○	◯					●				◯
5	Texture	smooth		•	○							◯					
		textured															
6	Complexity	off/on	•					•					•				
		discrete settings	•	○	•			○					●				

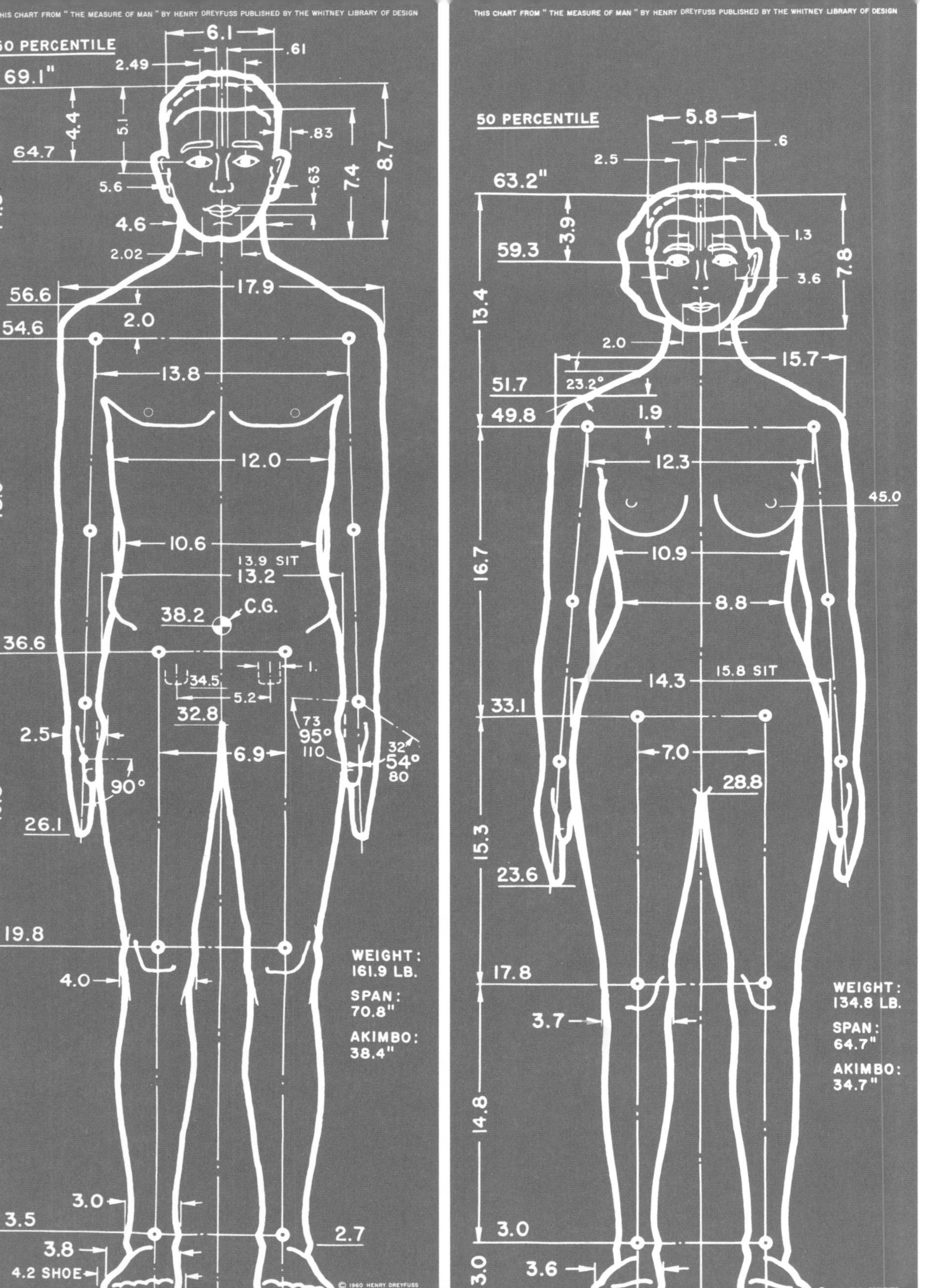
THIS CHART FROM " THE MEASURE OF MAN " BY HENRY DREYFUSS PUBLISHED BY THE WHITNEY LIBRARY OF DESIGN
50 PERCENTILE
69.1"
64.7
56.6
54.6
36.6
19.8
WEIGHT: 161.9 LB.
SPAN: 70.8"
AKIMBO: 38.4"
4.2 SHOE
© 1960 HENRY DREYFUSS
THIS CHART FROM " THE MEASURE OF MAN " BY HENRY DREYFUSS PUBLISHED BY THE WHITNEY LIBRARY OF DESIGN
50 PERCENTILE
63.2"
59.3
51.7
49.8
33.1
17.8
WEIGHT: 134.8 LB.
SPAN: 64.7"
AKIMBO: 34.7"

designing for people

When designers create products, spaces, or media, they inevitably ask along the way how human beings will interact with their work. Indeed, many designers believe that addressing human needs is design's fundamental mission. In the words of Bill Moggridge, "Engineers start with technology and look for a use for it; business people start with a business proposition and then look for the technology and the people. Designers start with people, coming towards a solution from the point of view of people."[1]

Who are these people that designers try so hard to understand? USERS have played various roles in the design process. They have been represented and addressed as ideal or normative types, as people of diverse sizes and abilities, as CONSUMERS to be observed, measured, and even manipulated, and as dynamic partners in the art of problem solving. Today, the divide between designer and user, subject and object, is breaking down as users become a creative force in their own right. The phrase "designing *for* people" is giving way to "designing *with* people" as creative teams seek more egalitarian relationships with an increasingly well-informed public.

Isn't all design centered around users? No. In fact, the forces that drive product development range from the short-term economic interests of manufacturers to the expressive or theoretical intent of designers to a community's entrenched habits and customs. Sometimes things look the way they do because that's the cheapest and fastest way to make them, sometimes because that's how the designer or client chose to express a personal vision or creative impulse, sometimes because that's how things have always been.

Amid such competing motivations, organizing the design process around users is a vital vein of contemporary practice. Compelled by this powerful ethical outlook, USER-CENTERED DESIGN strives to enhance the lives of stakeholders and to discover surprising solutions. Searching for unmet human wants and needs opens up the outcomes of the design process to include experiences, systems, and services as well as physical things.

***The Measure of Man* Posters, 1969.** Authored by Henry Dreyfuss (American, 1904–72). Designed by Alvin R. Tilley (American, 1914–93), Henry Dreyfuss & Associates (USA). Published by Whitney Library of Design (USA). Offset lithograph. Collection Cooper Hewitt, Smithsonian Design Museum, Henry Dreyfuss Archive, gift of Henry Dreyfuss, 1954–68. Photography: Matt Flynn.

Model 302 Telephone, 1937. Designed by Henry Dreyfuss (American, 1904–72) for Bell Telephone Company (USA). Manufactured by Western Electric Manufacturing Company (USA). Cast metal, enamel-coated steel, paper, rubber-sheathed cord, electronic components. Collection Cooper Hewitt, Smithsonian Design Museum, museum purchase from the Decorative Arts Association Acquisition Fund, 1994-73-2. Photography: Hiro Ihara.

Model 500 Telephone, 1953 (introduced in 1949). Designed by Henry Dreyfuss (American, 1904–72), Henry Dreyfuss & Associates (USA) for Bell Laboratories (USA). Manufactured by Western Electric Manufacturing Company (USA). Molded plastic, metal, rubber, electronic components. Collection Cooper Hewitt, Smithsonian Design Museum, 2009-50-1-a/c. Photography: Ellen McDermott.

The evolution of the telephone in the mid-twentieth century tells a story about designers' changing view of users. In the 1930s, Bell Labs asked Henry Dreyfuss to create a new telephone set, to be used across AT&T's vast phone system. Dreyfuss was a young man and an emerging voice in the field of industrial design, a profession that was taking flight alongside mass marketing and mass advertising in the burgeoning consumer economy. Designers including Dreyfuss, Raymond Loewy, and Walter Dorwin Teague were reinventing the point of contact between people and equipment, often by unifying mechanical parts inside smooth, sculptural shells.[2]

Dreyfuss and Bell Labs unveiled their Model 302 telephone in 1937.[3] The object's curving sidewalls swoop upward from a square base to cradle the graceful arc of the handset. Indebted to Jean Heiberg's 1931 phone for the Swedish company Ericsson, the Model 302 is a functional artifact of extraordinary beauty.

Elegant and useful as the Model 302 may have been, it had usability problems. The triangular profile of the handset caused the device to turn when cradled against the shoulder—the design didn't account for people's intuitive desire to talk hands-free. Dreyfuss addressed this issue with the Model 500, introduced in 1949. To create the next-generation device, Dreyfuss's design team and the engineers at Bell Labs started by working on the handset. They studied measurements of over two thousand human faces to determine the average space between the mouth and the ear. They gave the Model G handset a flattened, squared-off profile, fondly calling it the "lumpy rectangle."

Princess Telephone Advertisement, 1959. Telephone designed by Henry Dreyfuss & Associates (USA) and Bell Labs (USA). Manufactured by Western Electric Manufacturing Company (USA). Thermoplastic case, steel base, electronic components.

Alvin R. Tilley, an engineer in the Dreyfuss office, exclaimed that "a design that is neither concave nor convex and without sex is the darnedest thing!"[4] The new handset was smaller, lighter, and less likely to turn in the hand, and it stayed in place when cradled against the shoulder. The designers derived this homelier but more functional object from human habits and anatomy rather than from an abstract play of angles and curves.

The phone's rotary dial is a complex point of human contact. When first introduced, the Model 500 took longer to dial than the older model. John E. Karlin, an industrial psychologist at Bell Labs, moved the numbers and letters from inside the finger holes to outside. The change prevented the graphics from rubbing off over time and kept them visible while the dial turned. Karlin also placed a white dot inside each finger hole to give users a visual target.[5] According to Dreyfuss, these simple "aiming dots" reduced dialing time by seven-tenths of a second.[6]

Bell Labs manufactured phones for AT&T, a monopoly that delivered phone service across the U.S. When a subscriber signed up for phone service, the telephone came with it, and the devices were standard issue, designed for durability and function rather than consumer appeal. In order to expand its business, AT&T encouraged users to install multiple extensions or to enhance their service for an added charge. The decision in 1953 to produce phones in a range of colors transformed the telephone from a basic technology into an alluring consumer product. Ad campaigns encouraged women to see the phone as an element of home decoration.[7]

What if new phone models could target specific demographic groups? In the 1950s, advertisers and manufacturers discovered in teenagers a lucrative market for consumer goods; and in 1959, the Dreyfuss office introduced a glamorous new icon of phone design: the Princess. Its seductively anthropomorphic name mirrored its youthful market. With its small footprint, pretty colors, and light-up dial, the Princess appealed to young women as a bedside accessory. The design team had observed users lying in bed with the base of the Model 500 resting heavily on their torso; the Princess's lighter, more portable design responded to this unanticipated use.

By endowing the Princess with a standard Model G handset, the Dreyfuss team introduced a dramatically new product while minimizing manufacturing costs. Dreyfuss called the existing handset a "survival form"—a familiar element incorporated into an updated product. The designers moved the numbers and letters back inside the finger holes, deeming efficiency less important than saving space. The light weight proved to be a liability, however, as users commonly pulled the phone off its table by the cord; later designs feature a weighted base.

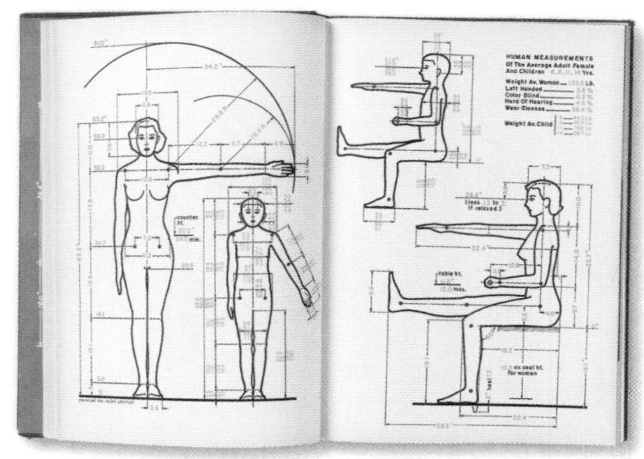

***Designing for People*, 1955.** Authored by Henry Dreyfuss (American, 1904–72). Drawn by Alvin R. Tilley (American, 1914–93), Henry Dreyfuss & Associates (USA). Published by Whitney Library of Design (USA). Offset lithograph. Collection Cooper Hewitt, Smithsonian Design Museum, Henry Dreyfuss Archive, gift of Henry Dreyfuss, 1954–68. Photography: Matt Flynn.

***Bauentwurfslehre (Architects' Data)*, 1938** (opposite page, left). Designed by Ernst Neufert (German, 1900–86). Published by Bauwelt-Verlag (Germany); first published in 1936. Offset lithograph.

***Anatomy for Interior Designers*, 1948** (opposite page, right). Authored by Francis de N. Schroeder. Illustrations by Nino Repetto. Published by Whitney Library of Design (USA). Offset lithograph.

This trilogy of Dreyfuss phones—from the classic Model 302 to the research-driven Model 500 to the glamorous Princess—shows the designer's shift in focus from shaping the sculptural integrity of the object to studying the anatomy and behavior of the typical user to targeting a consumer demographics.

Dreyfuss used the terms HUMAN FACTORS and HUMAN ENGINEERING to name his philosophy of "fitting the machine to the man rather than the man to the machine." He promoted this principle in his 1955 book, *Designing for People*, an anecdotal guide directed at general readers.[8] Human factors, also called ERGONOMICS, combine knowledge of bodily dimensions with an understanding of psychology. *Designing for People* also introduced Tilley's famous drawings of a typical American couple, dubbed "Joe" and "Josephine." To create the drawings, Tilley studied data employed by the U.S. military (for men) and the fashion industry (for women). His drawings were later published as lifesize wall charts in the Dreyfuss office's publication *The Measure of Man*.[9] Tilley determined a range of percentiles from 1 to 100; *The Measure of Man* wall charts represent the mean (50th percentile). Drawings depicting low and high percentiles appear in the portfolio of prints accompanying the full-scale charts.

The Measure of Man, which enabled designers to create products that fit average bodies with a greater degree of comfort, built on the international standards movement that took shape in the 1910s. The standards movement was concerned with improving efficiency in design and manufacturing more than with enhancing comfort. Measuring human movement and anatomy (ANTHROPOMETRICS) was a key component of Taylorization, which employed time-and-motion studies to maximize the productivity of factory workers. The human worker became a moving part within the machinery of modern industry.[10]

German architect Ernst Neufert was a student at the Bauhaus and collaborated with Walter Gropius on the design of the Bauhaus buildings in Dessau in 1925. Embracing the era's fascination with global standards for design and manufacturing, Neufert sought to coordinate standard measurements for objects, rooms, and buildings with the dimensions of typical bodies. Neufert's book, *Bauentwurfslehre (Architects' Data)*, first appeared in Germany in 1936; it is still used by architects and designers around the world today, and it has been published in countless editions and translations.[11]

Initially, Neufert employed the classical proportions of the Golden

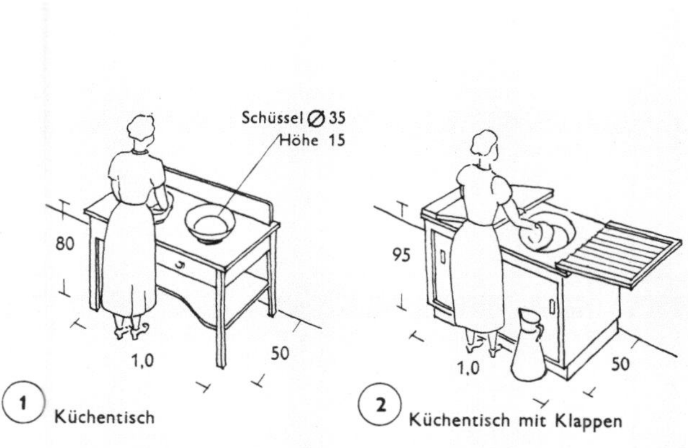

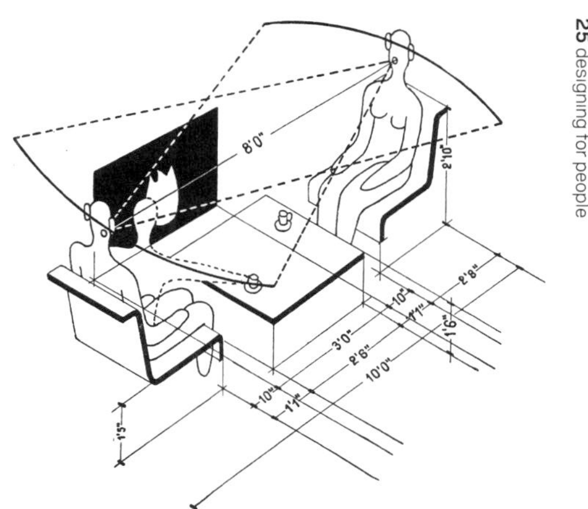

Section to diagram the ideal human body. As design historian Nader Vossoughian has pointed out, Neufert later adjusted his data on human dimensions to reflect a standardized unit he called the "octametric brick." This brick was the basis of a universal grid that could generate dimensions for any part of a building, from construction materials to furniture and appliances. Over time, Neufert's publications helped establish standard dimensions for a wide range of products, fixtures, and building components. Ultimately, he sought to make the body conform to industrial norms rather than deriving such norms from the body.[12]

Treating the body as an industrial component broke with the classical notion that "man is the measure," memorialized in Leonardo da Vinci's iconic cosmological diagram of a man's body inscribed in a circle and square. Da Vinci visualized a passage by the ancient Roman architect Vitruvius (*Ten Books of Architecture*), who wrote that buildings and cities should be fashioned in units that relate to the scale of the body, yielding environments well suited to human habitation and locomotion.[13]

A more playful humanism permeates Francis de N. Schroeder's 1948 guide, *Anatomy for Interior Designers*, based on measurements gathered from existing architectural standards and insurance statistics. Nino Repetto's whimsical yet informative illustrations depict people engaged in a range of social situations, from passing each other in a hallway to flirting in a cocktail lounge. This influential book presented a gentle view of people interacting with architecture.[14]

Niels Diffrient worked in the office of Henry Dreyfuss from 1955 through 1980, leading the design of such legendary products as the Princess phone and the Polaroid SX-70 camera.[15] Together with Tilley and research assistant Joan Bardagjy, Diffrient coauthored the *Humanscale* series of rotary selectors, beginning in 1974. A wheel grommeted inside each of these printed plastic guides coordinates a figure's height with various other dimensions, such as shoulder width, head width, and thigh length. The small circles in the *Humanscale* diagrams represent "pivot points," simplifications of the motions in bone joints. Diffrient's selectors were a triumph of user-centered design in their own right, collapsing massive printed volumes filled with dense linear charts into light, interactive, easy-to-use tools.

Whereas the earlier drawings of Joe and Josephine emphasize the dimensional mean, the *Humanscale* selectors document a diverse continuum. The drawings depict bodies in the 50th percentile of

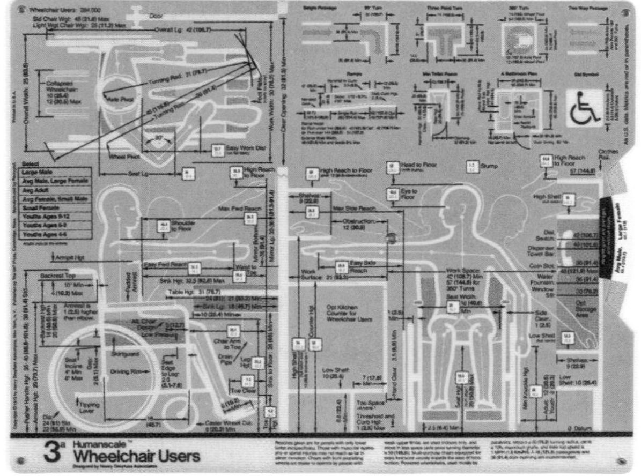

***Humanscale* Body Measurements Selector, 1974.** Authored by Niels Diffrient (American, 1928–2013), Alvin R. Tilley (American, 1914–93), and Joan C. Bardagjy, Henry Dreyfuss & Associates (USA). Graphic design by Valerie Pettis (American, b. 1946). Published by MIT Press (USA). Offset lithograph on plastic with rotary wheel. Photography: Matt Flynn.

standing height; this is midpoint in a range encompassing 95 percent of U.S. females and males. The diagrams also present dimensions for the bottom (2.5) and top (97.5) percentiles. These extremes are indicated with numbers, not drawings; excluded altogether are those falling outside the 95 percent range. The greatest variations in human size occur within the population of outliers at the edges of the anthropometric scale.

The authors of *Humanscale* acknowledged that the diagrams account for variations in height but not weight: in their "fleshy areas," populations feature broader individual differences than they exhibit in their height. The limb dimensions are averages; actual measurements vary from individual to individual. The goal in creating a standard system of measure—even an inclusive one like *Humanscale*—constantly comes up against human particularity.

The *Humanscale* project responded to the UNIVERSAL DESIGN movement. In the late 1960s and early 1970s, the newly vocal disability community compelled designers, builders, manufacturers, and lawmakers to accommodate the needs of a greater diversity of bodies. Humans face physical limitations throughout their lives, from childhood through the aging process. Some disabilities are permanent and others are temporary, but all are exacerbated by poor design decisions.

The Museum of Modern Art's 1988 project *Designs for Independent Living* was one of the first museum exhibitions dedicated to universal design. As curator Cara McCarty pointed out, people are "disabled" by obstacles in the environment; once those obstacles are removed, disability falls away. McCarty wrote, "It is imperative to involve the user in the design process, for the objective is to develop aids that will make maximum use of a person's abilities.... In the past, the tendency was to focus on what a person could *not* do, and products required assistance for use, encouraging dependency."[16] Ten years later, under the leadership of director Dianne Pilgrim, Cooper-Hewitt, National Design Museum opened its exhibition *Unlimited by Design*, which promoted the commercial viability of universal design strategies.[17]

Universal design wants to empower individuals to work, live, and travel as independently as possible. Well-designed objects humanize the experience of assistive devices, enhancing the environment not only for people with impairments but for other users as well. When mobility aids and medical products are beautiful and convenient, people are more likely to use them and thus enjoy improved health and independence. The

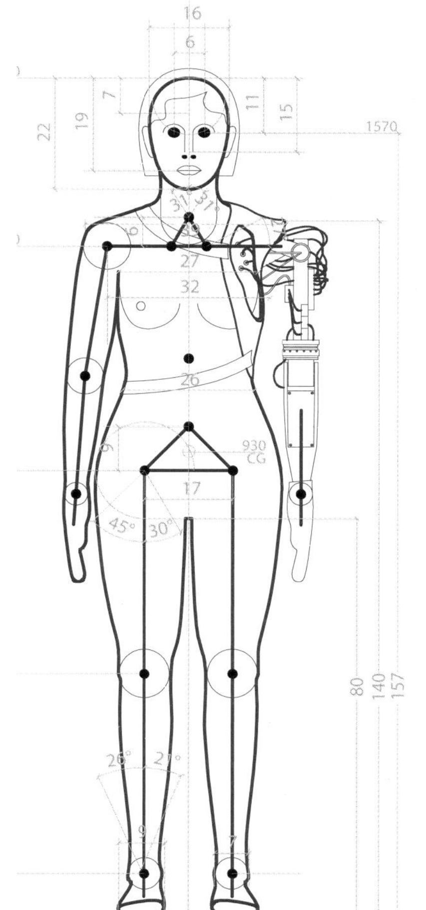

The Measure(s) of Man, 2011. Designed by Thomas Carpentier (French, b. 1986). Degree project, École Spéciale d'Architecture, Paris. Courtesy of the designer.

stigma of an unsightly walking aid or the annoyance of an impenetrable pillbox discourages users from benefiting from these products.

Design historian Bess Williamson has critiqued the urge to assimilate products for people with disabilities into the consumer mainstream: "In its commercial success, universal design found an irony: seamlessly integrating features related to disability into mass-market products could amount to hiding or ignoring actual people with disabilities."[18] By promoting products such as canes or bathroom grab bars as lifestyle accessories that work for everyone, companies contribute to society's desire to make disability disappear.

Some recent designs for prosthetics openly celebrate the visibility of mechanically augmented bodies. From a hi-tech digital limb engineered at Johns Hopkins University to a 3D-printed hand designed by Richard van As, these wonders of ingenuity proudly flaunt their technological identity. Indeed, the uncanny effect of lifelike prosthetics can be more unsettling to observers than a frank display of disability.

Mary Jane Lupton is a writer born with a deformed right hand. As she was coming of age in the 1950s, her family urged her to conceal her misshapen limb inside a naturalistic but rigid cosmetic prosthesis. The artificial hand's sole function was holding a purse or a cigarette. Realizing that the prosthetic "helped" only the people who didn't want to see her deformity, she eventually abandoned it altogether.

Thomas Carpentier has imagined new products and spaces for such extreme users as a bodybuilder, an amputee, a pair of conjoined twins, and Borg Queen, a character from *Star Trek* who has a living, biological head and a mechanical body. As people embrace technology's ability to enhance life, assistive devices will celebrate the aesthetics of the cyborg rather than assimilating bodies to norms.

By focusing on points of friction between people and devices, the Dreyfuss office pioneered the field of INTERFACE DESIGN. Early practitioners of ergonomics started in the 1940s using the word *interface* to describe the plane of connection between humans and machines.[19] Dials, buttons, and levers invite

GRiD Compass Laptop Computer Prototype, 1981. Designed by Bill Moggridge (English, 1943-2012). Manufactured by GRiD Systems Corporation (USA). Die-cast magnesium, injection-molded plastic. Collection Cooper Hewitt, Smithsonian Design Museum, gift of Bill Moggridge, 2010-22-1. Photography: Matt Flynn.

***Designing Interactions*, 2007** (opposite page). Authored by Bill Moggridge (English, 1943-2012). Published by MIT Press (USA). Offset lithograph. Photography: Matt Flynn.

users to operate complex, hidden systems. Some controls are direct and physical, such as the steering wheel of a car, whereas others rely on graphic representations, such as the "buttons" on a touch screen. Controls model how a device works, and they limit how people affect its actions.[20]

Dreyfuss's Honeywell Round, introduced in 1953 after ten years of development, remains the most widely used thermostat on the planet. A thermostat is pure interface: it is a switch for turning a system on and off, and it is a display that communicates the system's current and future state. Users operate the Honeywell Round with a simple twist of the dial, and they can intuitively compare the set temperature and the room temperature. The Honeywell Round replaced clunky boxes that users often mounted crookedly on the wall. Dreyfuss reinvented the lowly thermostat—produced with little consideration for users—by subjecting it to his process of designing for people.

Improving users' experience with hardware and software has become a crucial field of design practice. Interface design, pioneered by Dreyfuss in the 1940s and 1950s, has expanded to become INTERACTION DESIGN. As products ranging from medical devices to remote controls become staggeringly complex, designers are addressing more than the point of contact between people and devices. They are seeking, in the words of designer Brenda Laurel, ways "for humans and computers to construct actions together."[21] Interaction designers explore dynamic exchanges between users and systems. Both the human and the interface are actors sharing the stage in a dramatic narrative.

The Nest Learning Thermostat exemplifies the software-integrated products of today. Although many homes are equipped with energy-saving, programmable thermostats, countless users—perplexed by the interface—fail to implement all the features of such devices. The simple, round Nest uses sensors, software, smartphone apps, and touch-and-turn interaction to respond to users and encourage device programming.

One of the great pioneers of interaction design was Bill Moggridge. In 1980, GRiD Systems Corporation commissioned Moggridge, an industrial designer, to create what became the first laptop computer. The GRiD Compass has a screen that flips up to reveal a keyboard. Priced at approximately $8,000 a unit, the GRiD was reserved for elite business, government, and military applications and for NASA space missions. As Moggridge began using the GRiD himself, he realized that the relationships

Here are two stories of personal experiences that led me to start working toward a new design discipline, eventually called "interaction design." The first, about buying a digital watch for my son, made me see that I needed to learn how to design controls for products that contain electronics. The second, about designing the first laptop, made me see that I needed to learn how to design user interfaces for computers. The next nine chapters contain thirty-seven interviews, both in the book and on the DVD, with people who have made interesting or important contributions to this field. In chapter 10, "People and Prototypes," I expand my personal point of view about designing interactions.

The Radio Watch

The author with his son, in front of the Southland Runabout trailer where many of the ideas for this book were formed

Photo Catherine Ledner, published in Dwell magazine

I WAS BROWSING in the duty-free store in Narita airport outside Tokyo while waiting for my flight back to San Francisco in 1983. When I was on business trips, I tried to find gifts to bring home for my two sons, aged thirteen and ten at the time. I already had a Yomiuri Giants hat for the baseball-crazed ten-year-old but still needed something for the teenager, who was starting to get interested in heavy metal music and realizing that dad was not necessarily always right about everything. He was saving the money from his paper route to buy his first electric guitar.

I drifted across to a large array of glass-topped cases and found in them a seemingly endless collection of watches. My designer soul was mesmerized. How could there be so many great looking watches in the world? As well as the international brands that I was used to, there was case after case of beautiful and innovative designs from Japanese manufacturers. Some were for running or swimming, some had interchangeable dials with alternative functions, and many were just elegant. Then I saw a digital watch

Introduction | 3

among the user, the software, and the physical object were more compelling than the physical device. Moggridge cofounded IDEO, a design firm known for developing technology-integrated products and for disseminating the DESIGN THINKING methodology.[22]

Today, interaction design fits within the broader field of EXPERIENCE DESIGN. To shape an experience is to script a series of narratives around a person's encounters with a product or service.[23] Negative experiences, too, can inspire concepts for new products. Entrepreneur Andy Katz-Mayfield (cofounder of the eyeglass company Warby Parker) was dismayed one day at the high price and low value of a drugstore razor—in his frustration, he recognized the potential to transform an everyday product category. Users find little joy in the hyperstyled, blister-packed plastic razors sold in drugstores. In response, the Harry's design team reinvented not only the physical product but also the system for packaging, distributing, and marketing it. Harry's sells its attractive, pleasant-to-use razors directly to customers via the company's website, creating an enhanced experience at a reasonable price.

An object's capacity to support action is called an AFFORDANCE. The dial of a thermostat affords turning, whereas the pages of a book afford flipping, fanning, folding, tearing, and marking. From open doors and climbable steps to looming objects and the sudden drop-off of a cliff, some features of the environment are recognizable to nearly any creature as sources of danger or opportunity. An affordance can trigger an intuitive response—the crotch of a tree offers birds a safe, stable site to build a nest, whereas a flat surface raised to a certain height offers humans a convenient place to sit. An object doesn't need arms or legs to become a chair.[24]

Some affordances can be learned (and unlearned) culturally. The rotary phone dial that appeared self-evident to generations of users bewilders people weaned on buttons and keypads. Humans and other creatures interact with features of their environment in a continuous

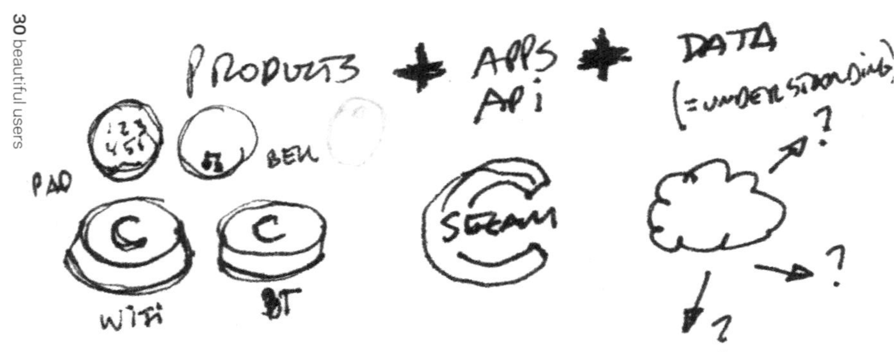

exchange. A person becomes a user in relation to those features of an object that invite action (handle, dial, switch, armrest). Likewise, these affordances come into being in response to the stream of action. Affordances exist as relationships between creatures and their environment. A crack in a wall becomes a doorway when it reaches sufficient size in relation to a creature that might pass through it. A saucer is designed to rest beneath a cup; it becomes a lid when someone sets it on top, changing its intended function. Affordances are not absolute or objective features of the environment but exist in relationship to agents. As people age, affordances that once invited action or mobility become obstacles and limitations.

Objects and their affordances belong to larger systems. In order to fully function, a wheelchair needs ramps, elevators, and paved roads. Pills need bottles, bikes need racks, and locks need keys—as well as locksmiths, key-cutting machines, and doormats for hiding spares. The August Smart Lock replaces the traditional key with a smartphone app. The user attaches an electronic device to an ordinary deadbolt; the device recognizes the owner's smartphone as well as the phones of users who have been granted "keys" to the lock. The owner of the lock can revoke a key at any time as well as create keys that automatically expire. At once a physical product and a digital service, August aims to streamline a routine annoyance without compromising the user's security.

For some people, a lock is not a symbol of safety and closure but a provocation to break and enter. Whether seeking intellectual adventure or political or economic advantage, HACKERS unravel secret codes and expose hidden gears. Interface design grew out of the need for understandable controls on systems that defy understanding; OPEN-SOURCE DESIGN lays bare the mechanisms behind the curtain of the interface.

The hacker—dressed in the gentler guise of MAKER—is conquering the realm of products. The term *maker* went mainstream when Dale Dougherty, publisher of a successful series of software guides, launched the magazine *Make* in 2005.[25] *The Maker's Bill of Rights* includes such slogans as "screws not glues," asserting the user's desire to take things apart and reassemble them in new ways.[26] *Make* triggered a groundswell of maker faires, maker lounges, and roving maker mobiles. Banished from this DO-IT-YOURSELF culture is the passive user, whose needs exist to be mapped out or manufactured.

An amateur zeal drives much open-source design. Turning your robotic vacuum cleaner into a cat mobile (Roomba hacking) or converting a Lack side table into a standing desk (IKEA hacking) doesn't solve existential problems, but

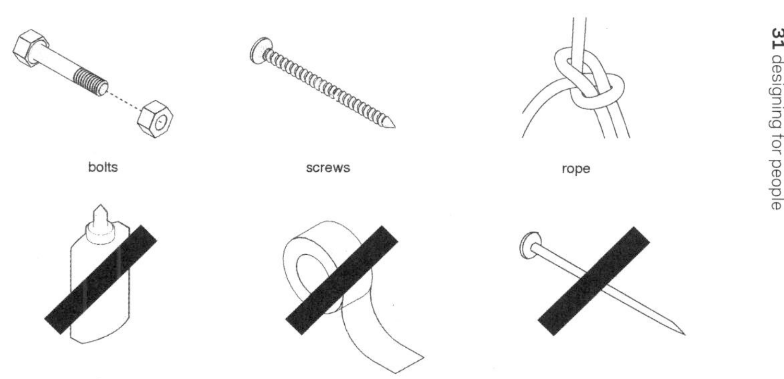

August Smart Lock Concept Drawing, 2013 (opposite page). Designed by Yves Béhar (Swiss, b. 1967), fuseproject (USA). Courtesy of the designer.

OpenStructures (OS) Diagram: Preferred and Non-Preferred Assembly Techniques, 2009 (right). Designed by Thomas Lommée (Belgian, b. 1979). Courtesy of the designer.

it does empower people to understand technology, constraints, and problem solving. Although most IKEA hacks yield awkward results, skilled designers such as Andreas Bhend have created graceful new products at a low cost, sharing the instructions with the public.

The design BRICOLEUR views IKEA's warehouse as a kit of parts rather than a menu of finished goods. OpenStructures (OS), founded by Thomas Lommée, is a system of interlocking components that can be freely downloaded and 3D-printed by any designer. Jesse Howard's Transparent Tools combine OS parts with standard wheel assemblies, repurposed motors, and glass and plastic containers. These open-source objects subvert the industrial designer's traditional task—exemplified by the work of Henry Dreyfuss—of masking technology with an opaque interface.

Who is the user of the future? Affordable 3D printing promises a new era of personal design and manufacturing. As this promise unfolds, professional designers will create libraries of forms and tools for combining and recombining elements. As products seek out an audience of one, designers may become therapists and soothsayers who lead makers through the process of uncovering their needs and motivations.

What lies beyond usability? In *Designing Interactions* (2007), Moggridge mapped out a hierarchy of human factors research that puts the dimensions of human anatomy (anthropometrics) at the very bottom of a sequence that moves upward and outward in complexity and reach. Anthropometrics is followed by physiology (how the body works), cognitive psychology (how the mind works), and cultural anthropology (understanding the human condition). Occupying the top of the human factors hierarchy is ecology, devoted to the interdependence of all living things. Thinking past the user, Moggridge recognized that the lens of individual need is too narrow for the future of design thinking. He saw the limits of user-centered design even while becoming one of the field's leading theorists.

We are moving towards a more holistic view of design and its impact on the larger person, community, and world.
—*Bill Moggridge*

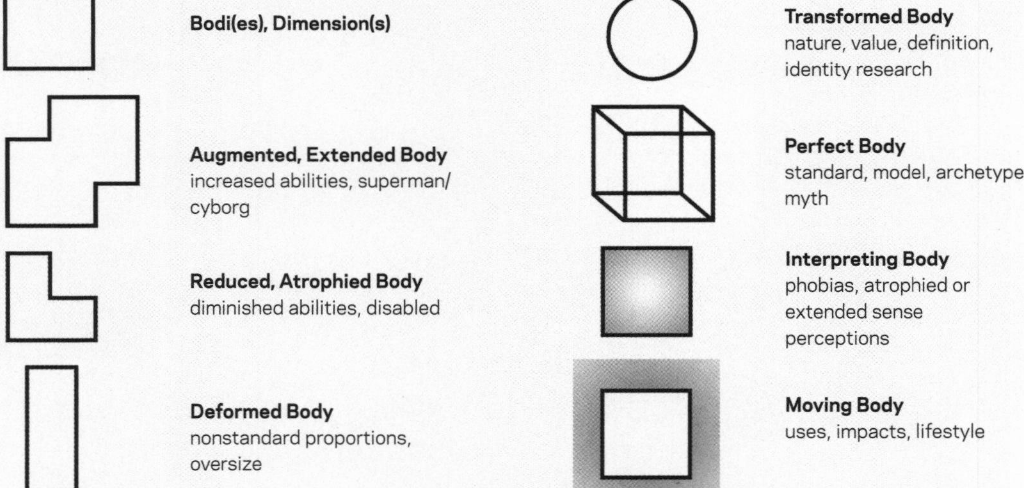
Bodi(es), Dimension(s)
Augmented, Extended Body
increased abilities, superman/
cyborg
Reduced, Atrophied Body
diminished abilities, disabled
Deformed Body
nonstandard proportions,
oversize
Transformed Body
nature, value, definition,
identity research
Perfect Body
standard, model, archetype,
myth
Interpreting Body
phobias, atrophied or
extended sense
perceptions
Moving Body
uses, impacts, lifestyle

Thomas Carpentier

the measure(s) of man: *architects' data* add-on

All images in this project designed by Thomas Carpentier (French, b. 1986) for his degree project at the École Spéciale d'Architecture (Paris, 2011).

Modern society seeks to rationalize, classify, and standardize goods and services of every kind. Architecture cannot escape from this agenda: spaces, programs, uses, dimensions, individuals, values, and thinking tend to conform to standards rather than explore the possible. Human bodies, as the basis of this larger system, are also subject to standardization. Do ERGONOMICS and linear spaces generate sameness?

The manual *Bauentwurfslehre (Architects' Data)*, first published by Ernst Neufert in 1936, is the Bible of architectural standards, adopted globally by generations of students and practitioners. Although the book has been updated over the decades, *Architects' Data* continues to carry modernism's founding dream of universality. By its account, architecture is always and everywhere experienced through the same tool: the human body. No single normative body can express the range of architectural experiences derived from humankind's countless cultural, personal, physiological, and morphological variations.

The body is not standard. It can be tall, short, fat, thin, wizened, deformed, or twisted. This project imagines architectural forms and spaces for extraordinary bodies.

Le Corbusier's Modulor, a modernist model of architectural proportions, employs the human body as a standard measure. In reality, this model does not express the range of human singularities.

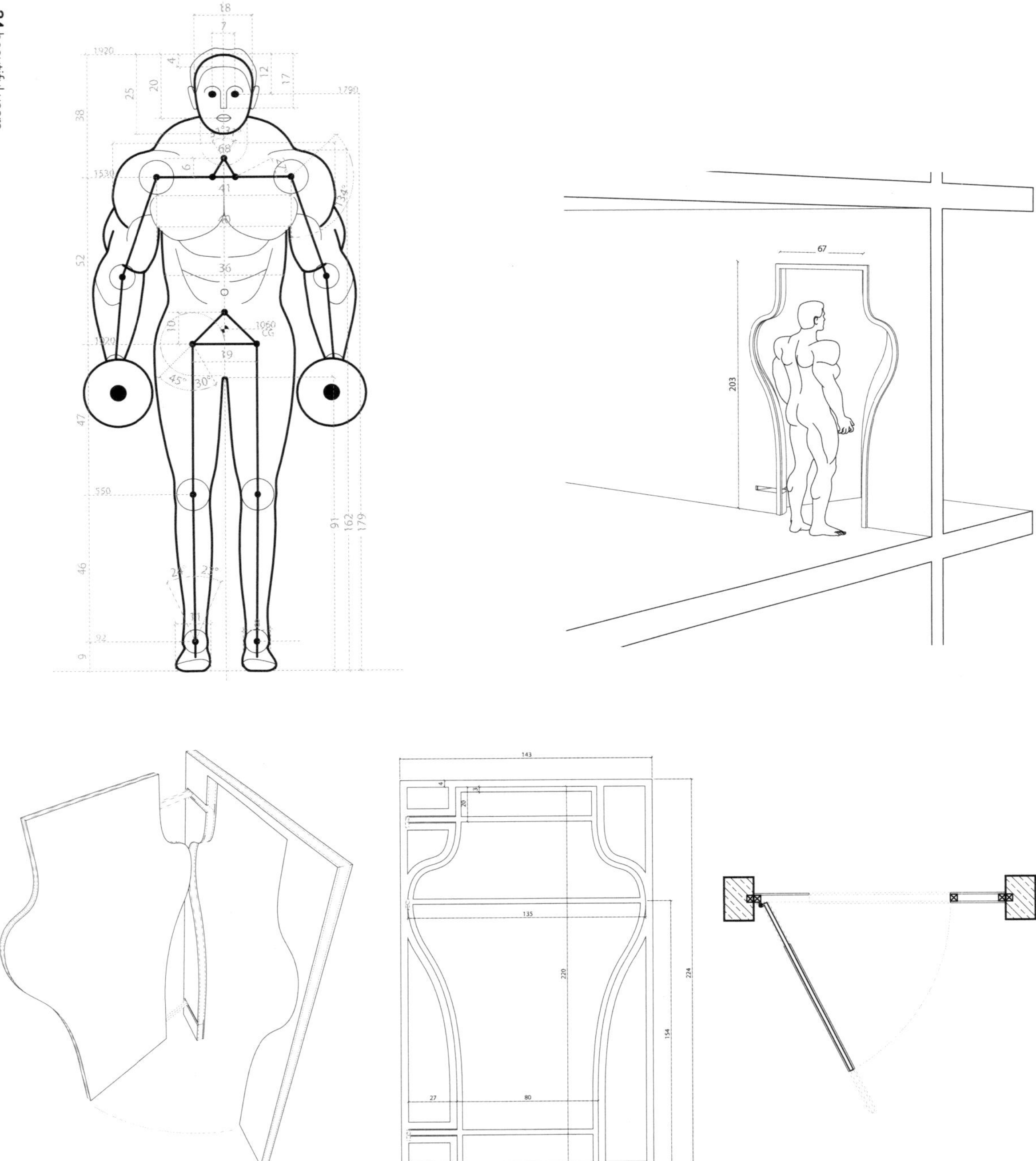

Arnold is a body builder with prominent shoulders. The entrance to his house offers an extra-wide opening at shoulder height. The resulting door requires a custom frame with extended hinges.

Borg Queen (opposite) has only a head and chest. The rest of her body is an accessory for simulating a human appearance. At home, an electric rail allows her to glide from room to room. She no longer has contact with the ground, only with the ceiling.

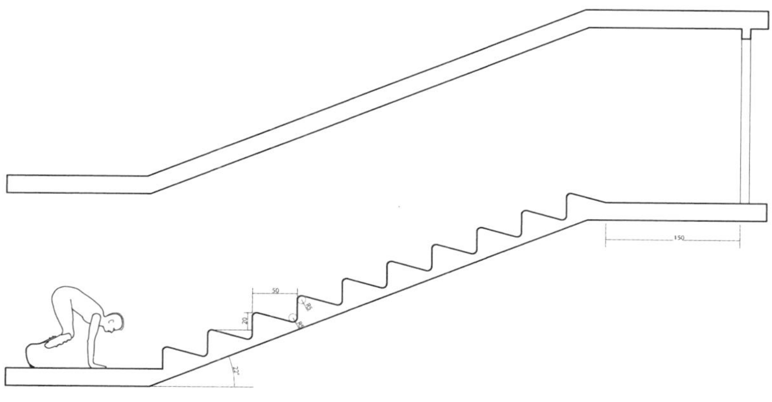

Oscar is one of the fastest men on Earth despite his physical difference, but his athletic prostheses are designed only for running, not for walking or even turning. When he uses them, a stairway serves as a running track. Its angle is flattened, and the stairs' edges are rounded off.

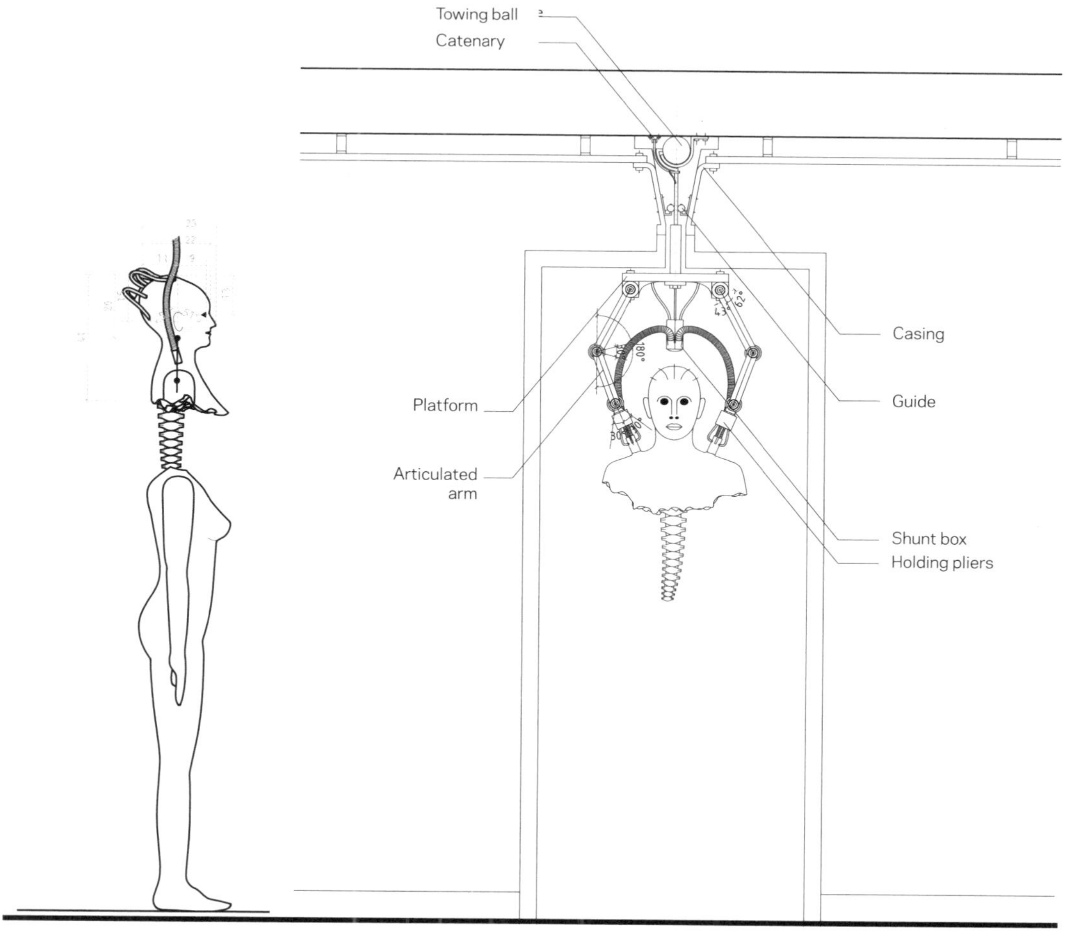

Towing ball
Catenary
Casing
Platform
Guide
Articulated arm
Shunt box
Holding pliers

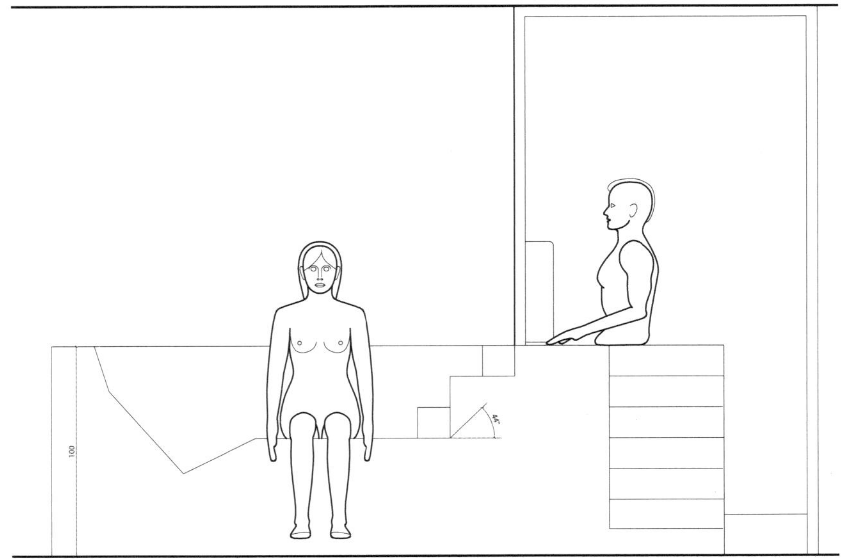

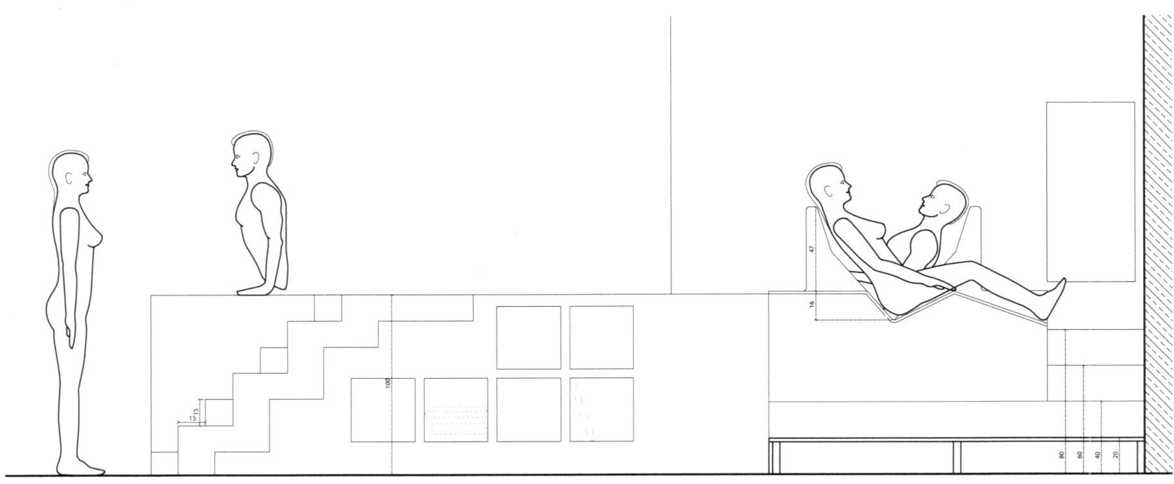

David is a legless dancer. He and his wife don't live at the same altitude: he moves along the floor, whereas she is one meter higher. By raising David's level, this furniture installation creates a continuous landscape in which their bodies can interact and mingle without difference.

bedroom

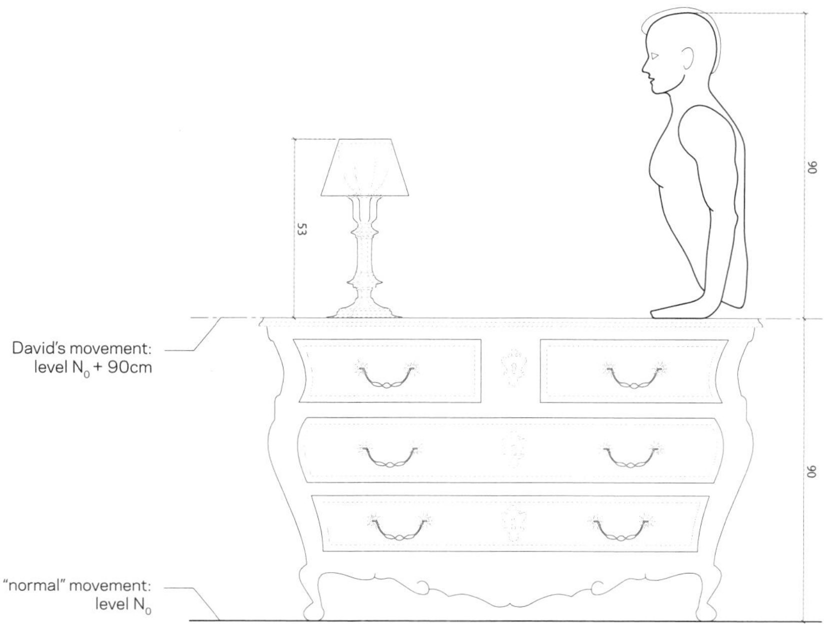
53
90
90
David's movement:
level N_0 + 90cm
"normal" movement:
level N_0

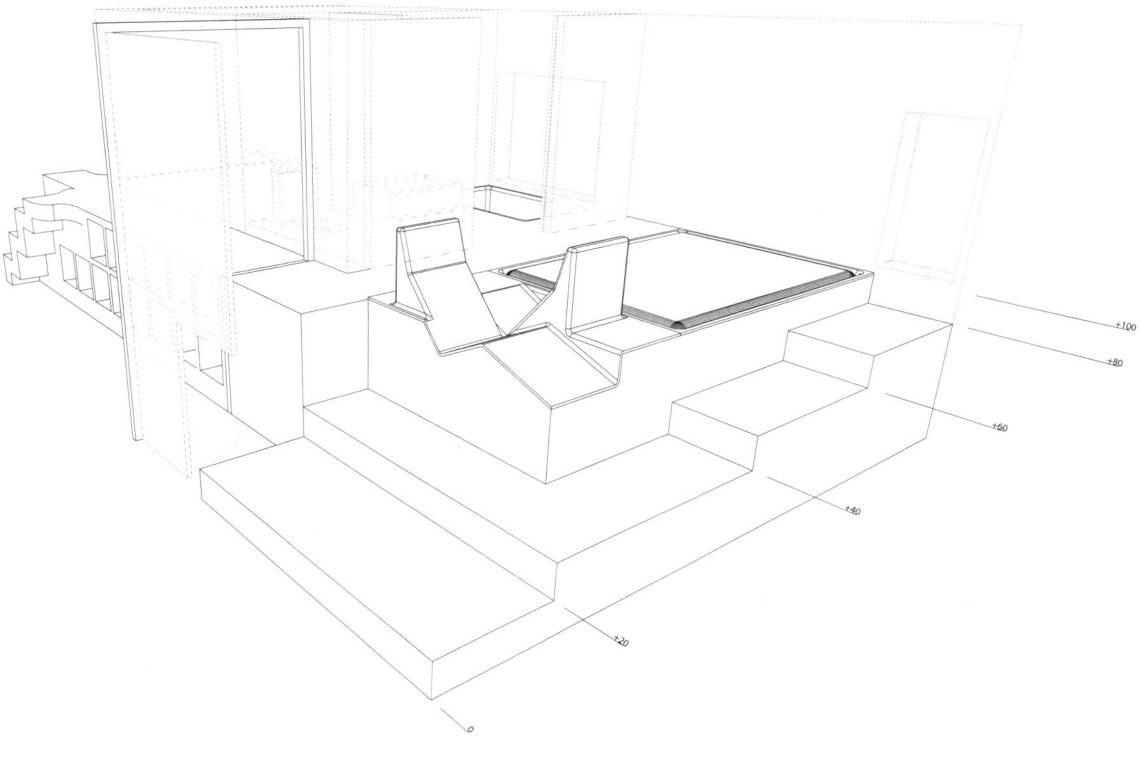

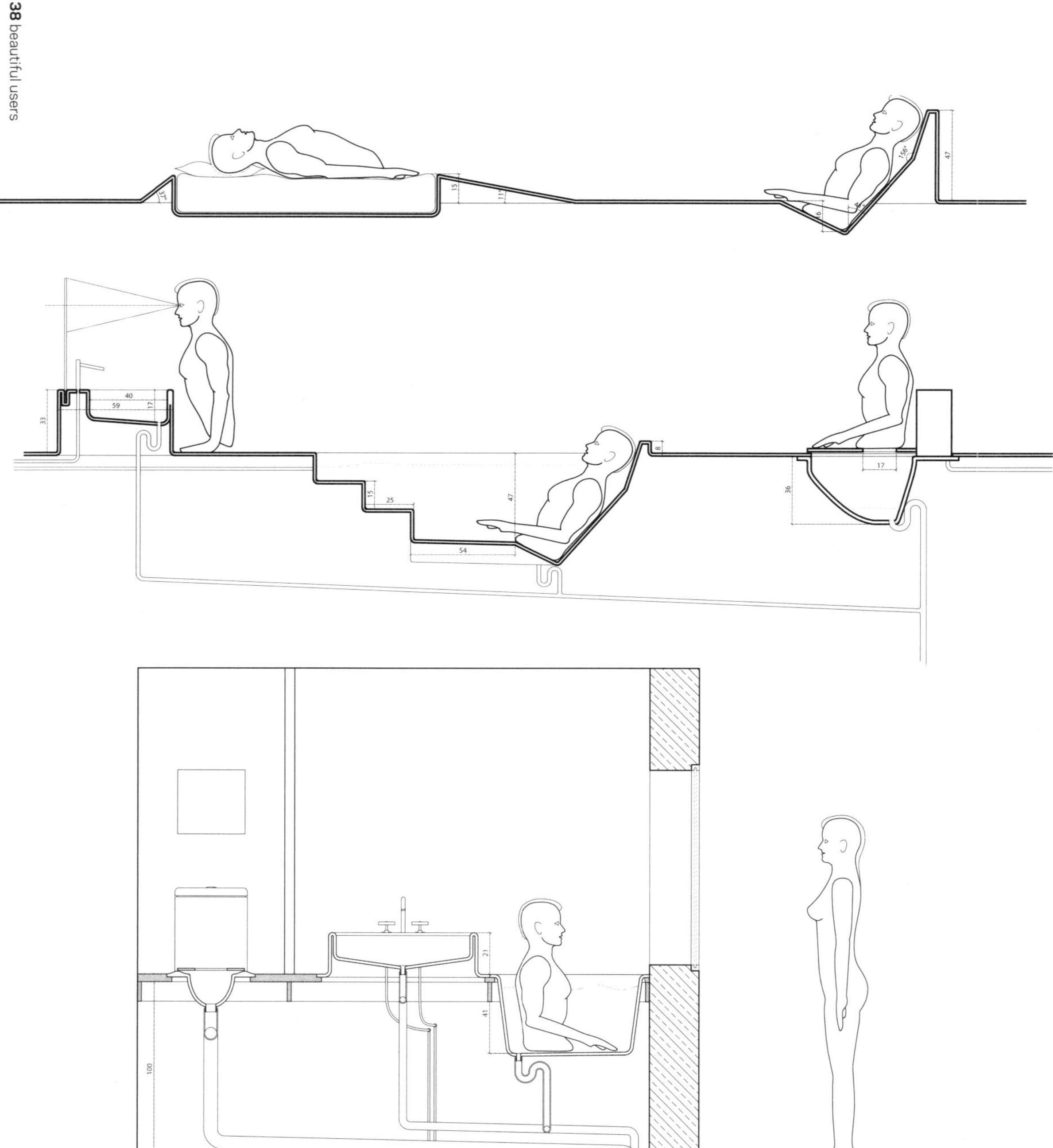

Changing levels could be uncomfortable for David. To limit level changes, why not bring all the furnishings and sanitary fixtures to the same level? The result is a new architectural landscape that moves up and down from a zero level.

bathroom

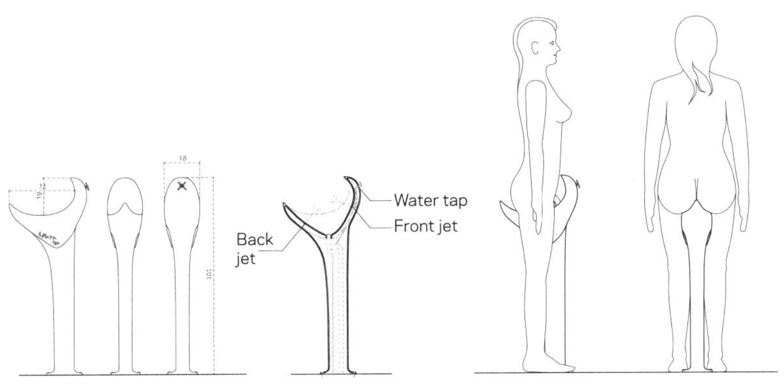

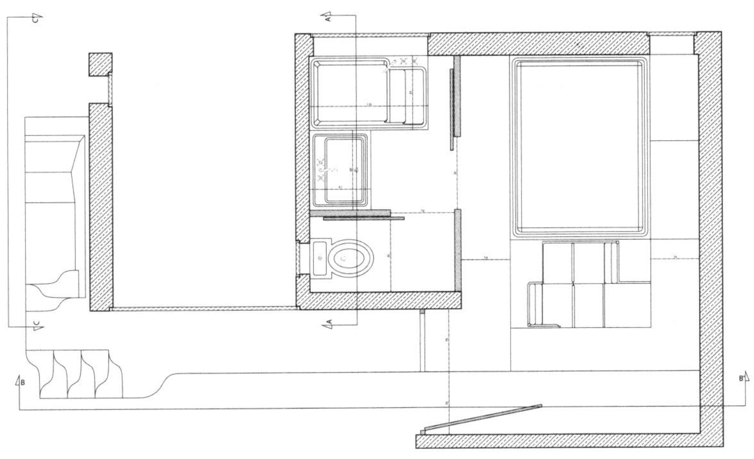

Hermaphroditus has both male and female genitalia. A high bidet allows him/her to clean the female organs while standing in a male position, thus respecting his/her double identity. The sanitary unit stands in the middle of the living room in the tradition of Louis XIV, who gave his *gentilhommes* the privilege of witnessing the king's affairs. The most intimate space becomes public.

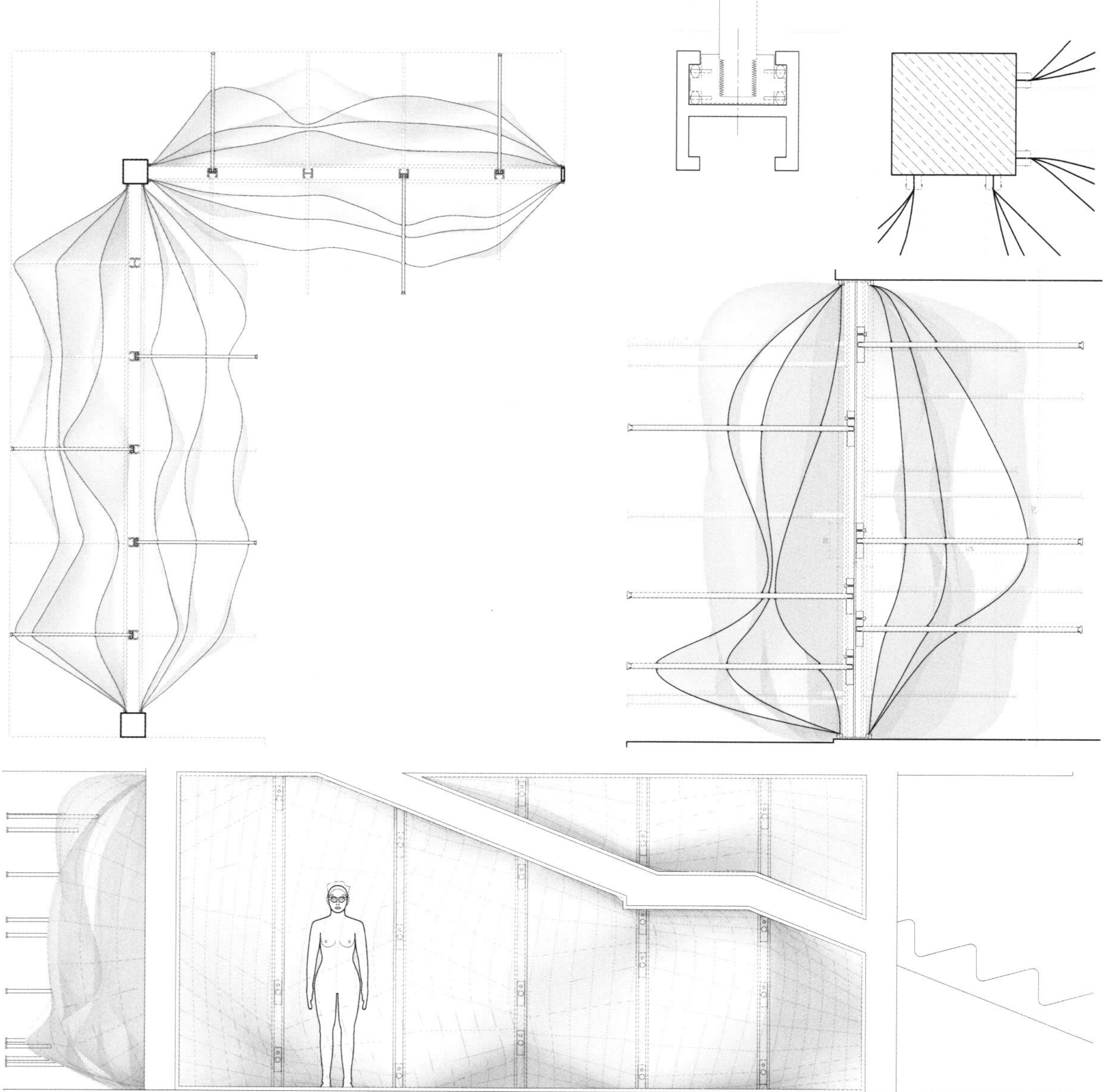

Orlan is a French artist who inhabits her skin by transforming it with surgeries and procedures. Similarly, the walls of this structure are a series of transparent fabric layers that allow Orlan to recompose the building into new spaces, extending and modifying them for her own uses.

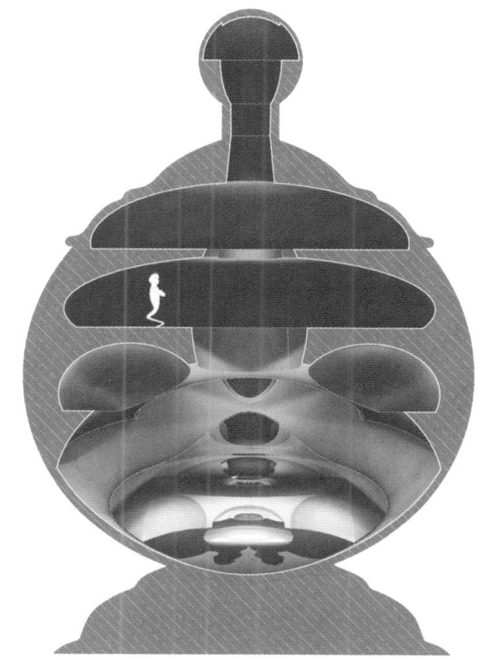

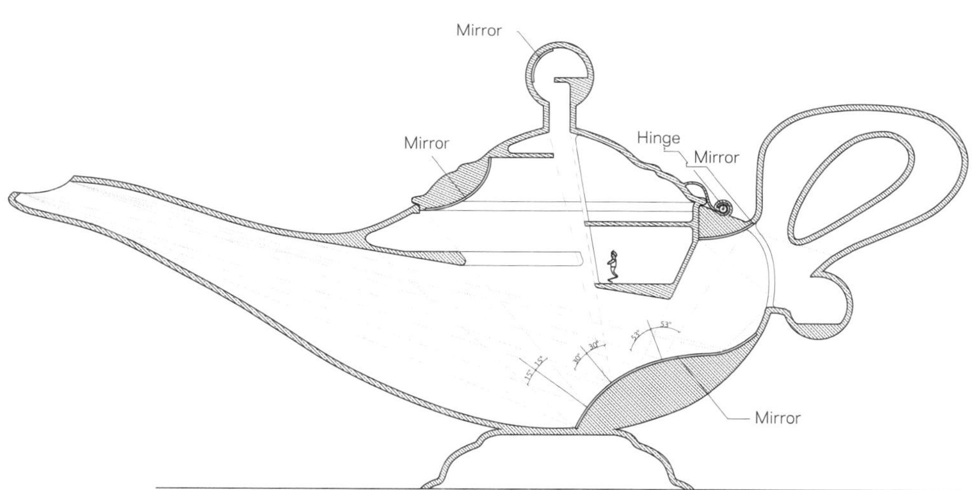

Genie lives inside an oil lamp. The only opening that admits light to the inside is the hole for the flame. Bulging mirrors in the rooms inside the lamp allow light to permeate the house.

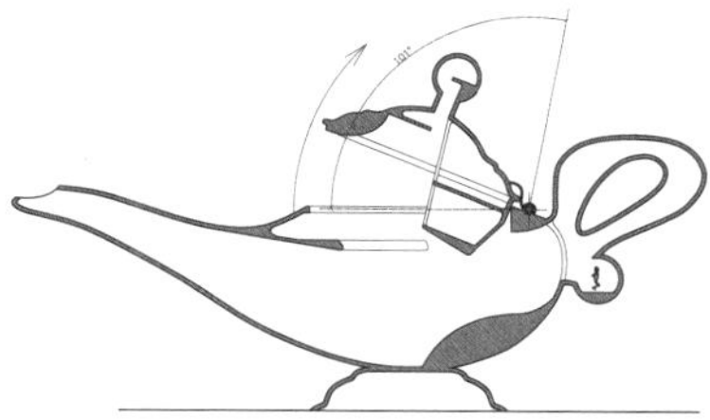

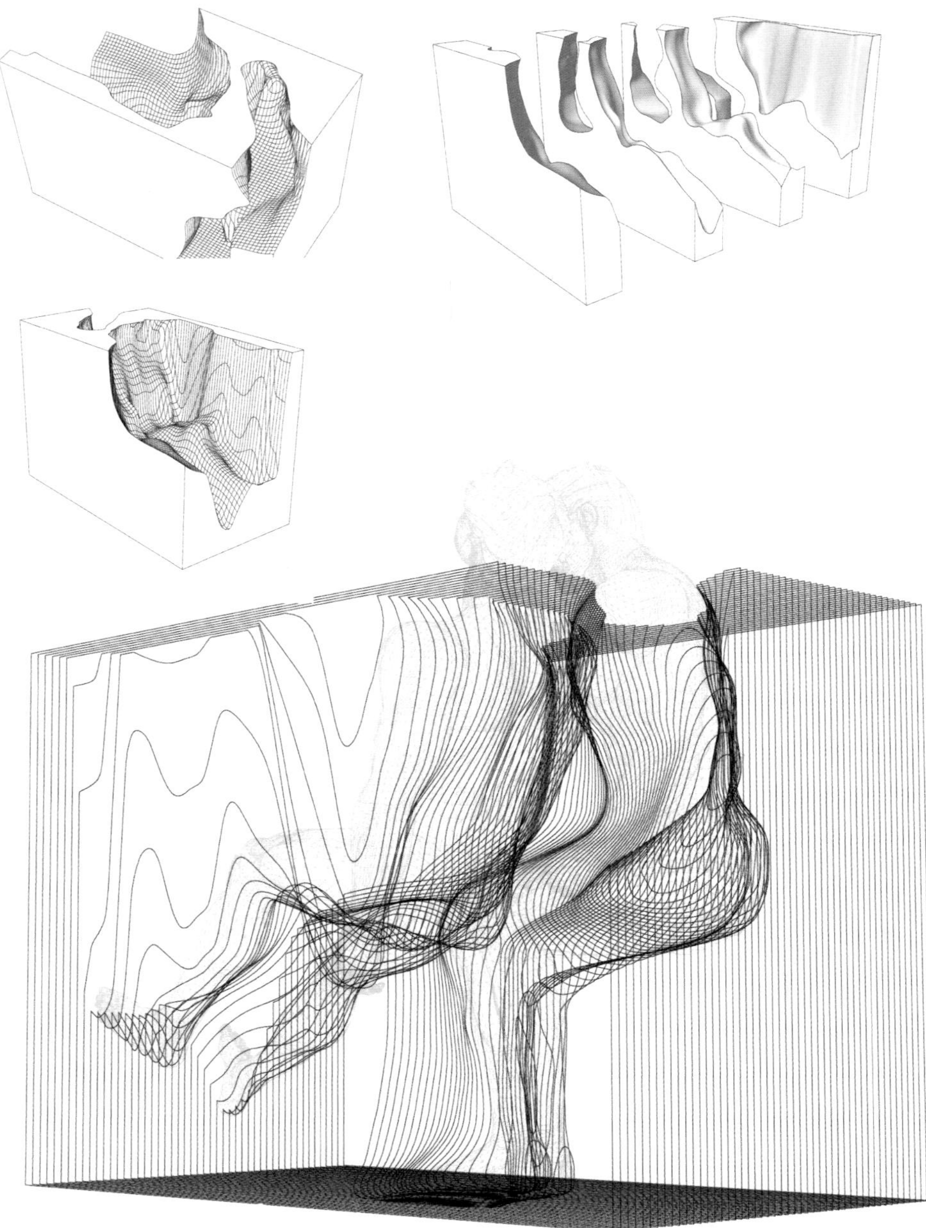

Dracula would like to sit comfortably while having a drink. This double-molded armchair supports his victim's body while he enjoys a taste.

living room

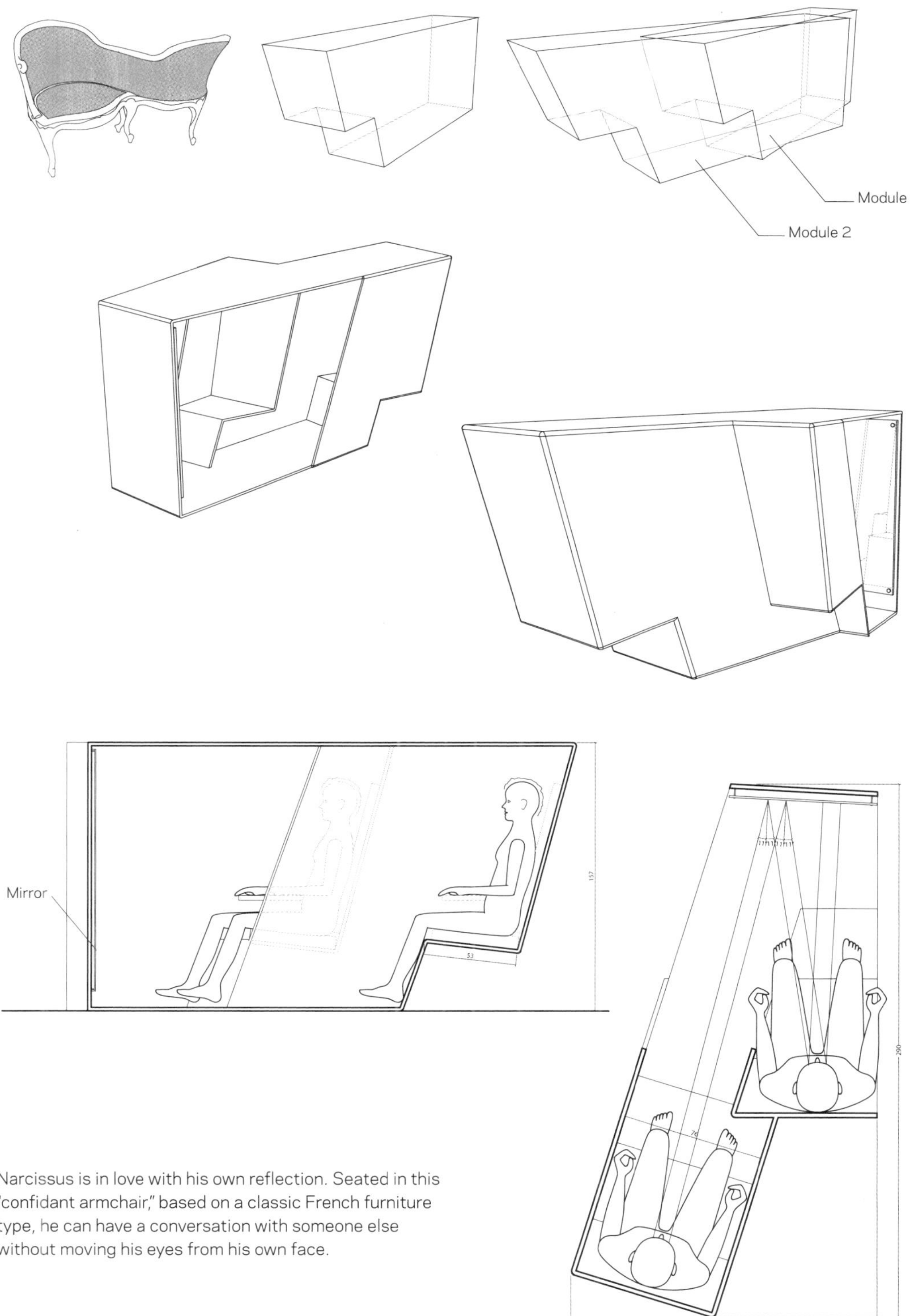

Narcissus is in love with his own reflection. Seated in this "confidant armchair," based on a classic French furniture type, he can have a conversation with someone else without moving his eyes from his own face.

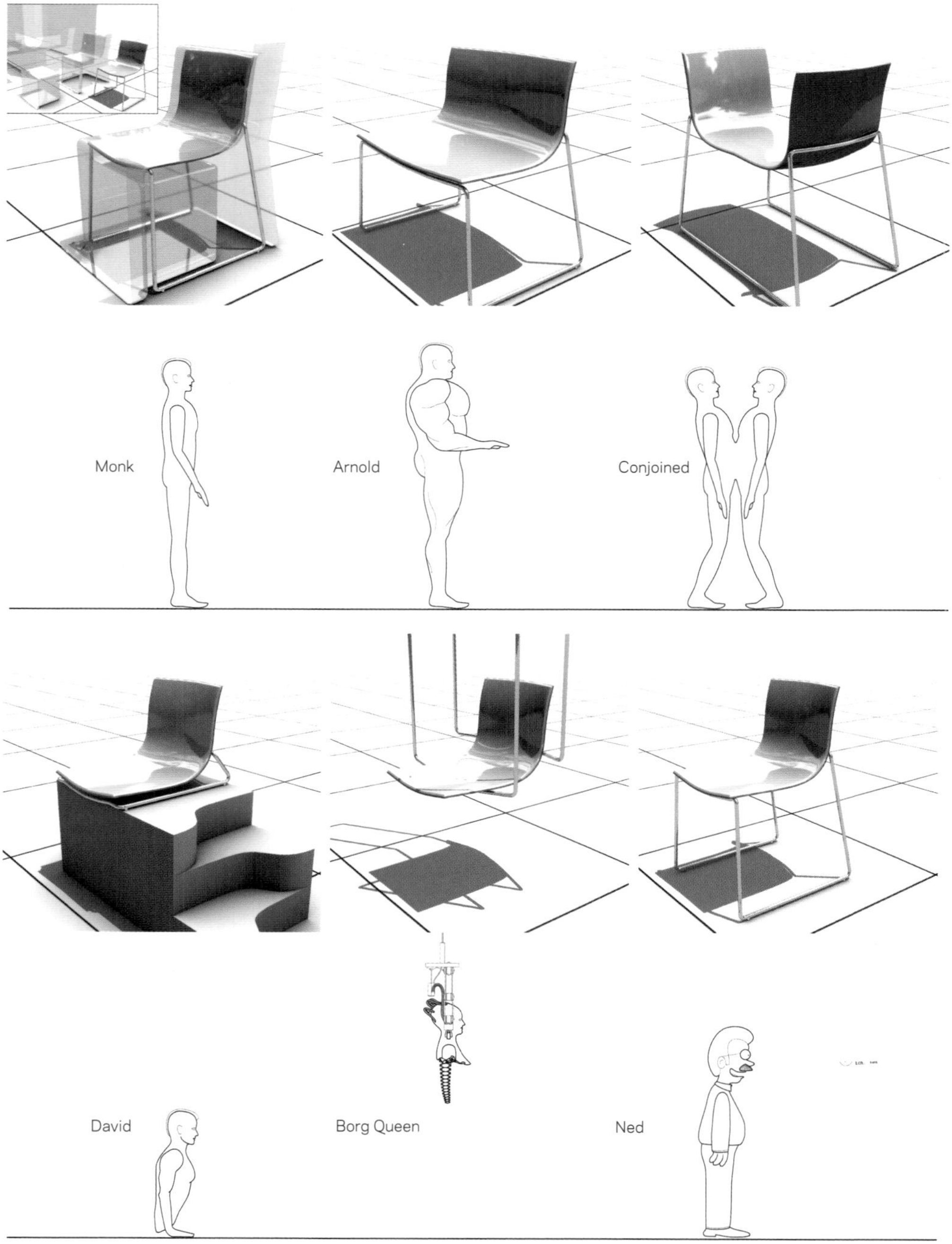

Monk

Arnold

Conjoined

David

Borg Queen

Ned

A recomposed family with multiple singularities should be able to dine together at the same table. Here, each chair has been specially designed for a specific user, resulting in variations on an initial model.

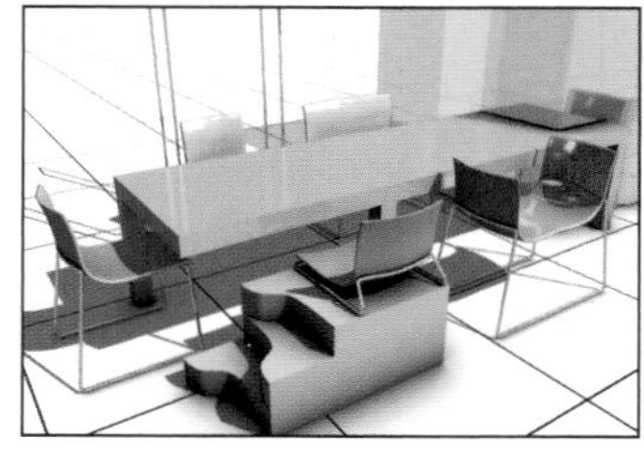

dining room and kitchen

Alice has followed the white rabbit and entered a space opposite her own multiphase reality: the housewife's Wonderland. The kitchen shown here is the product of one of the world's most "thinking standard" companies, and it was designed with its web tool. It is the counterpoint of this research on nonstandards.

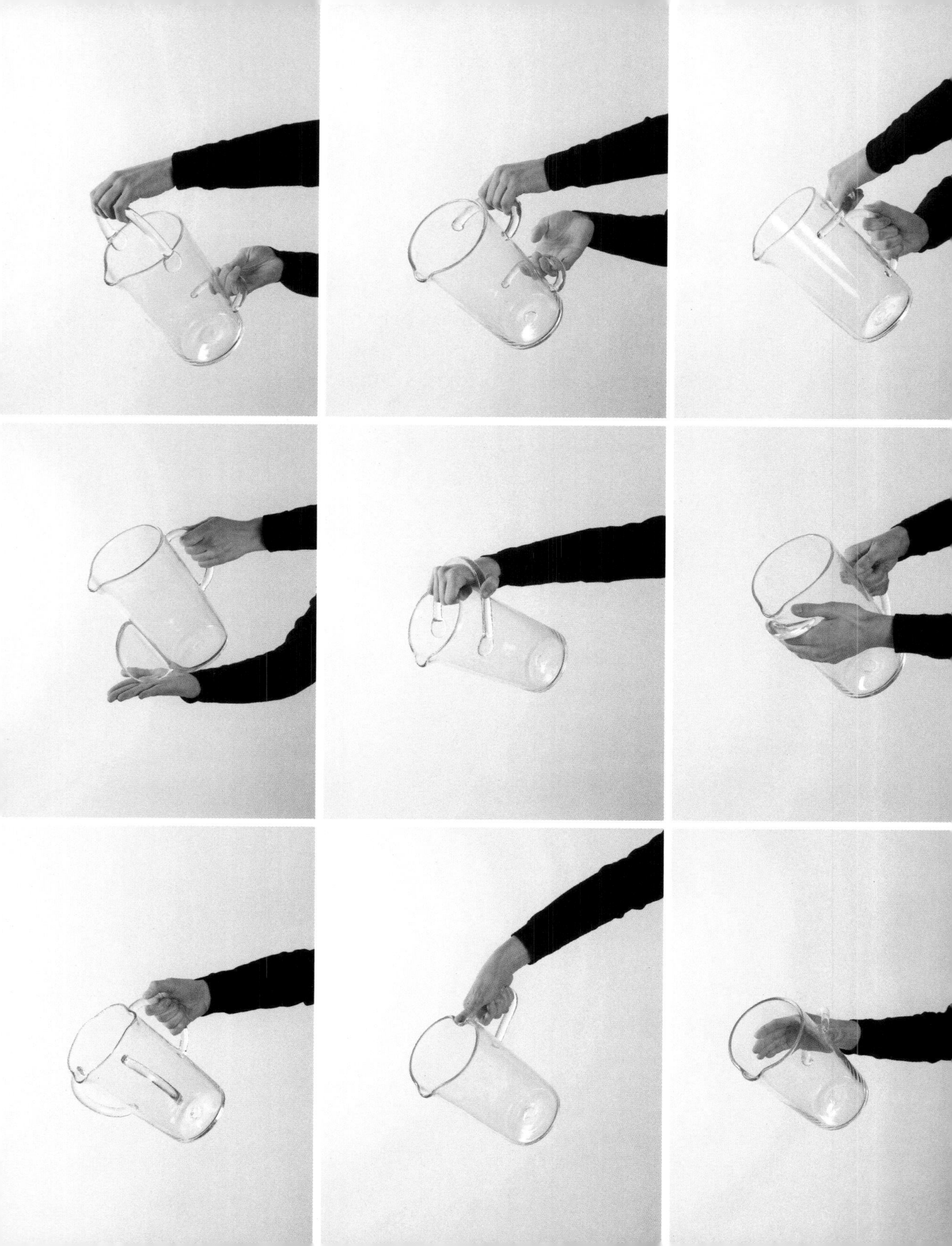

handle

The word *handle* is both a noun and a verb. As a physical thing, a handle invites human grasp. It is a point of connection between people and products. From the molded grip of a bicycle to the delicate loop of a teacup, handles are examples of what cognitive psychologists call AFFORDANCES: features of the environment that trigger or invite specific behaviors or actions. A thoughtfully designed handle feels right in the hand; a poorly designed one provokes pain and discomfort.

The verb *to handle* means to feel, touch, or manipulate with the hands. The objects on the following pages explore handling as an active, lived exchange between creatures and things. In each of these projects, designers have invited USERS to touch, grasp, hold, push, squeeze, or otherwise implement an object in order to achieve goals of their own.

Nine Ways to Use a Pitcher, 2013. Designed by Leon Ransmeier (American, b. 1979). Manufactured by GlassLab, Corning Museum of Glass (USA). Handblown glass. Courtesy of the designer. Photography: Ransmeier, Inc.

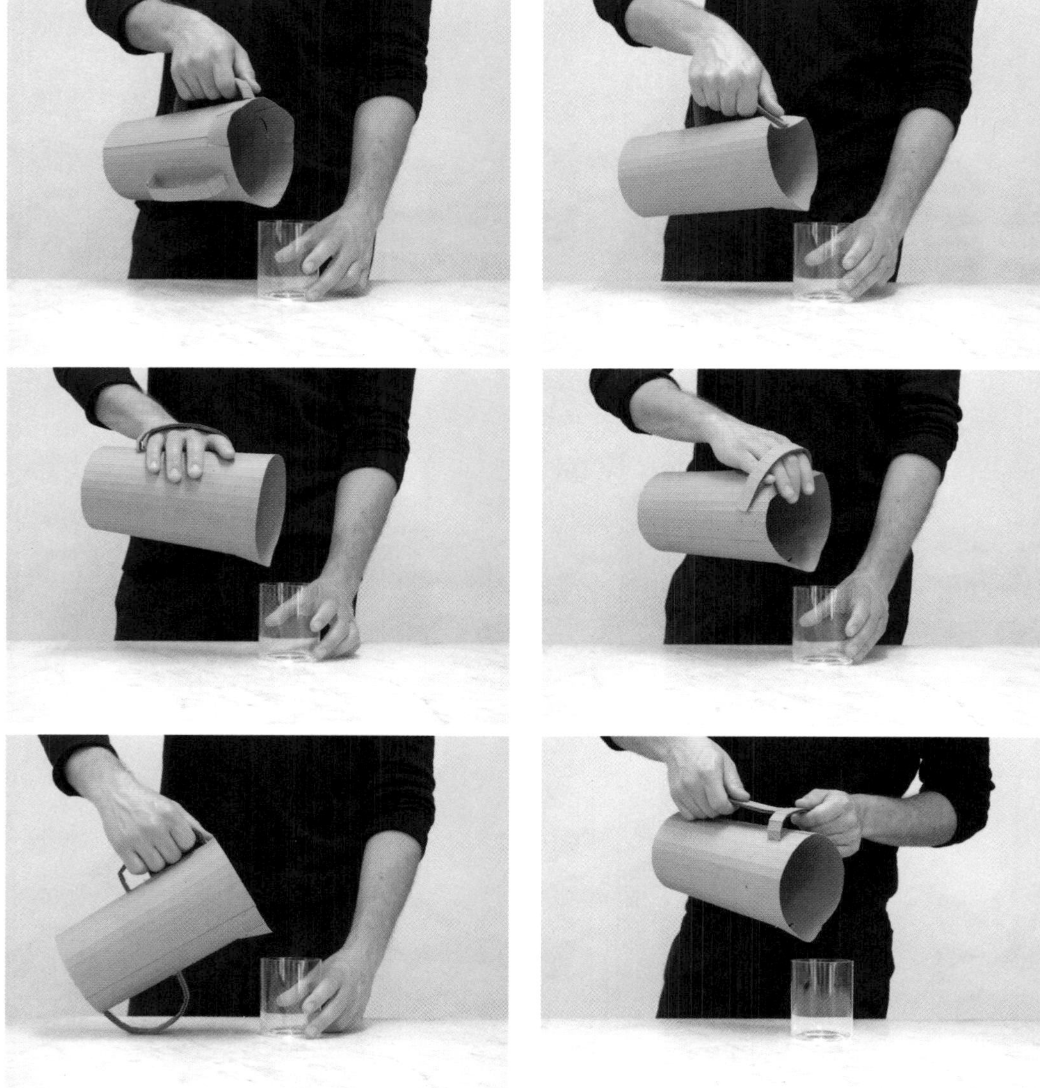

Each handle configuration in this series of pitchers affords a different set of behaviors from users. By starting with an archetypal, nearly generic vessel, Ransmeier focuses our attention on the elementary language of the handle and its communication with the human body. Ransmeier started by making prototypes in cardboard that established the basic shape and performance of each vessel. Over a period of several days in July 2012, he worked with artisans from GlassLab, a mobile hot-glass studio operated by the Corning Museum of Glass, to translate his initial prototypes into glass. He returned to the museum's glass-blowing studio in Corning, New York, the following year to create the full set of pitchers.

Nine Ways to Use a Pitcher Prototypes, 2013. Designed by Leon Ransmeier (American, b. 1979). Cardboard. Courtesy of the designer. Photography: Ransmeier, Inc.

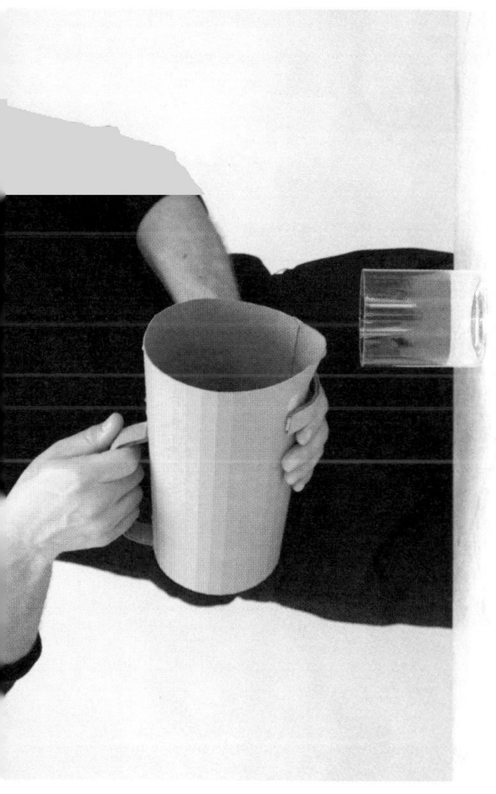

Whereas the cardboard handles in the prototypes are conducive to ribbonlike forms, the final handles are round. Ransmeier explains that glass "really likes to be round. It's a radial material, it's always spinning, and it's always being turned. And so because of that, the round cane handles feel a bit more natural, and they feel like they fit in your hand a little bit more nicely as well."

Nine Ways to Use a Pitcher, 2013. Designed by Leon Ransmeier (American, b. 1979). Manufactured by GlassLab, Corning Museum of Glass (USA). Handblown glass. Courtesy of the designer. Photography: Ransmeier, Inc.

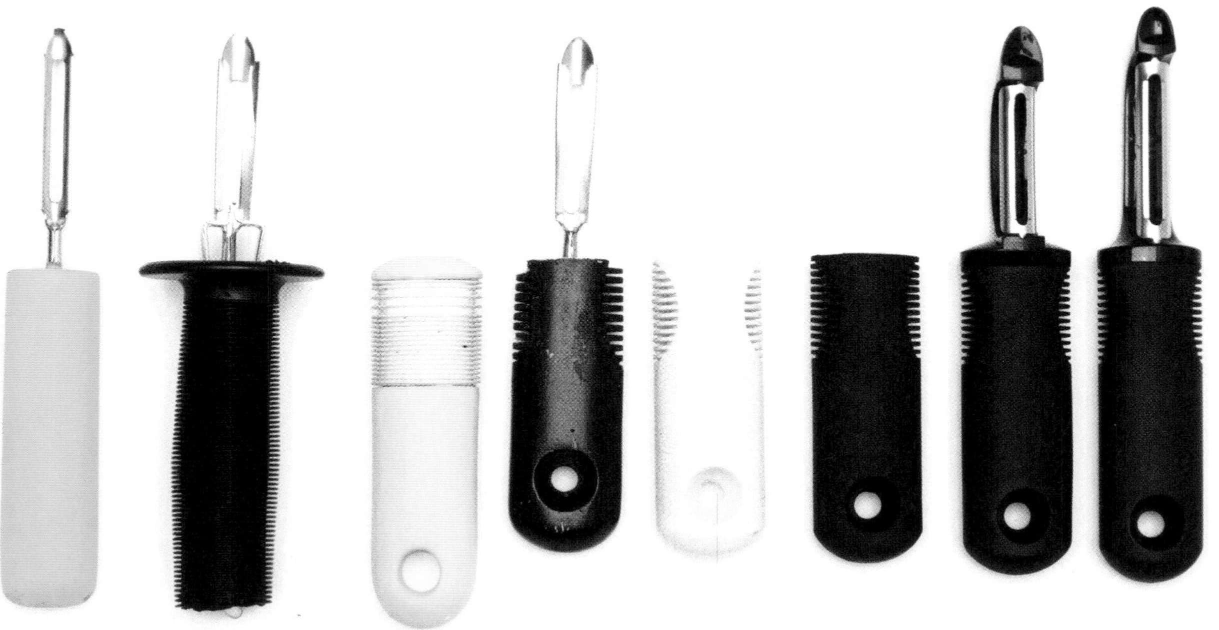

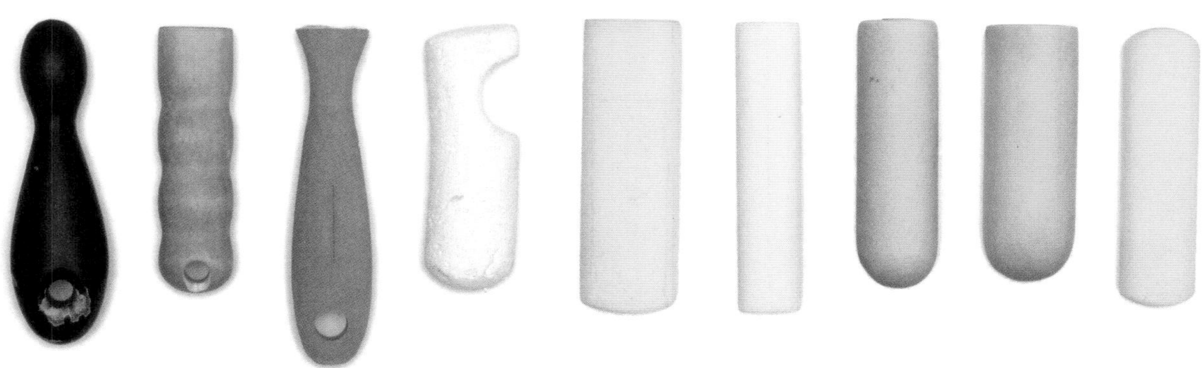

The OXO brand of kitchen tools was born when retired kitchenware designer Sam Farber began working with his wife, Betsey Farber, to create clay models of implements with thick, easy-to-grasp handles. Betsey suffered from arthritis, which made it painful to use an everyday vegetable peeler. Sam then partnered with Smart Design to develop the OXO Good Grips line.

The design team created dozens of handle prototypes out of materials including wood, rubber, plastic, and foam. The designers laid them out on a table to test and explore. Among the wooden and plastic prototypes was a standard rubber bicycle handle, which team members kept picking up and handling. That rubber handle became a key inspiration for the final product line. The OXO brand

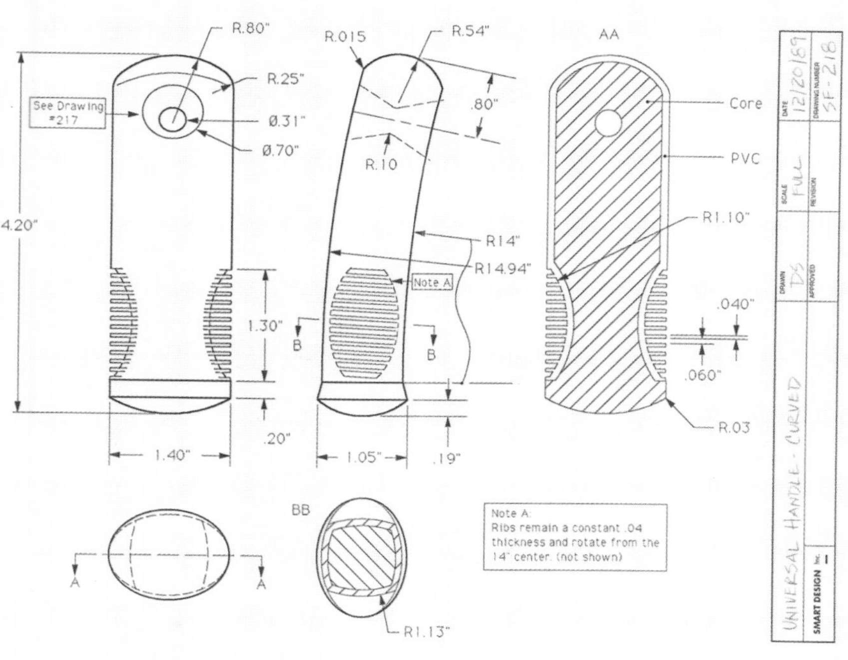

Good Grips Kitchen Tools, Prototypes, and Drawing, ca. 1990. Designed by Smart Design (USA). Design directors: Davin Stowell, Daniel Formosa. Team members: Tucker Viemeister, Stephen Russak, Stephen Allendorf, Michael Calahan, Jürgen Laub, Stephen Wahl. Manufactured by OXO (USA). Stainless steel, Santoprene (thermoplastic rubber), carved foam, plastic, wood, plaster, polypropylene, graphite on pre-printed white wove paper. Collection Cooper Hewitt, Smithsonian Design Museum, 1992-52-1/10, 25; 2011-50-1/9, 11/20; 2011-50-24. Photography (drawing): Matt Flynn.

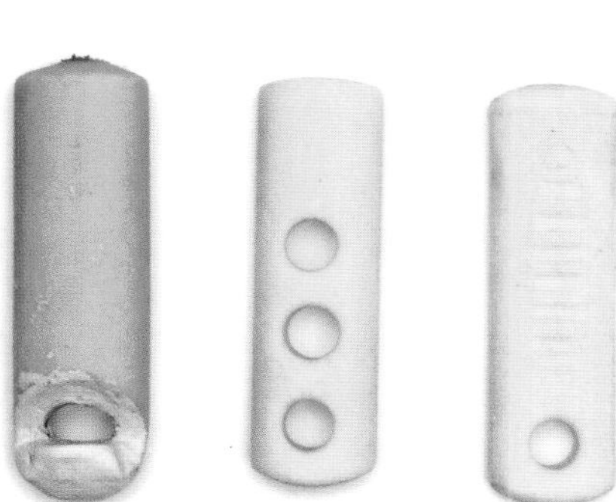

now encompasses a broad range of products, including medical devices and tools for small children, and the chubby, black rubber handle has become an icon of comfort and ease of use. OXO embraces a core principle of universal design: that improving access for disabled users improves the experience of those of ordinary ability.

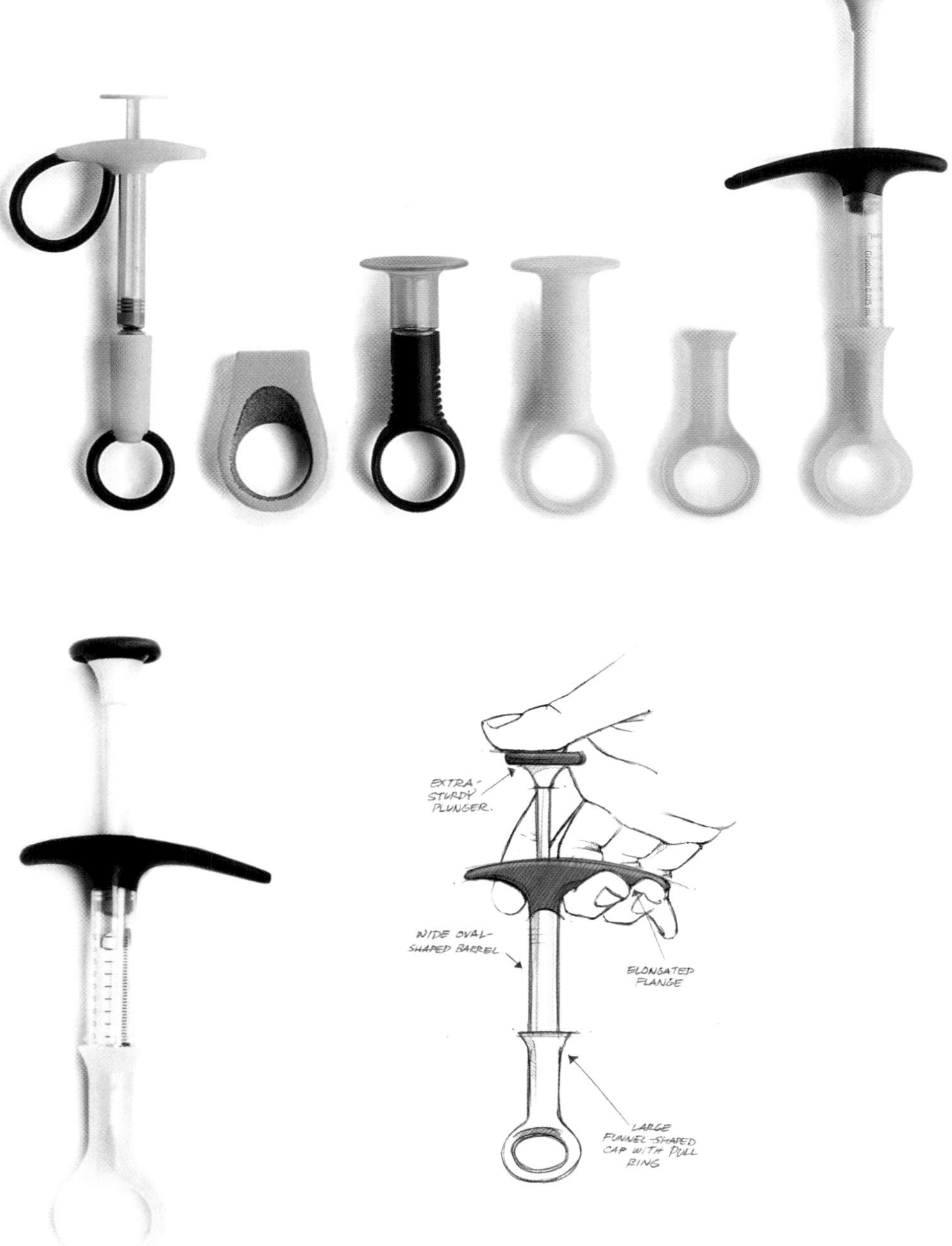

Cimzia Home Injection Experience Prototypes, 2010. Designed by Smart Design (USA). Manufactured by UCB Pharmaceuticals (Belgium). Polycarbonate plastic. Courtesy of the designers.

Cimzia is a medication for people suffering from rheumatoid arthritis. RA patients are sensitive to sharp objects and have 25 to 30 percent of the hand and finger strength of healthy people. Smart Design created numerous prototypes to improve the patient experience and encourage compliance. The three-finger flange and soft, large thumb pad reduce contact with pointy elements. The plunger enables users to apply greater effective force. The product accommodates fourteen different grip styles, and the oval-shaped barrel resists spinning when grasped. The looped needle cover is easy to remove; its flared shape minimizes recoil and thus helps prevent accidental sticks. The product's perceived ease and comfort reinforces its proven functionality.

***One of the very last times I touched my grandmother*, 2003.**
By Elinor Carucci (American, born Israel, 1971). Photograph. Courtesy of the artist/INSTITUTE (USA).

Photographer Elinor Carucci has chronicled the life of her family through intimate images of the varied textures of human lives and bodies.

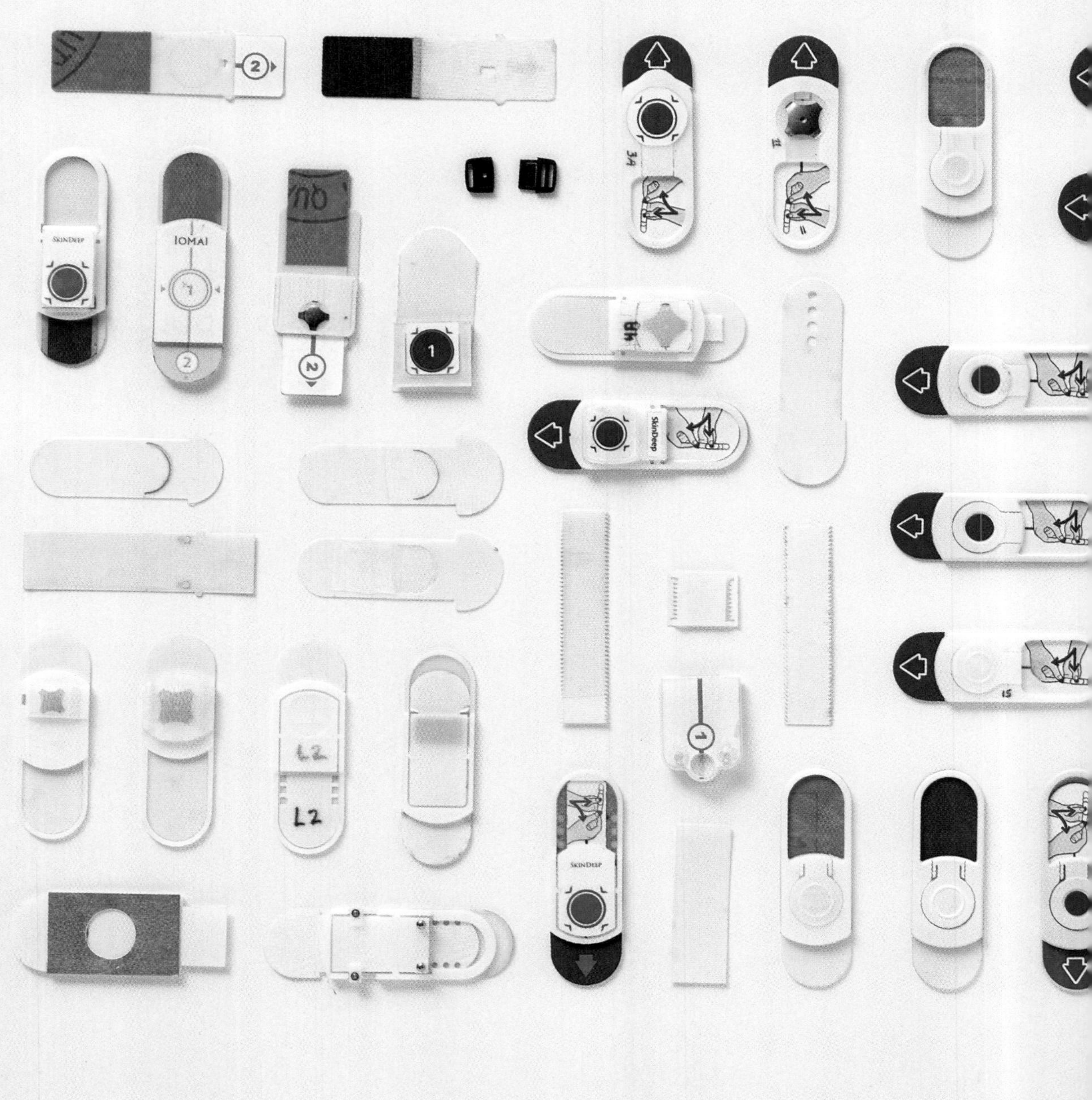

In 2006 delivering vaccines to patients required a skilled technician and a sterile needle. Iomai, a company that specialized in transcutaneous immunization, commissioned IDEO to develop a user-centered needle-free vaccine-delivery system. Testing determined that forty microns of skin—equivalent to the thickness of a plastic bag—must be removed to prepare skin for the vaccine. IDEO produced hundreds of prototypes to test ways that users could disrupt their skin and accurately place the patch over the prepared area. After many rounds of prototyping and user testing, IDEO created a design that uses sandpaper to remove the top layer of skin, a bistable button to provide both visible and audible feedback, and ink to leave behind guides for the patch

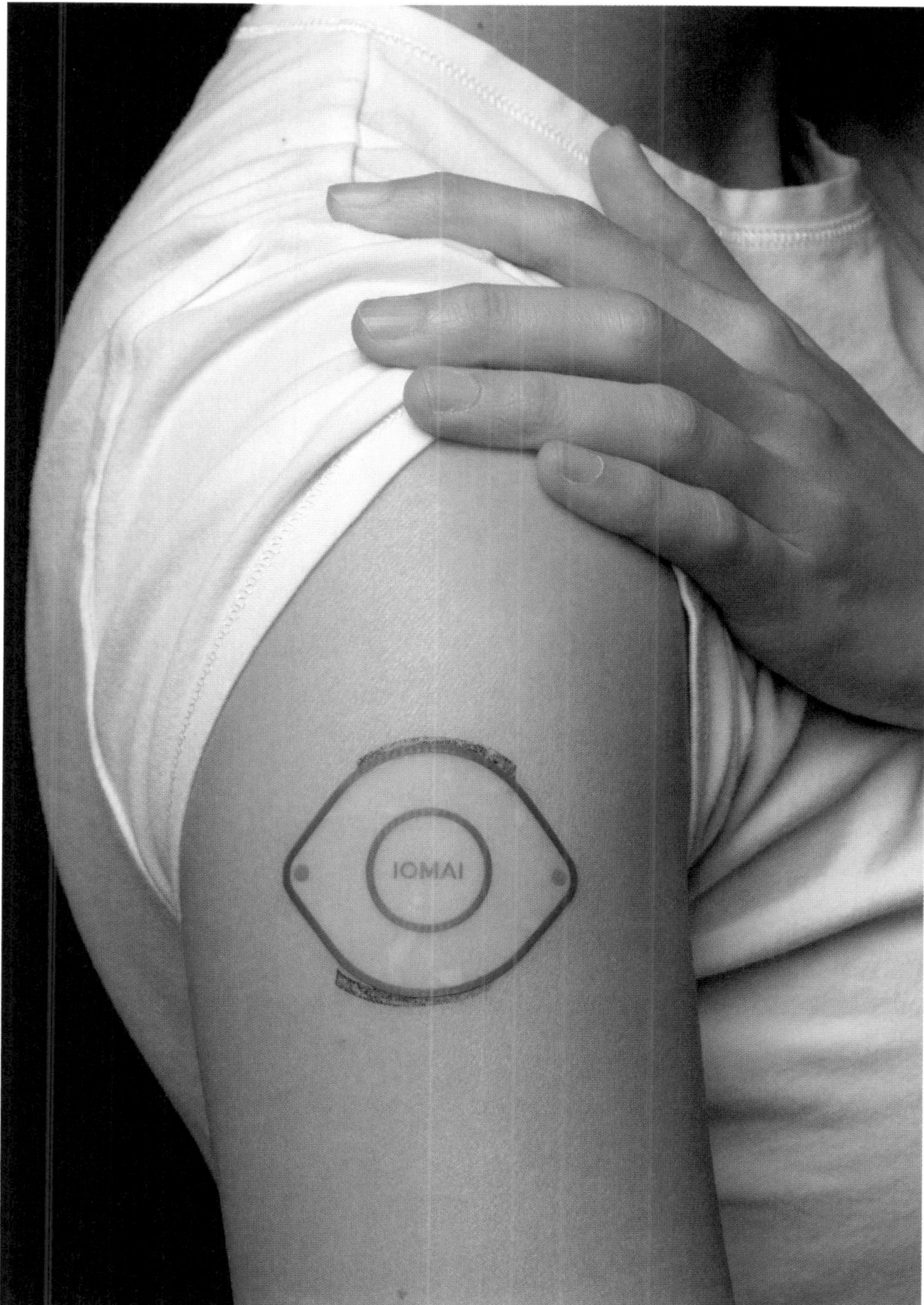

Iomai Needle-Free Vaccine Delivery Prototypes, 2006. Designed by IDEO (USA). Bistable spring steel, medical-grade sandpaper, woven adhesive tape, laminate graphics, plastic sheet, 3D-printed ABS plastic fasteners. Courtesy of the designers.

placement. The final design is a production-ready model for a device that could revolutionize vaccine delivery. The patch has a stable shelf life and can be shipped through the mail and self-applied by users; it is designed for ease of manufacture with standard materials and processes. The product thus addresses such urgent human needs as pandemic vaccination and large-scale vaccination in emerging economies. Iomai completed its IPO in 2006 and was funded under a contract with the Department of Health and Human Services directed toward its pandemic flu program. Iomai was acquired by Intercell in August 2008.

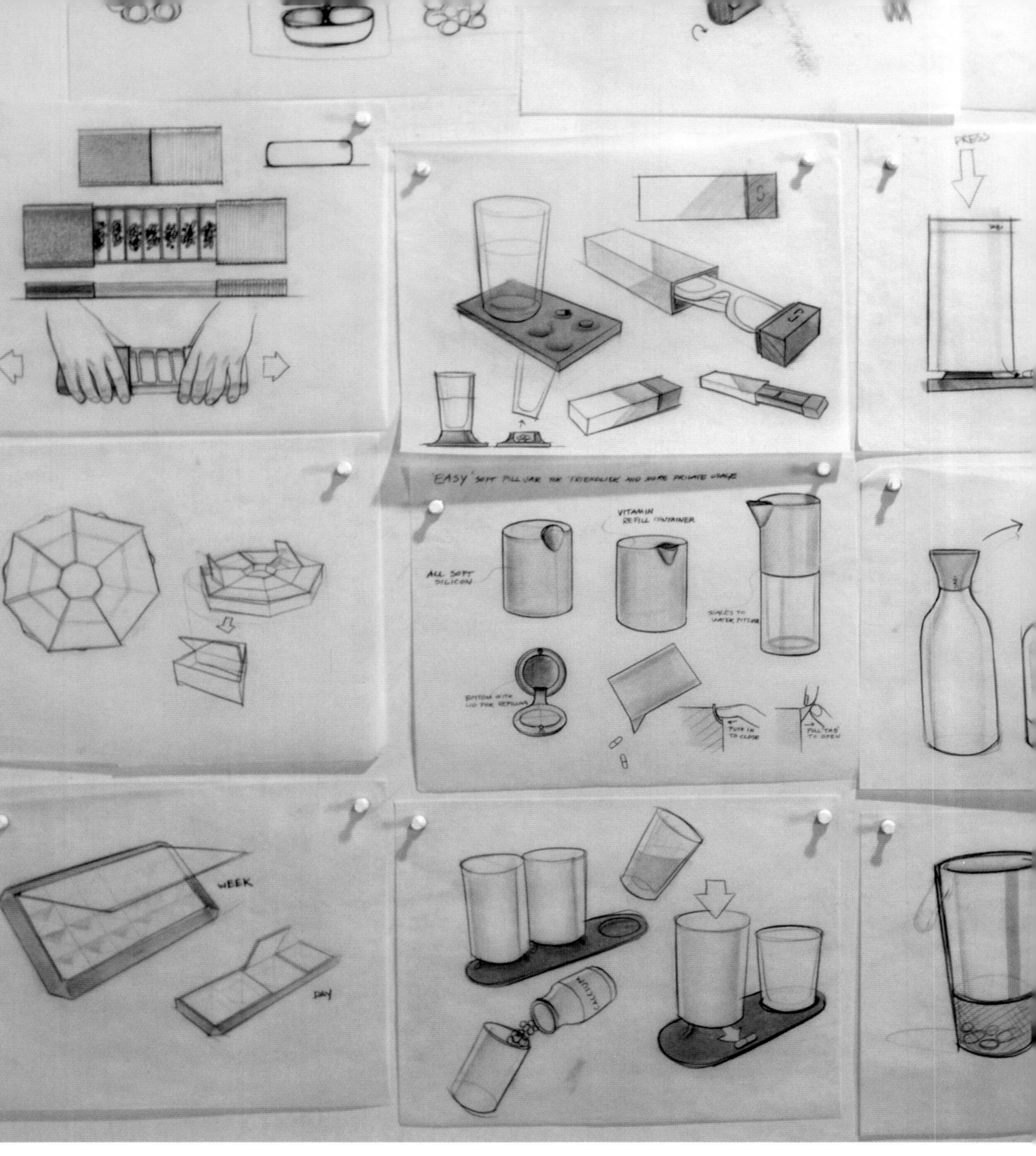

Sabi THRIVE products encourage compliance by making pill use a more positive experience. In the words of Sabi founder Assaf Wand, "These stealthy, whimsical products take the shame out of pill use." The designers' process drawings explore various directions for integrating pill use into daily life, including containers for organizing pills, dispensing pills, and carrying pills and water together. The FOLIO pill carrier looks like a personal notebook, providing privacy, convenience, and a tailored appearance. The SPLIT Pill Cutter has no metal blade, which means it doesn't have to be sold behind the counter in drugstores; a soft surface inside the cutter allows the plastic blade to cut through hard pills with ordinary palm pressure and provides the user with haptic feedback.

Sabi THRIVE Pill Organizers and Accessories, 2011. Designed by Yves Béhar (Swiss, b. 1967), fuseproject (USA). Manufactured by Sabi (USA). Plastic (ABS, TPE, PET, PP, and others). Courtesy of Sabi.

Sabi seeks direct feedback from users. The company learned that many people were using the CARAFE for dietary supplements, requiring a bigger storage cap; users wanted to put the larger cap in the dishwasher, and they wanted to be able to sip from the water container without removing the cap. Sabi incorporated these user suggestions into the CARAFE grande.

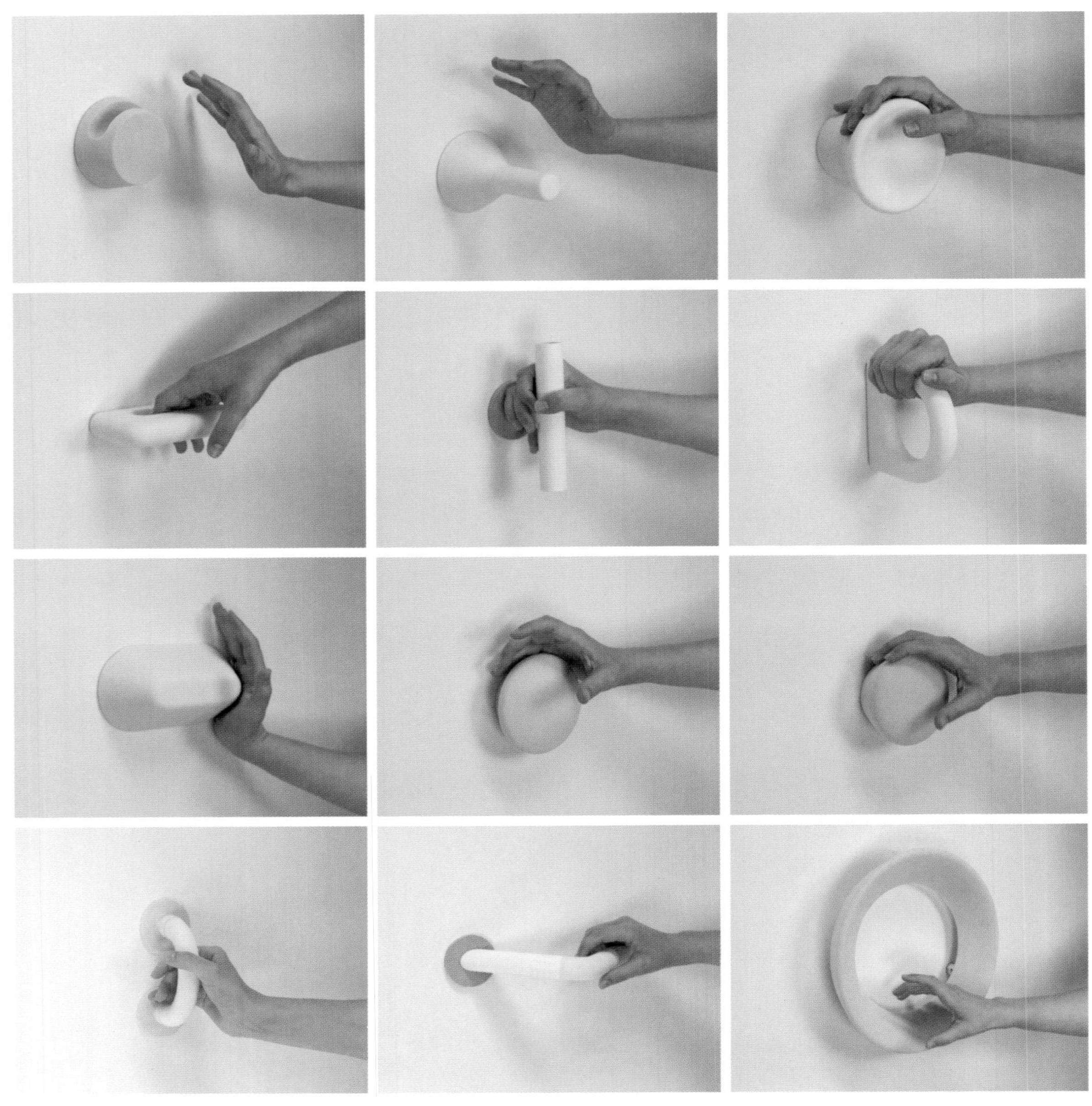

The Sabi HOLD is a no-stigma approach to helping people get in and out of the bath or shower. The easy-to-install fixture also functions as a towel holder, which integrates it into the bathroom decor. The prototypes reveal how the designers explored a variety of handle shapes before arriving at HOLD's serene circular form. The final product is comfortable to grasp and intuitive to use while avoiding reference to conventional grab bars. Seventy percent of bathroom falls occur getting in and out of the bath or shower. Grab bars have become an important feature of fall-prevention programs. Studies show that users typically employ grab bars to steady their balance as they get in and out of the bath, rather than to pull the body up or lower it down.

Sabi HOLD Bathroom Prototypes, 2014. Designed by MAP (UK), founded by Edward Barber (British, b. 1969) and Jay Osgerby (British, b. 1969). Polyurethane model board, sintered nylon. Manufactured for Sabi (USA). Courtesy of Sabi.

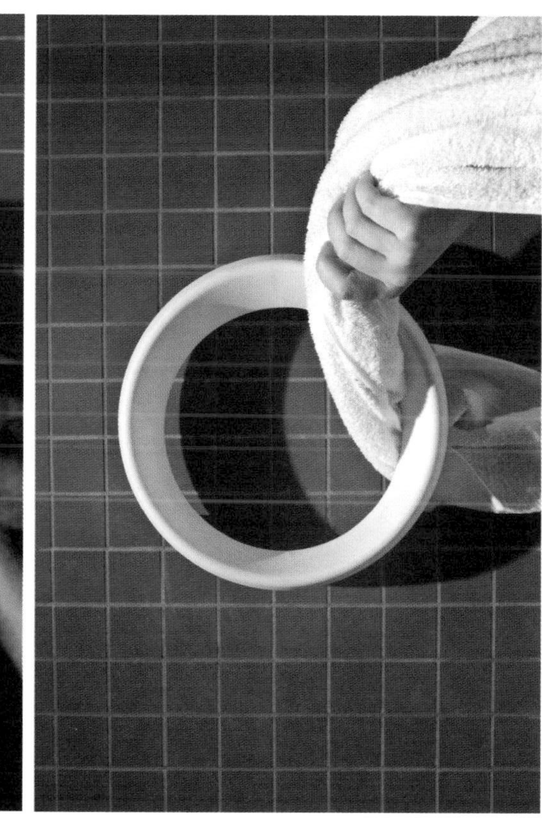

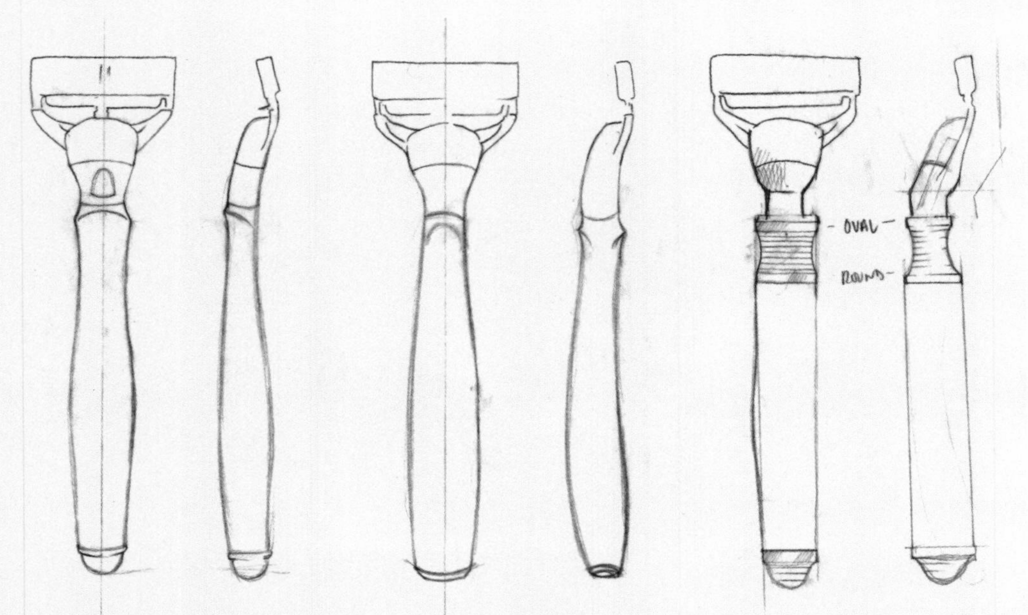

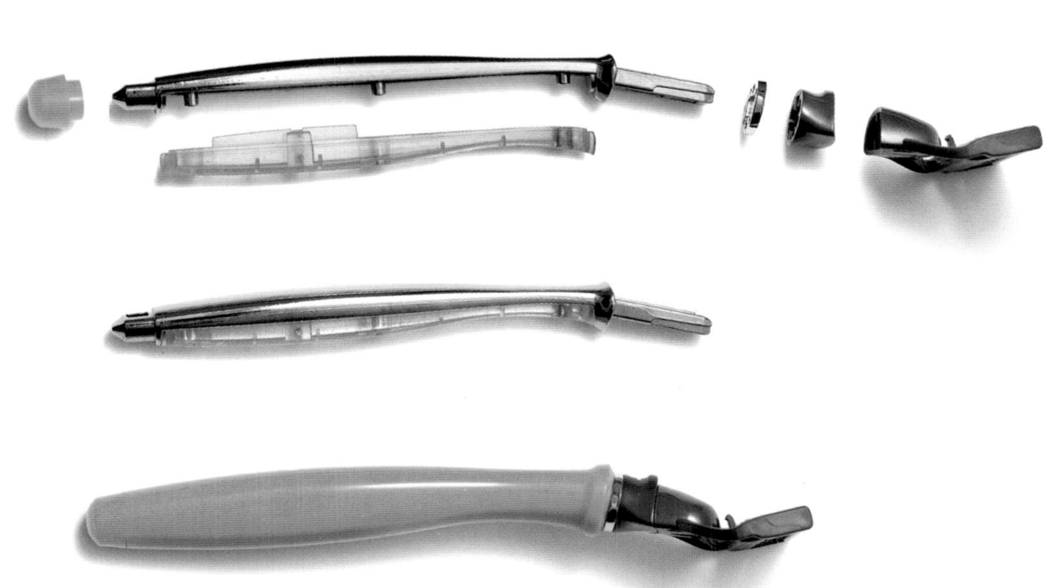

Andy Katz-Mayfield was tired of paying high prices for shaving products that didn't appeal to him as a user. He and his partner, Jeff Raider, set out to build a brand dedicated to customer experience and predicated on high-quality, thoughtfully designed products delivered at fair prices. They worked with branding agency Partners & Spade and industrial designers Stuart Harvey Lee and Jochen Schaepers of Prime Studio. Lee and Schaepers designed dozens of prototypes in order to create a handle both classic and ergonomic. The drawings and prototypes shown here tested and explored various shapes, finishes, materials, and colors while studying the angle of connection between the product and the user's skin.

Harry's Shaving Drawings and Prototypes, 2013. Designed by Stuart Harvey Lee (British, b. 1965) and Jochen Schaepers (German, b. 1968), Prime Studio (USA). Manufactured for Harry's (USA) by Zhuhai Technique Plastic Container Factory Co., Ltd. (China) and FeinTechnik GmbH Eisfeld (Germany). Painted polymer, ABS, polycarbonate, TPR, stainless steel, chrome-plated zinc alloy, chrome-plated aluminum alloy, brass. Courtesy of Harry's.

1 Concept sketches
2 Internal components
3 First appearance model
4 First factory prototype
5 Surface-finish exploration
6 Cartridge connection optimization
7 Some rejected colors
8 Final Harry's Truman assortment

Left to right, top to bottom: Schaepers and Lee sort through a box of shaving products purchased from local drugstores—the razors are packaged in hard-to-open plastic bubbles and styled with swoopy curves and aerodynamic fins. "Nobody likes this stuff," says Lee. Harry's handles are produced by Zhuhai Technique Plastic Container Factory Co., Ltd. (China). The blades are made by FeinTechnik GmbH Eisfeld (Germany). In 2014, Harry's purchased the German manufacturer, a move designed to make Harry's more competitive with giants like Gillette.

Harry's Shaving Packaging (Winston Set), 2013. Packaging designed by Stuart Harvey Lee (British, b. 1965) and Jochen Schaepers (German, b. 1968), Prime Studio (USA). Branding and graphics designed by Partners & Spade (USA). Manufactured for Harry's (USA) by Zhuhai Technique Plastic Container Factory Co., Ltd. (China) and FeinTechnik GmbH Eisfeld (Germany). ABS, engineered paper. Courtesy of Harry's.

Harry's distributes its products primarily through direct sales on its website (harrys.com). The packaging, made from engineered paper and minimal plastic components, is the user's first point of contact with the physical product. A complete set, which includes a handle, three blades, and Harry's signature shave cream, costs from $15 to $25.

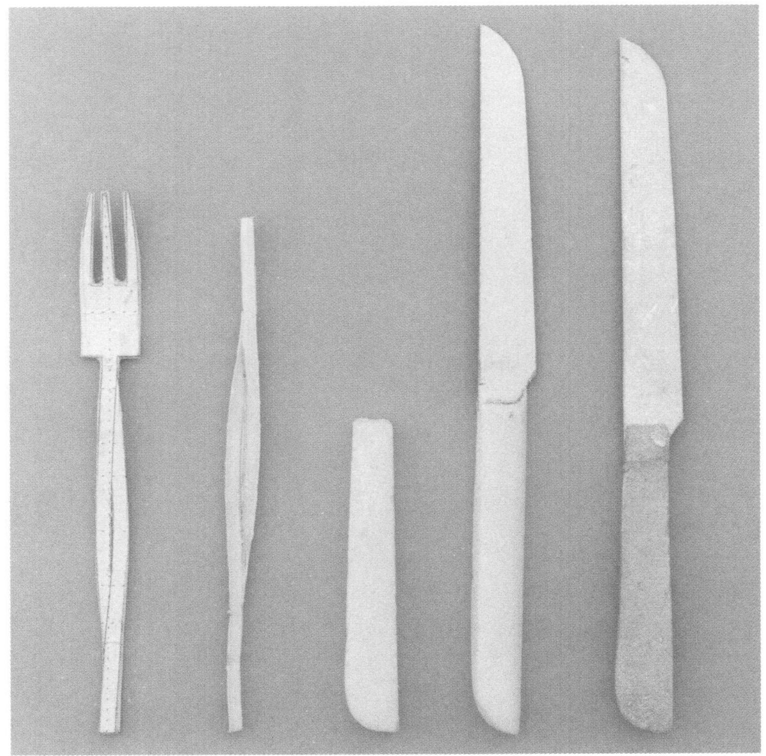

Hybrid Flatware and Prototypes, 2007. Designed by Constantin Boym (Russian, b. 1955) and Laurene Leon Boym (American, b. 1964), Boym Studio (USA). Manufactured by Gourmet Settings (Canada). Foam, foamcore, cardboard, stainless steel. Courtesy of the designers. Photography: Matt Flynn.

Constantin Boym and Laurene Leon Boym seek out new ideas by exploring popular culture and everyday life. In their design process, the Boyms often use existing things as models and inspiration. The series of flatware patterns they created for Gourmet Settings ask questions about function, play, narrative, and iconography. How do users actually live with their flatware? Over time, pieces go astray and matched sets make room for new arrivals. As a household evolves, so too does the mixed company of forks, knives, and spoons that inhabit the kitchen drawer. The Boyms' intentionally mismatched flatware pattern Hybrid emulates the social life of everyday things.

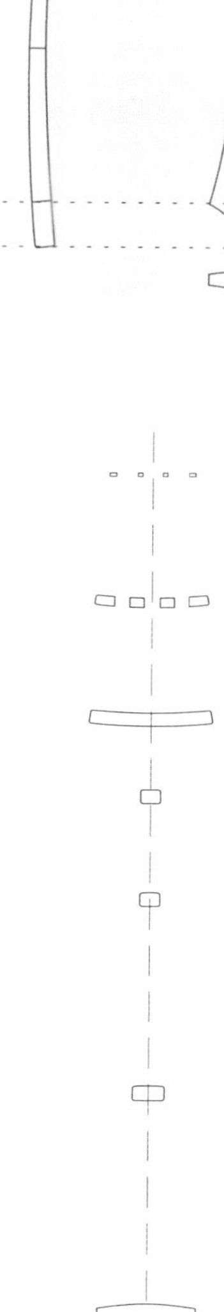

Goth Flatware, Prototypes, and Digital Drawings, 2007. Designed by Constantin Boym (Russian, b. 1955) and Laurene Leon Boym (American, b. 1964), Boym Studio (USA). Manufactured by Gourmet Settings (Canada). 3D-printed plastic, stainless steel. Courtesy of the designers. Photography: Matt Flynn.

Forks and knives play bit parts in many Hollywood horror films. Intrigued with the dark side of kitchen tools, the Boyms created Goth, whose sharp points and accentuated angles make reference to a neo-Gothic aesthetic that has been popular in fashion, art, and music since Victorian times. The flatware pattern thus brings an undercurrent of narrative and drama to the dining experience.

Colonial Ghost Flatware, Source Material, and Prototypes, 2007. Designed by Constantin Boym (Russian, b. 1955) and Laurene Leon Boym (American, b. 1964), Boym Studio (USA). Manufactured by Gourmet Settings (Canada). Plastic, cardboard, foamcore, 3D-printed plastic, stamped metal, stainless steel. Courtesy of the designers. Photography: Matt Flynn.

Initially, the pieces in Colonial Ghost were designed to hang from a rack. (Flatware from Laurene Leon Boym's childhood kitchen inspired the idea.) Although the Boyms later abandoned the rack, they kept the cutout shapes—each form is a "ghost" of an archetypal American flatware style. The cutouts reduce the weight of the pieces and create visual and tactile interest.

GS Army Flatware, Source Material, and Prototypes, 2007. Designed by Constantin Boym (Russian, born 1955) and Laurene Leon Boym (American, b. 1964), Boym Studio (USA). Manufactured by Gourmet Settings (Canada). Plastic, cardboard, foamcore, 3D-printed plastic, stamped metal, stainless steel. Courtesy of the designers. Photography: Matt Flynn.

The details of GS Army are inspired by cheap flatware purchased in an army surplus store. The designers were attracted to these simple, utilitarian pieces stamped out of thin metal. GS Army's raised lip thus makes subtle reference to military mess kits while providing an elegant, tactile frame around the handle of each piece.

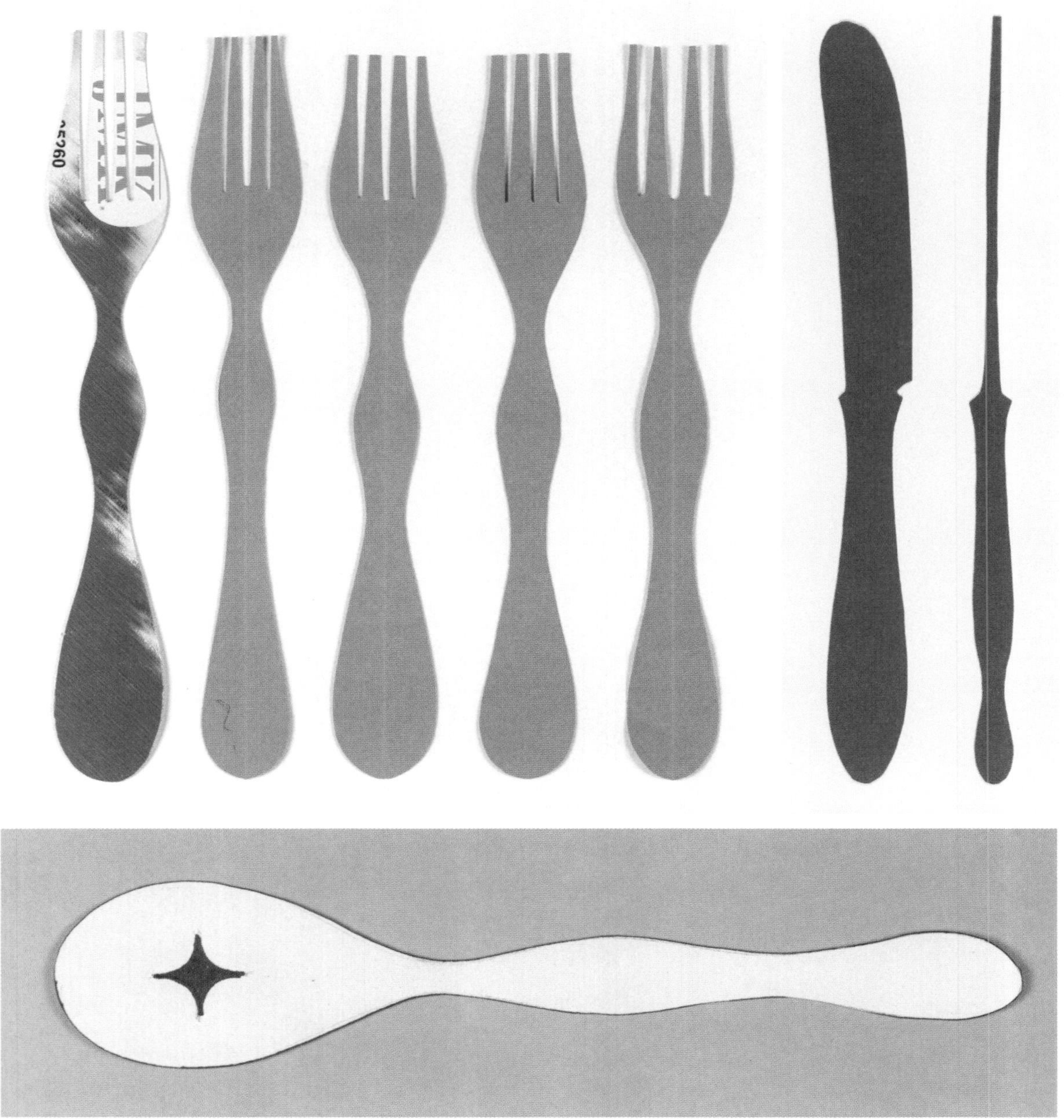

Born in Hungary in 1906, Eva Zeisel endured two world wars and the Soviet revolution. She spent sixteen months in a Russian prison and escaped Nazi persecution before immigrating to the U.S. in 1938. Best known for her ceramics, Zeisel called herself a modernist with a little *m*. She rejected doctrinaire geometries in favor of fluid forms and counterforms. Throughout her career, Zeisel employed cut paper in her design process. These cutouts enabled her to refine and emphasize the curving silhouettes that are the hallmark of her work. Her Eva flatware, created for the retailer Crate and Barrel, is among her last designs. Olivia Barry, Zeisel's design assistant, produced these cut-paper designs with Zeisel's guidance.

Cutouts: Designs for Eva Flatware, 2012. Designed by Eva Zeisel (American, born Hungary, 1906–2011) with Olivia Barry (American, born Canada, 1974). Cut paper, graphite. Collection Cooper Hewitt, Smithsonian Design Museum, gift of the Estate of Eva Zeisel, 2014-8-38/41, 2014-8-43/57, and 2014-8-60. Photography: Matt Flynn.

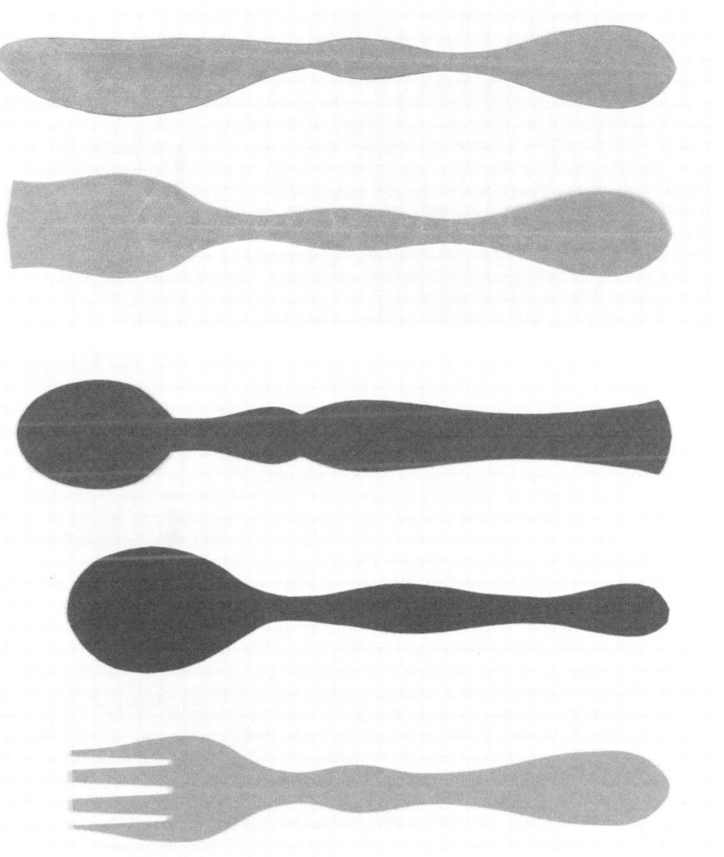

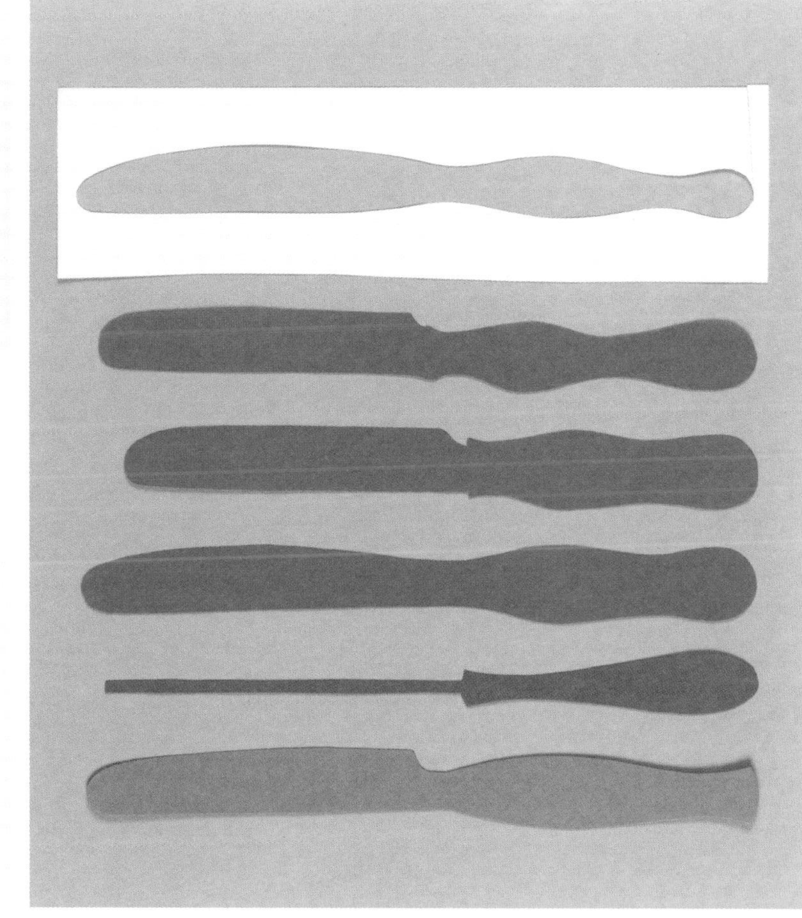

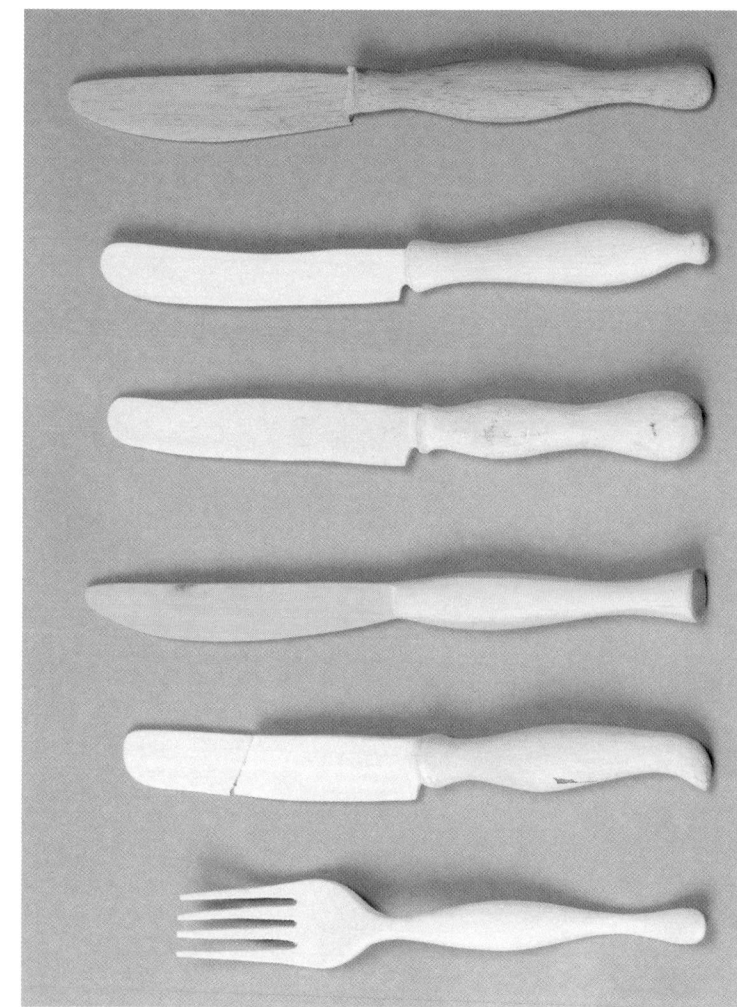

Eva Flatware Prototypes, 2012. Designed by Eva Zeisel (American, born Hungary, 1906–2011) with Olivia Barry (American, born Canada, 1974). Made by Olivia Barry (2014-8-3/9,11); Yamazaki Tableware, Inc. (2014-8-10,12,13). Carved and painted balsa wood. Collection Cooper Hewitt, Smithsonian Design Museum, gift of the Estate of Eva Zeisel, 2014-8-3/6,8/13. Photography: Ellen McDermott.

Eva Flatware, 2012. Designed by Eva Zeisel (American, born Hungary, 1906–2011) with Olivia Barry (American, born Canada, 1974). Manufactured by Yamazaki Tableware, Inc. (Japan) for Crate and Barrel (USA). Forged stainless steel. Collection Cooper Hewitt, Smithsonian Design Museum, gift of Crate and Barrel, 2014-8-1/5. Photography: Ellen McDermott.

A model maker produced three-dimensional prototypes based on Zeisel and Barry's paper cutouts. The prototypes were the basis of digital drawings Barry created for manufacturing.

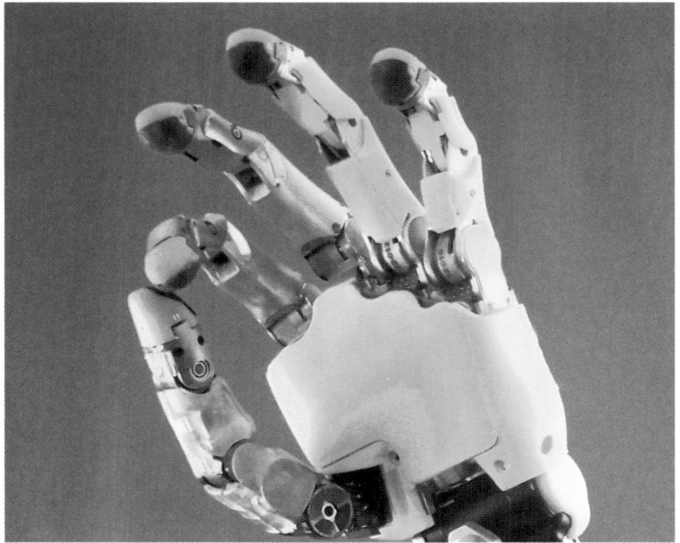

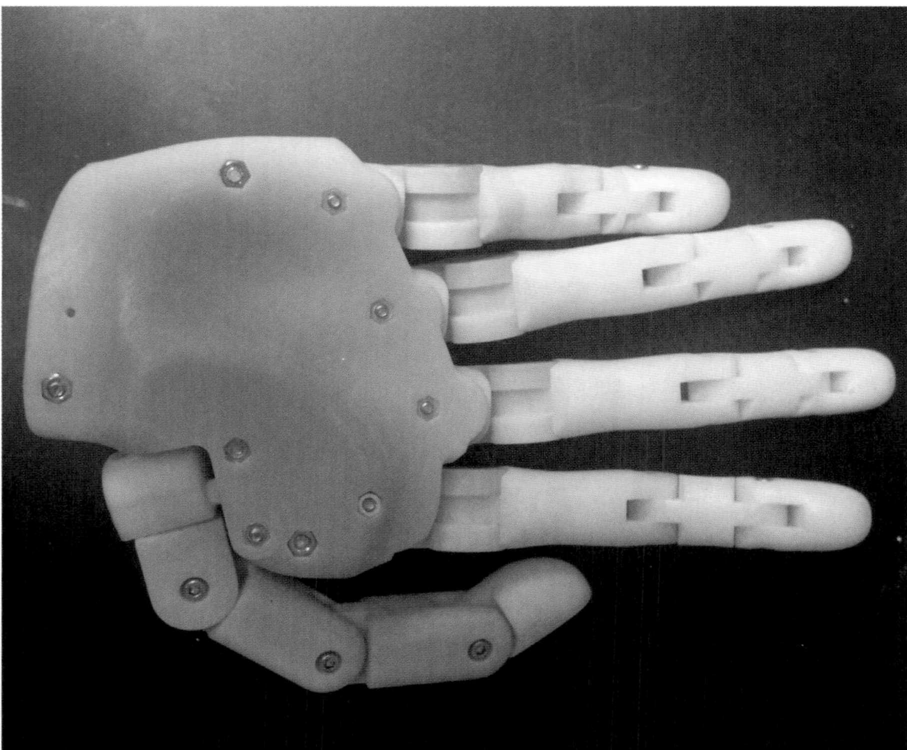

Modular Prosthetic Limb (MPL) v.1.0, 2009, and MPL Concept Prototype, 2009. Designed by Johns Hopkins University Applied Physics Lab and Hunter Defense Technologies (USA). Aluminum, steel, printed circuit boards, select polymers (MPL v.1.0); 3-D printed rapid prototype material (concept prototype). Courtesy of JHU Applied Physics Lab.

A human hand has twenty-eight moving, articulated joints. The Modular Prosthetic Limb (MPL) comes close, with twenty-six joints. These mechanical joints are operated by just seventeen motors, which keeps the fingers lightweight. Some of the joints move in concert with or in response to other joints or in response to external pressure/stimulus. The limb can be controlled remotely for completing human-hostile tasks such as bomb extraction. Amputees can control the device from sensors placed against the skin of their remaining limb; the sensors pick up electrical signals (myoelectricity) from the muscles that signal the desire to move the arm and hand. People suffering from paralysis or ALS can control the limb with their brains. These users have no

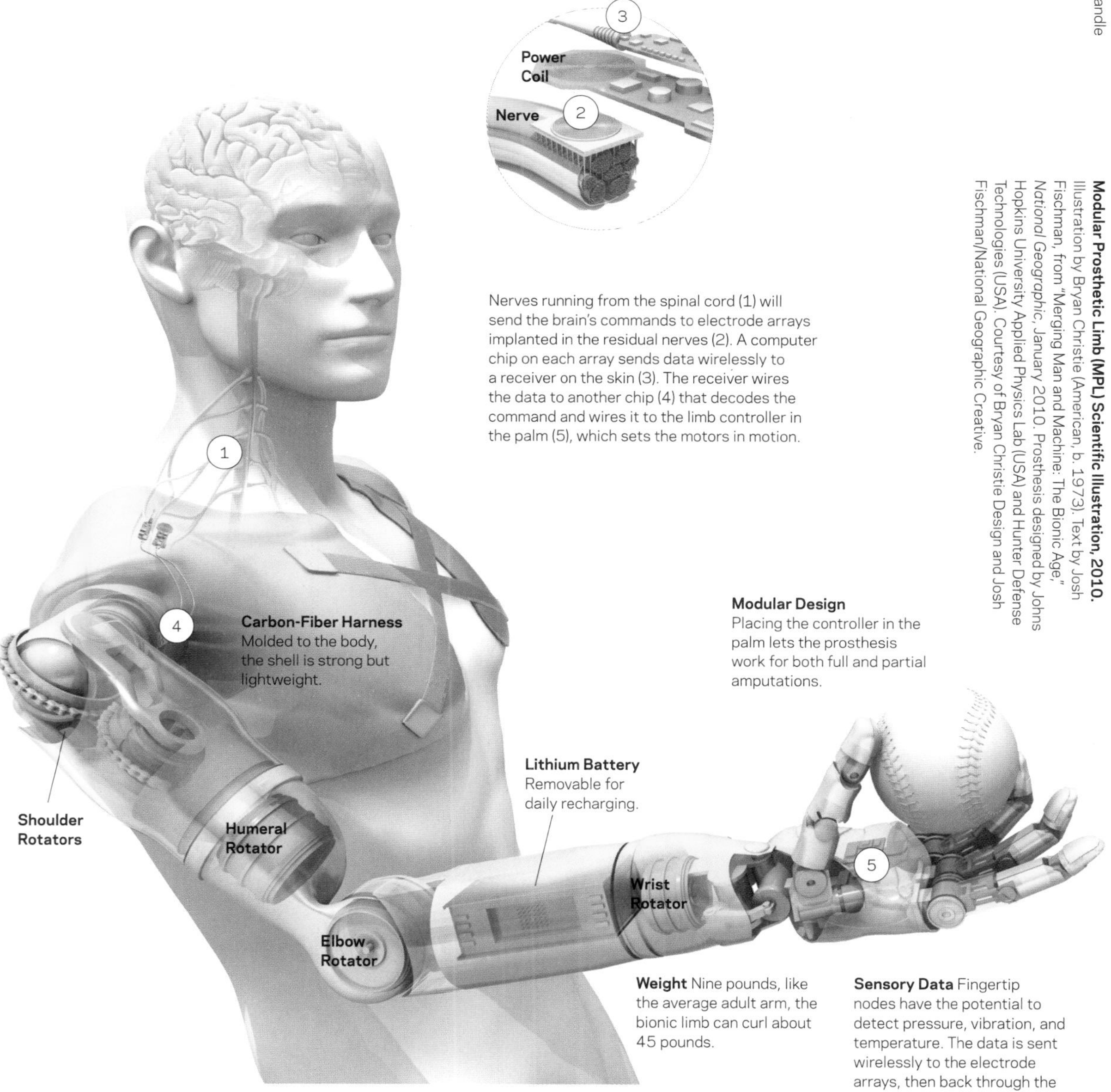

Modular Prosthetic Limb (MPL) Scientific Illustration, 2010. Illustration by Bryan Christie (American, b. 1973). Text by Josh Fischman, from "Merging Man and Machine: The Bionic Age," *National Geographic*, January 2010. Prosthesis designed by Johns Hopkins University Applied Physics Lab (USA) and Hunter Defense Technologies (USA). Courtesy of Bryan Christie Design and Josh Fischman/National Geographic Creative.

motor function and can't produce myoelectric signals. An "invasive array" of ninety-six tiny electrodes and multiples thereof can plug directly into a user's brain, tracking the ionic charge and discharge of neurons and allowing the user to control the position and orientation of the MPL hand as well as to shape multiple grasps. When the user's brain commands the hand to move forward, the hand takes the arm and elbow with it. Over time, the user's brain activity correlates with movements; the system and the brain learn to work together so that the appropriate brain impulses yield the desired motions.

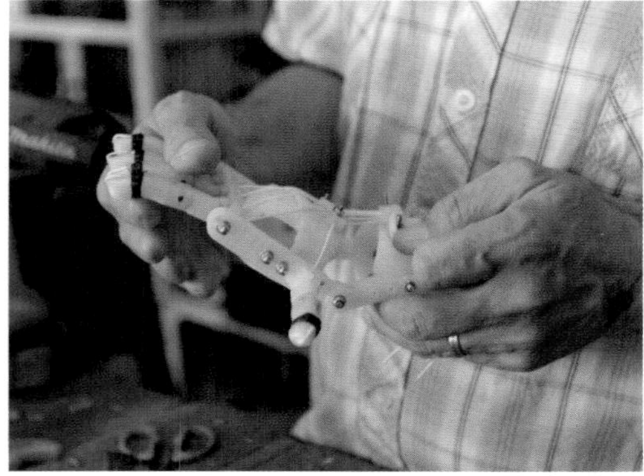

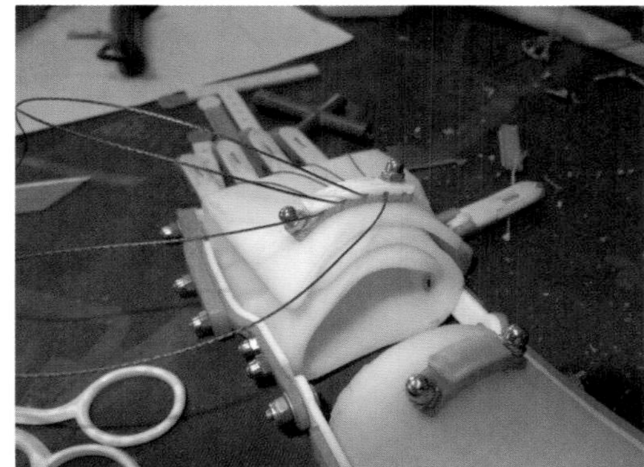

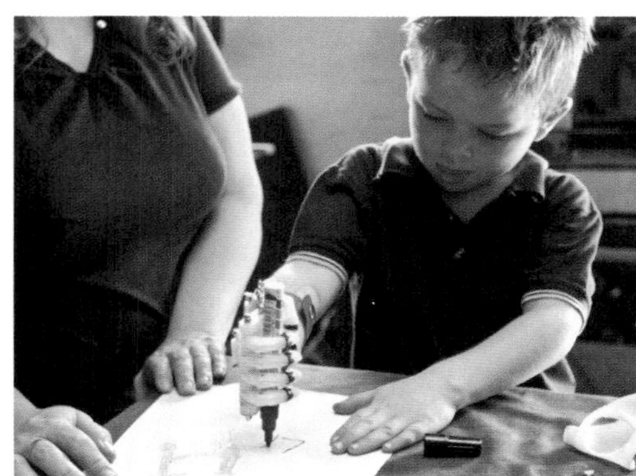

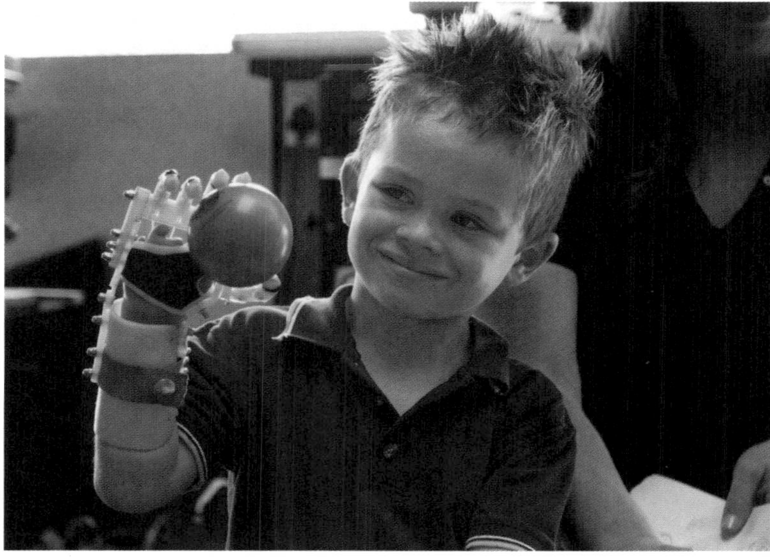

Richard van As, a South African woodworker, lost four fingers in a shop accident in 2011. Frustrated to learn that functional prosthetic fingers could cost more than $10,000 each, he sought to design an affordable prosthetic hand with functioning fingers. Using a MakerBot Replicator 2 Desktop 3D Printer (donated by MakerBot), he was able to prototype his device and create multiple iterations quickly and at low cost. How does the Robohand work? Cables attached to the base structure cause the prosthetic fingers to curl when the user's wrist folds and contracts, enabling the fingers to grasp objects. Seeing the humanitarian potential of his invention, van As began to develop prosthetic hands for other users. Liam, a six-year-old boy born with no fingers on his right

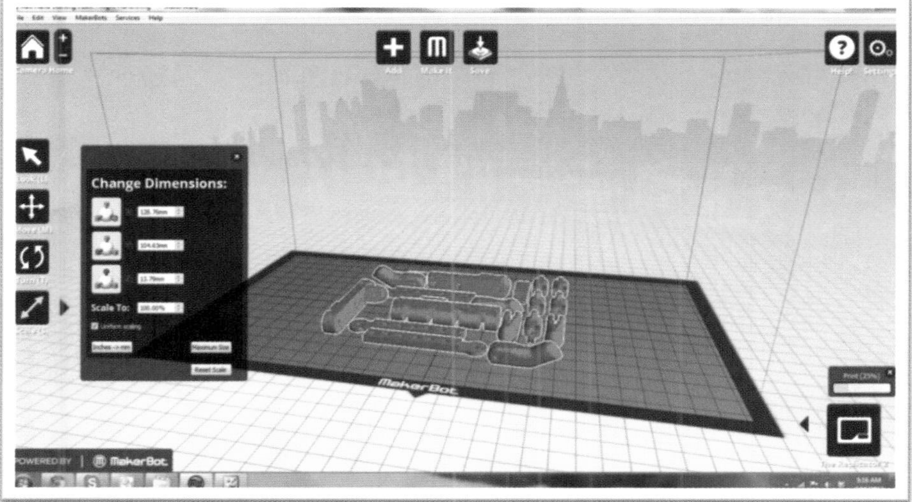

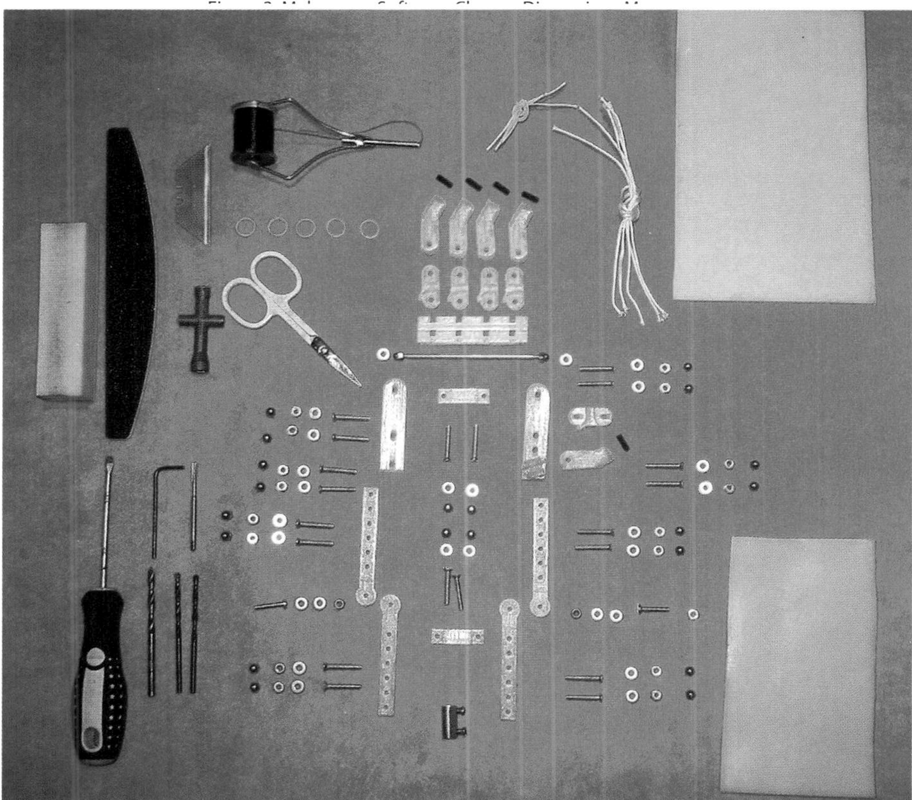

Robohand Prosthetic Hand, 2013. Designed by Richard van As (South African). 3D-printed PLA, stainless-steel parts. Courtesy of the designer.

hand, received his first Robohand in 2013. 3D printing technology is enabling Liam's family to replace the hand affordably as he grows. The files for Robohand are posted online on Thingiverse, allowing users around the world to produce and modify their own devices (thingiverse.com/robohand/designs).

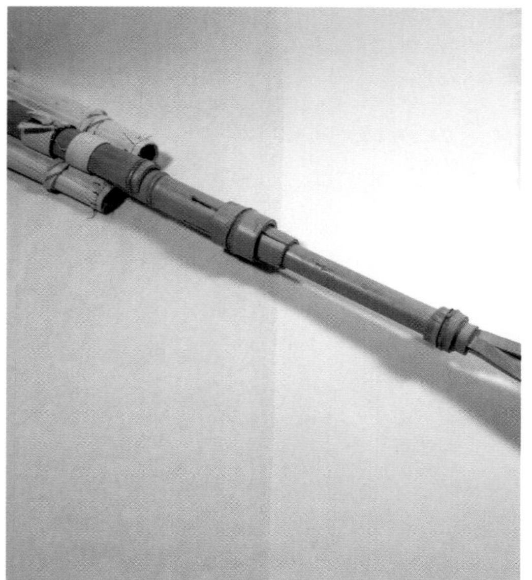

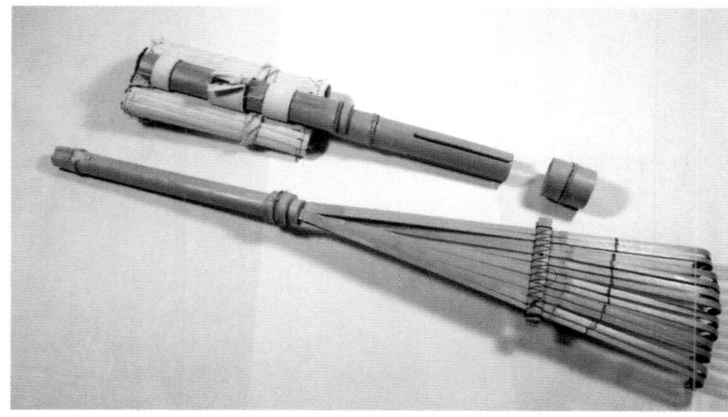

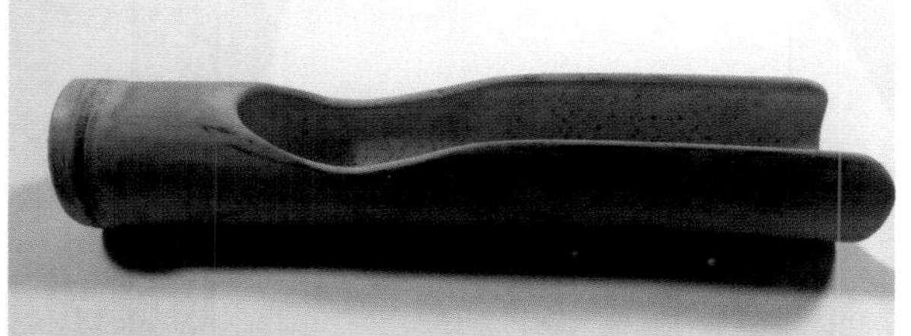

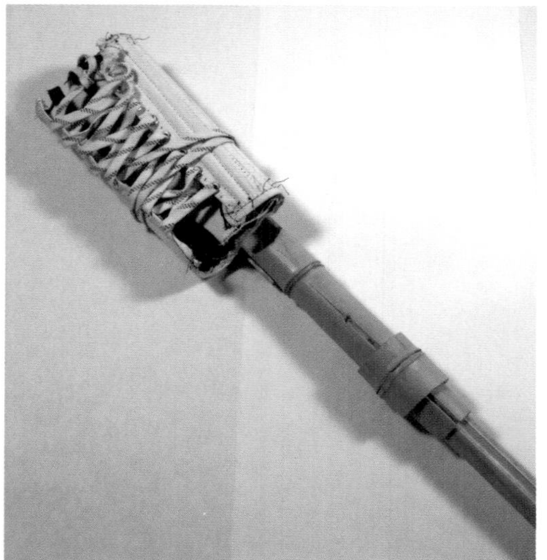

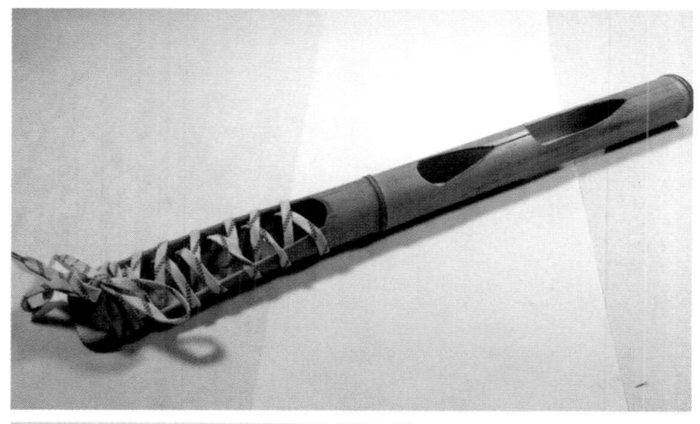

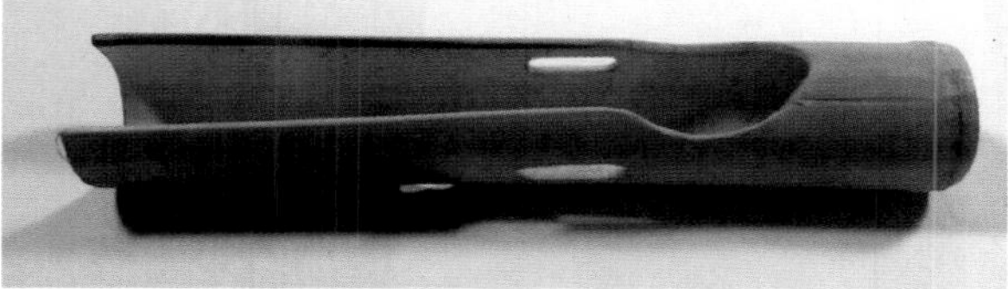

Nicholas Richardson designed his first prosthetic device after breaking his thumb in a skiing accident in fourth grade. He and his father hot-glued a Bic pen to a piece of salvaged plastic packaging; the device slipped over his index finger, allowing him to write. For his senior thesis at Maryland Institute College of Art (MICA), Richardson designed a prosthetic arm. He learned that 80 percent of all people with amputations live in developing countries, where even used or outmoded prosthetics are expensive and scarce—and usually don't fit the people who need them. Furthermore, they have to be custom-fitted and refitted over the course of the patient's life. Richardson decided to create an adjustable device that would be helpful to people with upper-body amputations living in

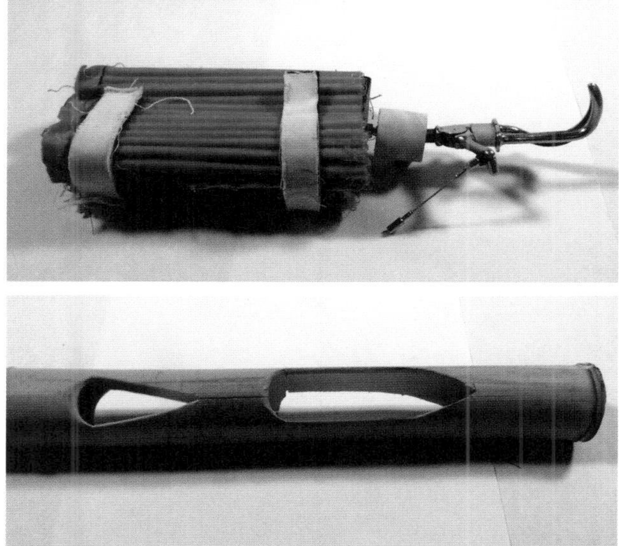

BamBam Prosthetic Limb Prototypes, 2012. Designed by Nicholas Richardson (American, b. 1984). Bamboo, canvas, plastic bottle, cotton laces, metal components. Courtesy of the designer.

agricultural communities. He experimented with recycled bottles and 3D printing before hitting on bamboo, a material that is strong, light, cheap, and easy to grow locally. Bamboo can be bent or shaped with basic tools, such as a machete, a rudimentary steamer, and sandpaper. Instead of trying to make a perfect hand that can do everything, he designed an adjustable "locking cuff" that connects to various tools, including a rake, a broom, and a shovel. A canvas sleeve, reinforced with bamboo ribs, secures the prosthetic to the user's stump. An artist in Providence, Rhode Island, has been testing the device. She reports that BamBam is more comfortable than traditional medical gear. Richardson is now seeking funding to develop his system further.

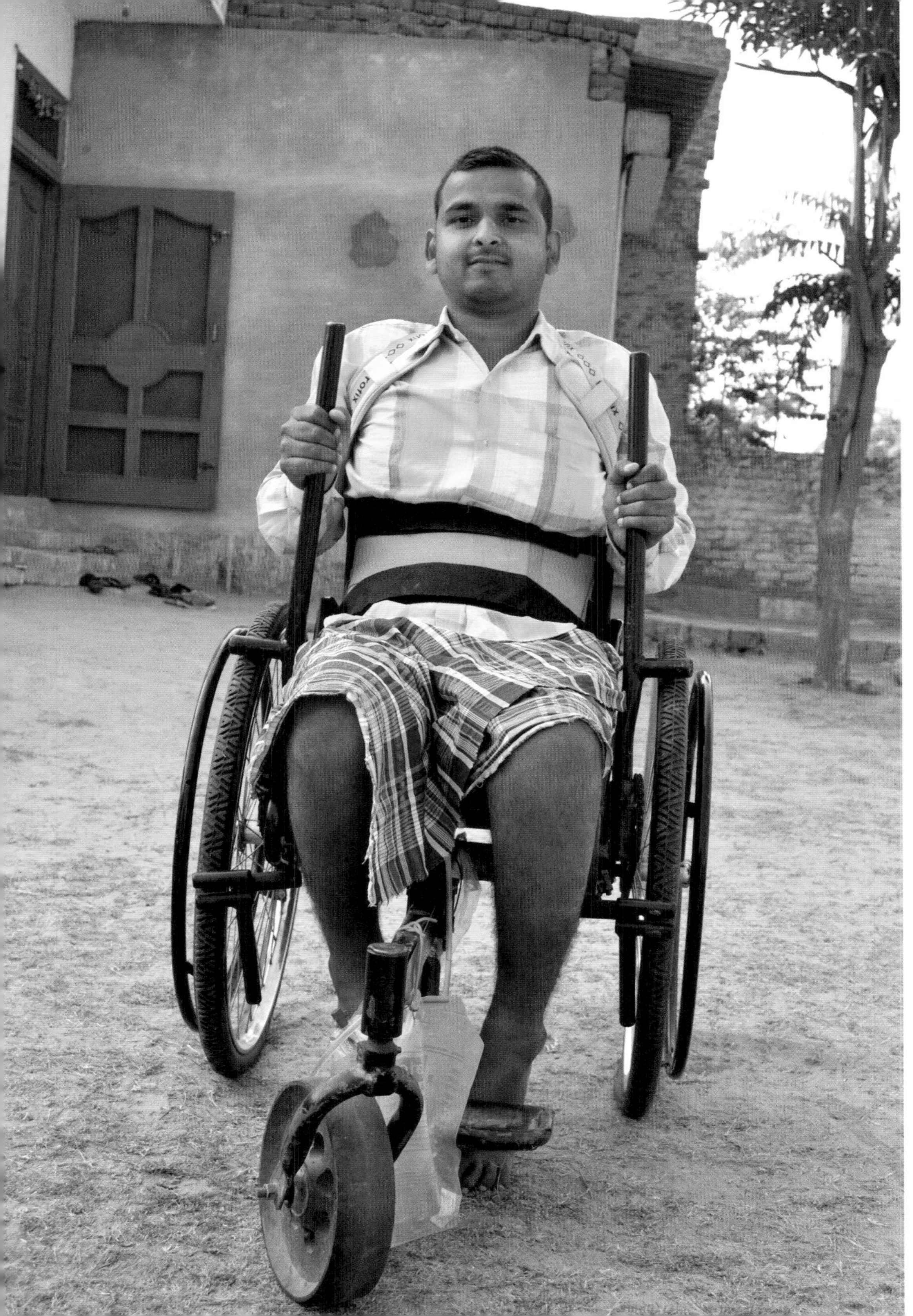

mobility

HUMAN-CENTERED DESIGN addresses the needs of global populations and people with diverse abilities. The freedom to move around one's home and community is key to achieving personal and economic independence. Bicycles, wheelchairs, and canes can transform USERS' lives and livelihoods. Each conveyance, however, exists within a broader system. Standard wheelchairs require smooth roads, ramps, and elevators; they can't function on the rough terrain that users face in many towns and landscapes around the world. Bicycles can be difficult to park, store, or carry indoors, creating problems for daily commuters. Some people avoid using canes and walkers that look like medical equipment; good design can make assistive devices more appealing to users by combining beauty and function. Advocates of UNIVERSAL DESIGN demand an improved experience and broader access for as many users as possible.

LFC Case Story: Panna Lal Sahu. Courtesy of GRIT.

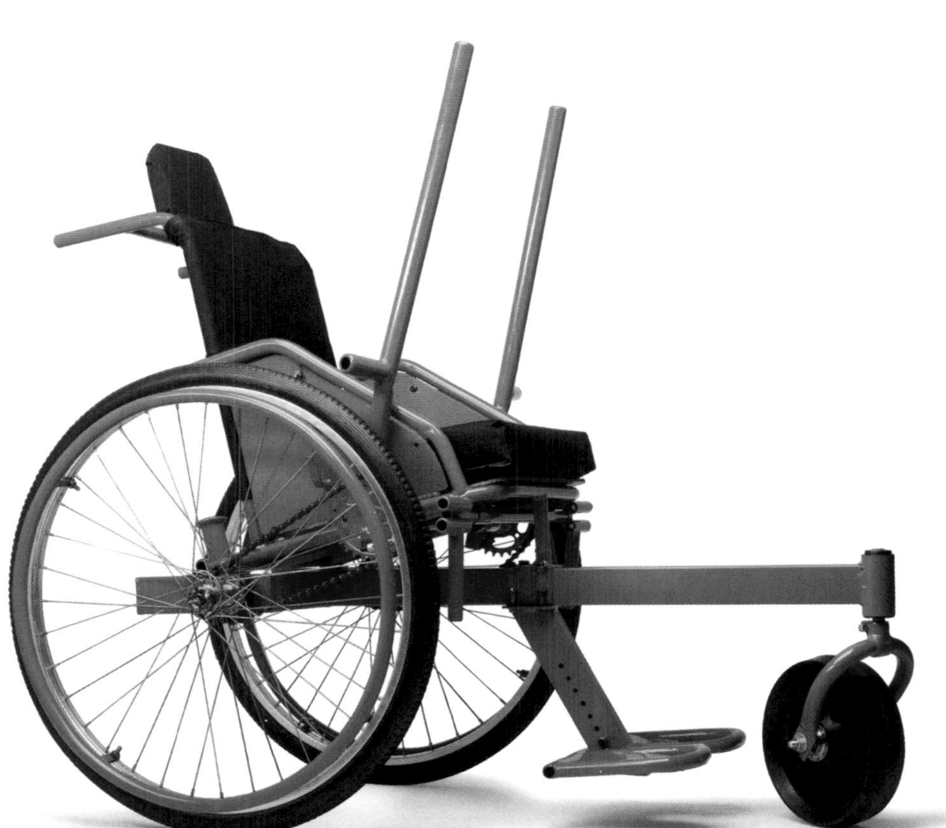

Leveraged Freedom Chair (LFC), 2013. Invented by Amos Winter, Mario Bollini, Tish Scolnik, Benjamin Judge, Harrison O'Hanley, Daniel Frey (MIT). Designed by Amos Winter, Mario Bollini, Benjamin Judge, Harrison O'Hanley (GRIT). Manufactured for GRIT (USA) by Pinnacle Industries (India). Mild steel, bicycle components. Courtesy of GRIT.

The Leveraged Freedom Chair (LFC) is designed to be manufacturable, repairable, and rideable throughout the world. Twenty million people around the globe need wheelchairs but don't have access to the ramps and paved roads required by traditional push-rim chairs. The LFC allows for off-road travel and uses human power more efficiently than standard wheelchairs. It combines the chain-and-sprocket drive train of a standard bicycle with two extended push levers to allow the user to move up to 80 percent faster on flat ground and to produce 51 percent higher torque on rough terrain. Users shift gears by moving their handhold along the length of the levers. The levers can be removed and stored on the frame of the chair, allowing it to be used comfortably

Leveraged Freedom Chair (LFC) Prime Prototype, 2012. Invented by Amos Winter, Mario Bollini, Tish Scolnik, Benjamin Judge, Harrison O'Hanley, Daniel Frey (MIT). Designed by Jake Childs and Jung Tak, Continuum LLC (USA). Aluminum, 3D-printed plastic. Courtesy of Continuum LLC.

indoors. The LFC was invented by Amos Winter and his students at the MIT Mobility Lab; the team later founded GRIT (Global Research Innovation and Technology). The LFC shown here was produced at GRIT's contract manufacturer in India. It is currently being distributed throughout India and other developing countries. The design firm Continuum LLC improved the aesthetics of Winter's invention and developed the LFC Prime (above). Building on the original's core gear-and-lever technology, the LFC Prime is a concept model for a high-performance wheelchair. GRIT is working with wheelchair users in the United States and building on this concept to develop a fully functional product, expected to be on the market in late 2014.

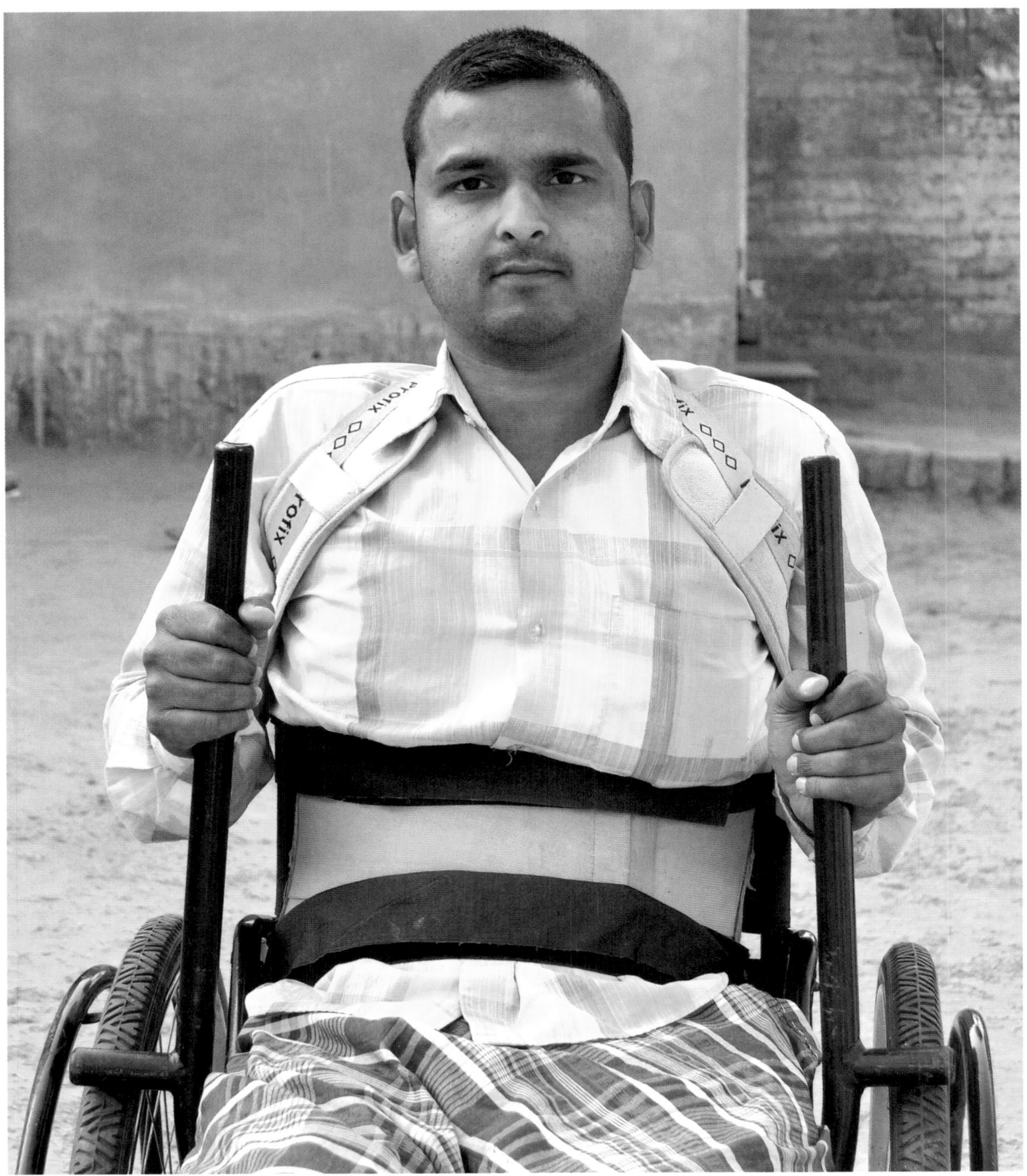

Living in Jaipur, India, Panna Lal Sahu was run over by a car, which damaged his spinal cord. After a year confined to a bed, he received a standard folding wheelchair, but he was unable to go outside without someone pushing the chair. In January 2011, he got an LFC. Panna Lal reports, "After my accident, I was bedridden for more than a year. I lost my job and used to be upset most of the time. After I got the LFC, I started going out on my own and started feeling better. Now I ride my LFC five kilometers a day. I meet and interact with people, which makes me feel good. I am inspired and want to start working again."

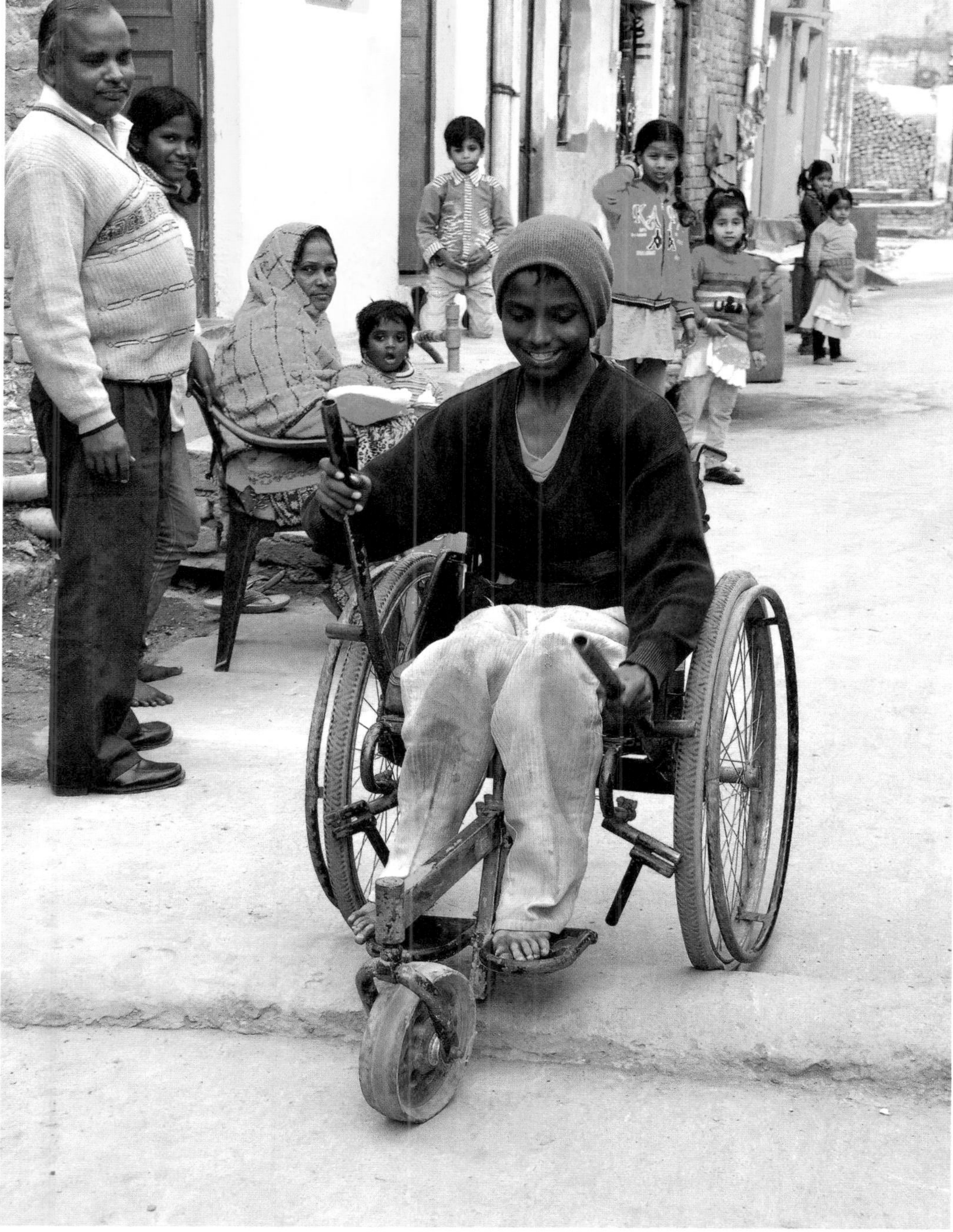

LFC Case Stories: Panna Lal Sahu and Ravi. Courtesy of GRIT.

Before Ravi got his LFC in March 2013 at age fifteen, his mobility was limited to his house. Living in Delhi, India, he could never go outside by himself. His parents got him crutches, but he was unable to use them. Now Ravi goes out unaccompanied and engages with the children in the neighborhood. Every day he spends four to six hours outside his home. His parents say that he understands and perceives things better now and is able to talk to others easily. He is happier and more confident. His hands have become stronger and his appetite has improved. Ravi reports, "It is a lot of fun to ride the LFC. I go around on my own, and I really like it. I go farther distances with my brother, and we play a lot. I go to shops and buy chocolates."

After studying and working in mechanical engineering, Mark Sanders sought to create a product that brings aesthetics and humanity to innovative engineering. In 1985, he designed the STRiDA bicycle for his industrial design thesis project at the Royal College of Art, in London. The STRiDA can be folded in less than ten seconds and is easy to move in its folded state—like a "rolling umbrella." The striking triangular profile enables users with a wide range of heights, from taller than six foot four inches down to five foot three inches or shorter, to ride the same model of bicycle. Sanders established MAS Design Products to manufacture the STRiDA. He later sold the design to Ming Cycle in Taiwan, which now distributes the bike worldwide.

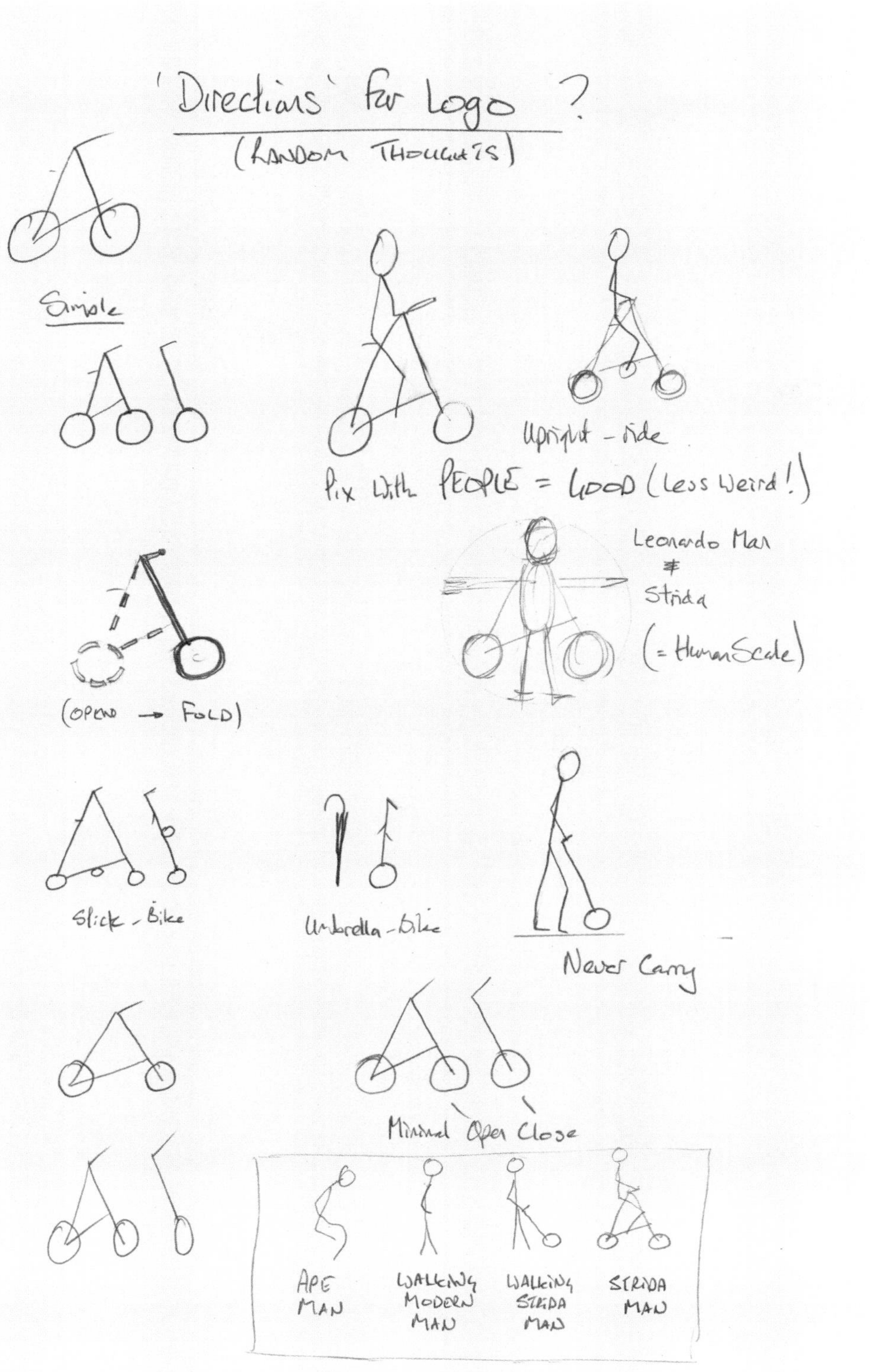

'Directions' for Logo ?

(RANDOM THOUGHTS)

Simple

Upright - ride

Pix With PEOPLE = GOOD (Less Weird!)

Leonardo Man ≠ Strida (= Human Scale)

(OPEN → FOLD)

Stick - Bike

Umbrella - bike

Never Carry

Minimal Open Close

APE MAN

WALKING MODERN MAN

WALKING STRIDA MAN

STRIDA MAN

STRiDA LT Bicycle and Logo Sketch, 1985–2009. Designed by Mark Sanders (British, b. 1958). Manufactured by Ming Cycle (Taiwan). Aluminum, plastic. Courtesy of Ming Cycle.

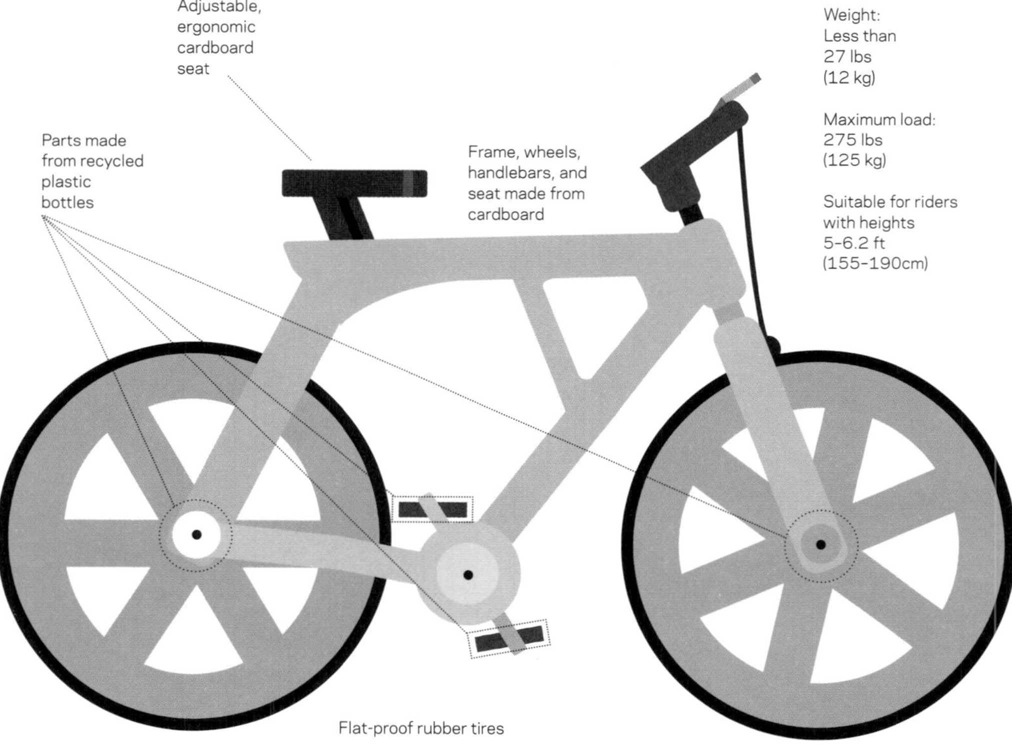

Israeli inventor Izhar Gafni has used the principles of origami—which builds strength into paper by folding it—to create a strong, durable bicycle from cardboard. The finished bike, which is sealed with glue and varnish, holds up to 500 pounds. After building an initial working prototype that looked like a "package on wheels," Gafni went on to produce a version that looks more like a typical bicycle. The resulting bike could retail for about $60; Gafni and his business partner Nimrod Elmish are developing plans for further reducing the cost, including on-bike advertising and green manufacturing subsidies.

Izhar Cardboard Bike, 2013. Designed by Izhar Gafni (Israeli, b. 1962). Manufactured by I.G. Cardboard Technologies (Israel). Cardboard, glue, varnish, recycled rubber. Courtesy of the designer.

Many people avoid using canes and walkers because they look like medical equipment. These prototypes are designed to be elements of domestic life, supporting rich social and mental activities while encouraging safe mobility. The T-Cane helps users serve tea and snacks. The U-Cane holds books, magazines, and supplies for knitting and crafting. The I-Cane doubles as an iPad stand.

No Country for Old Men: Together Canes, 2012. Designed and produced by Francesca Lanzavecchia (Italian, b. 1984) and Hunn Wai (British, b. 1980), Lanzavecchia + Wai (Italy). Maple, lacquered MDF. Courtesy of the designers. Photography: Davide Farabegoli (this spread and the following spread).

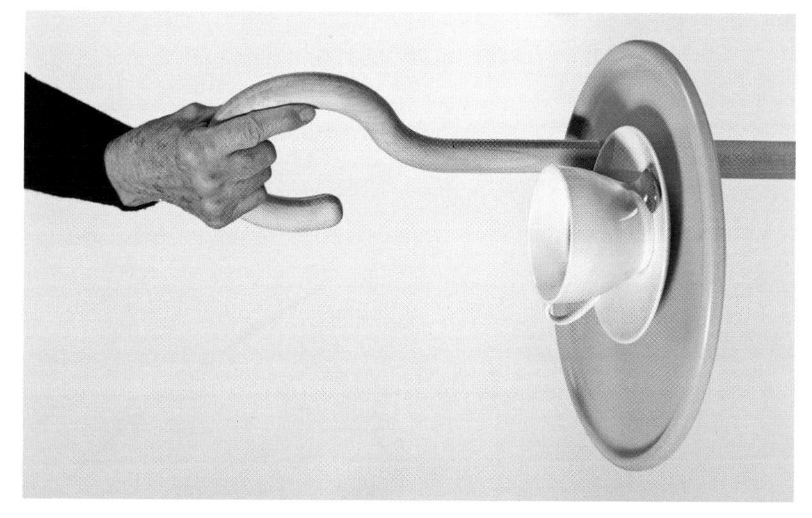

DWG. NO. 113
DATED 5-19-43
FOR ACRATHERM
W/CLEAR PLASTIC CAP

interface

Many contemporary products feature integrated hardware and software. An INTERFACE is a mix of inputs and outputs, signals and gestures, that allow humans and devices to communicate via sight, sound, touch, and even smell. As smart products begin to emulate human behavior, some people respond to them with emotions of attachment, trust, or empathy.

Henry Dreyfuss's Honeywell Round thermostat, which replaced earlier box-shaped models, operates with a simple turn of the outer ring. Recent products like the Nest Learning Thermostat and the August Smart Lock combine advanced digital technology with simple forms to merge seamlessly with daily activity. Such products belong to the broader fields of INTERACTION DESIGN and EXPERIENCE DESIGN, which consider the full narrative of a USER's engagement with a product or offering.

Design for Acratherm Gauge, 1943. Designed by Henry Dreyfuss (American, 1904–72), Henry Dreyfuss & Associates (USA). Rendered by Roland Stickney (American, 1892–1975). Brush and gouache on illustration board. Collection Cooper Hewitt, Smithsonian Design Museum, gift of Honeywell Inc., 1997-10-6. Photography: Matt Flynn.

Henry Dreyfuss began designing the Honeywell Round Thermostat in 1943. He observed that rectangular thermostats often sit crooked on the wall; a round device would be easier to install properly. The numerous drawings leading up to the completed product reveal Dreyfuss's attention to user interaction; some designs incorporate a clock face. The Honeywell Round, released in 1953, is remarkably simple. Temperature adjusts with a twist of the dial. Some models allow users to intuitively compare the set temperature and the room temperature. The product also invited customization: users could remove the protective cover and paint the device to match the room. The Honeywell Round remains one of the world's most commonly used thermostats.

T86 Round Thermostat, 1953 (opposite page). Designed by Henry Dreyfuss (American, 1904–72), Henry Dreyfuss & Associates (USA). Manufactured by Honeywell Inc. (USA). Metal, molded plastic. Collection Cooper Hewitt, Smithsonian Design Museum, gift of Honeywell Inc., 1994-37-1. Photography: Hiro Ihara.

Designs for Regulator, 1949. Designed by Henry Dreyfuss (American, 1904–72), Henry Dreyfuss & Associates (USA). Rendered by Roland Stickney (American, 1892–1975). Brush, gouache, and ink on illustration board. Collection Cooper Hewitt, Smithsonian Design Museum, gift of Honeywell Inc., 1997-10-15, 1997-10-18. Photography: Matt Flynn.

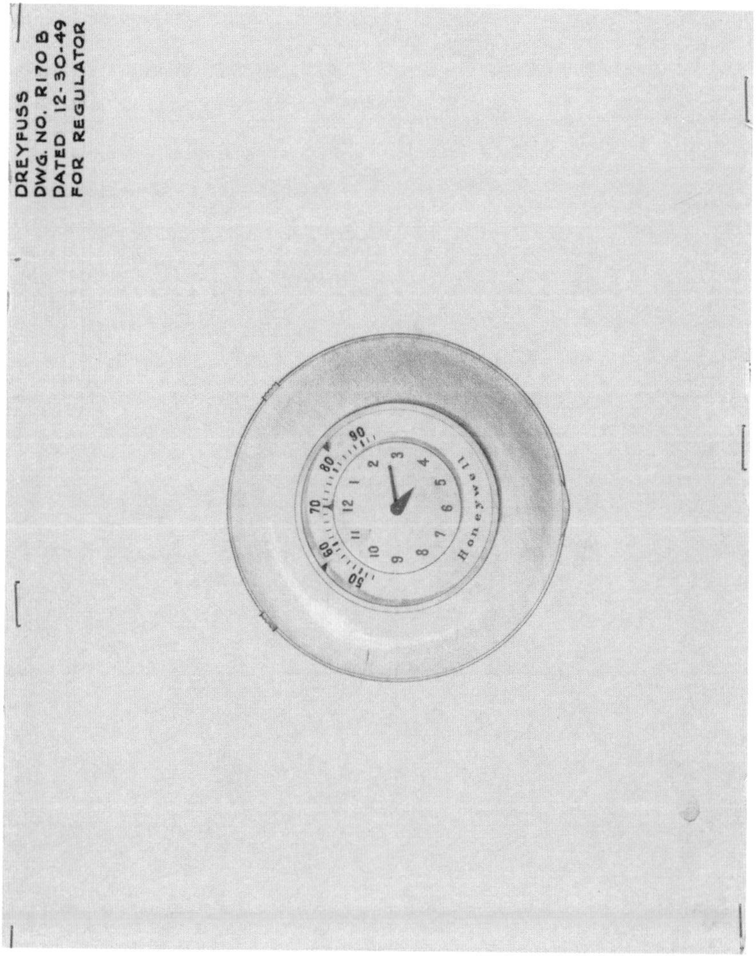

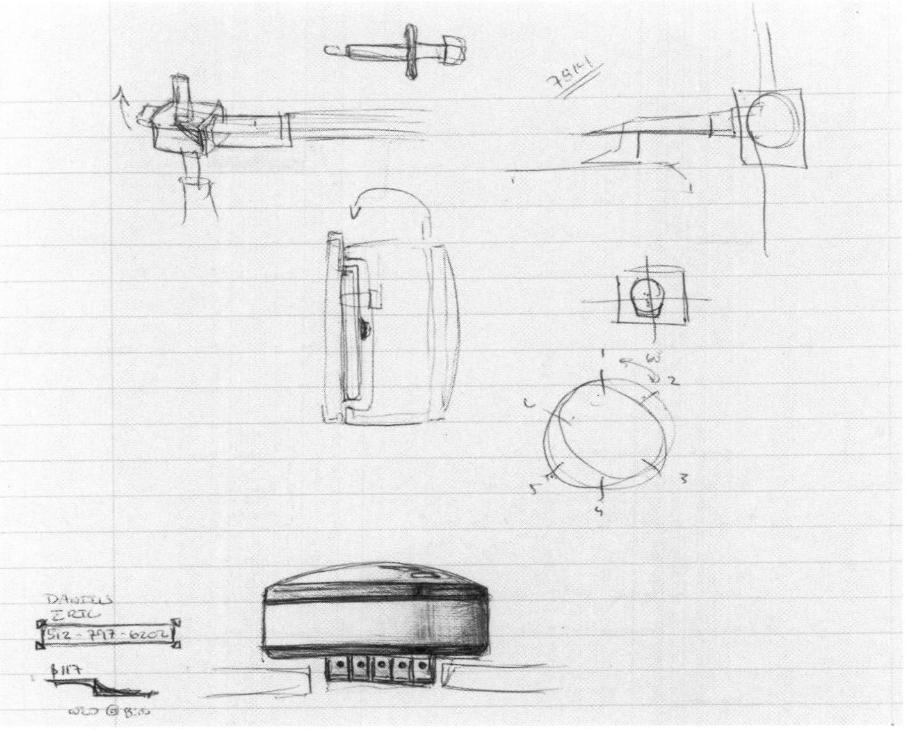

Preparatory Drawing for Nest Learning Thermostat: Proposed Design for Integration of Back Plate into Head Unit (detail), 2011. Designed by Eric Daniels (American, born Germany, 1974) for Nest Labs, Inc. (USA). Pen and blue ink on white lined paper. Collection Cooper Hewitt, Smithsonian Design Museum, gift of Nest Labs, Inc., 2014-9-2. Photography: Matt Flynn.

Two Preparatory Drawings for Nest Learning Thermostat: Proposed Design for Minimizing Motion Sensor Window and Cross Section of Wire to Board Connector, 2011. Designed by John Benjamin Filson (American, b. 1977) for Nest Labs, Inc. (USA). Pen and black ink on cream paper (2014-9-8). Pen and orange, green, red, and black ink, and graphite on cream paper (2014-9-5). Collection Cooper Hewitt, Smithsonian Design Museum, gift of Nest Labs, Inc., 2014-9-8, 2014-9-5. Photography: Matt Flynn.

The Nest Learning Thermostat brings advanced interaction design to a basic home device. The rotating interface recalls the classic design of Henry Dreyfuss's Honeywell Round. Turning the outer ring raises or lowers the temperature. The illuminated screen responds to motion in the room; the sensors signal Nest to adjust the temperature when people enter or leave the room.

Pushing the ring activates a menu of additional options, from programming the device to switching from heating to cooling. Smartphone apps allow users to program the thermostat remotely and to track energy use over time. The preparatory drawings reveal the task of integrating complex components into a unit that sits seamlessly against the wall.

Nest Learning Thermostat, Second Generation, 2012. Designed by Tony Fadell (American, b. 1969). Manufactured by Nest (USA). Glass, metal, electronic components. Courtesy of Nest Labs, Inc.

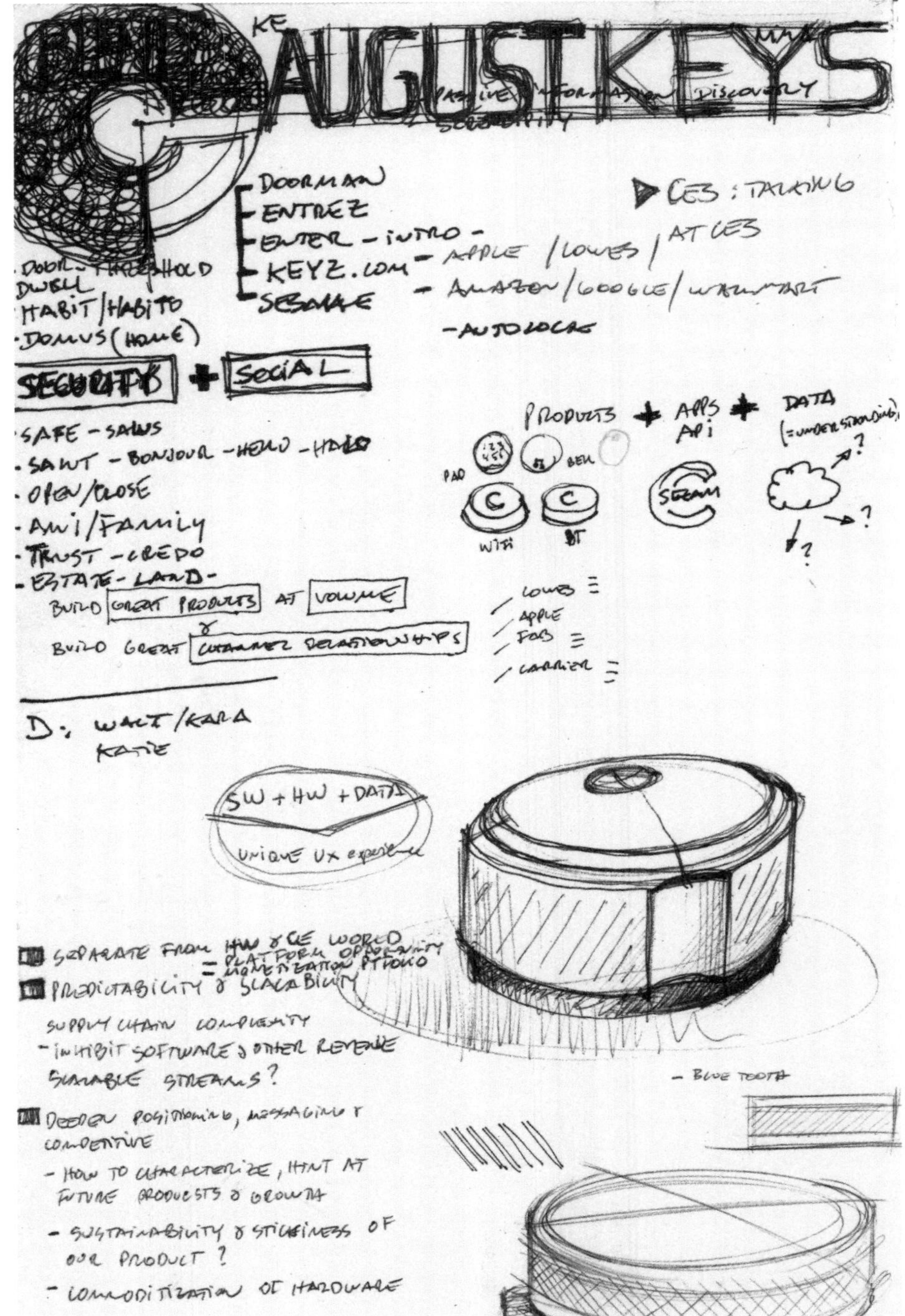

The August Smart Lock is an app-enabled device that fits over an existing single-cylinder dead bolt. The app allows the system owner to distribute virtual keys to guests, family members, service people, and others. The system owner can create keys with automatic expiration dates and disable keys at any time. The August Smart Lock recognizes key holders when their smartphone is in range of the lock. Whereas physical keys can be duplicated and distributed without the owner's knowledge, an August lock allows the owner to track who has access to a property and when someone has entered or departed. Users can still employ physical keys when needed. The sketch above, by designer Yves Béhar, shows early concept development for the product, diagramming the

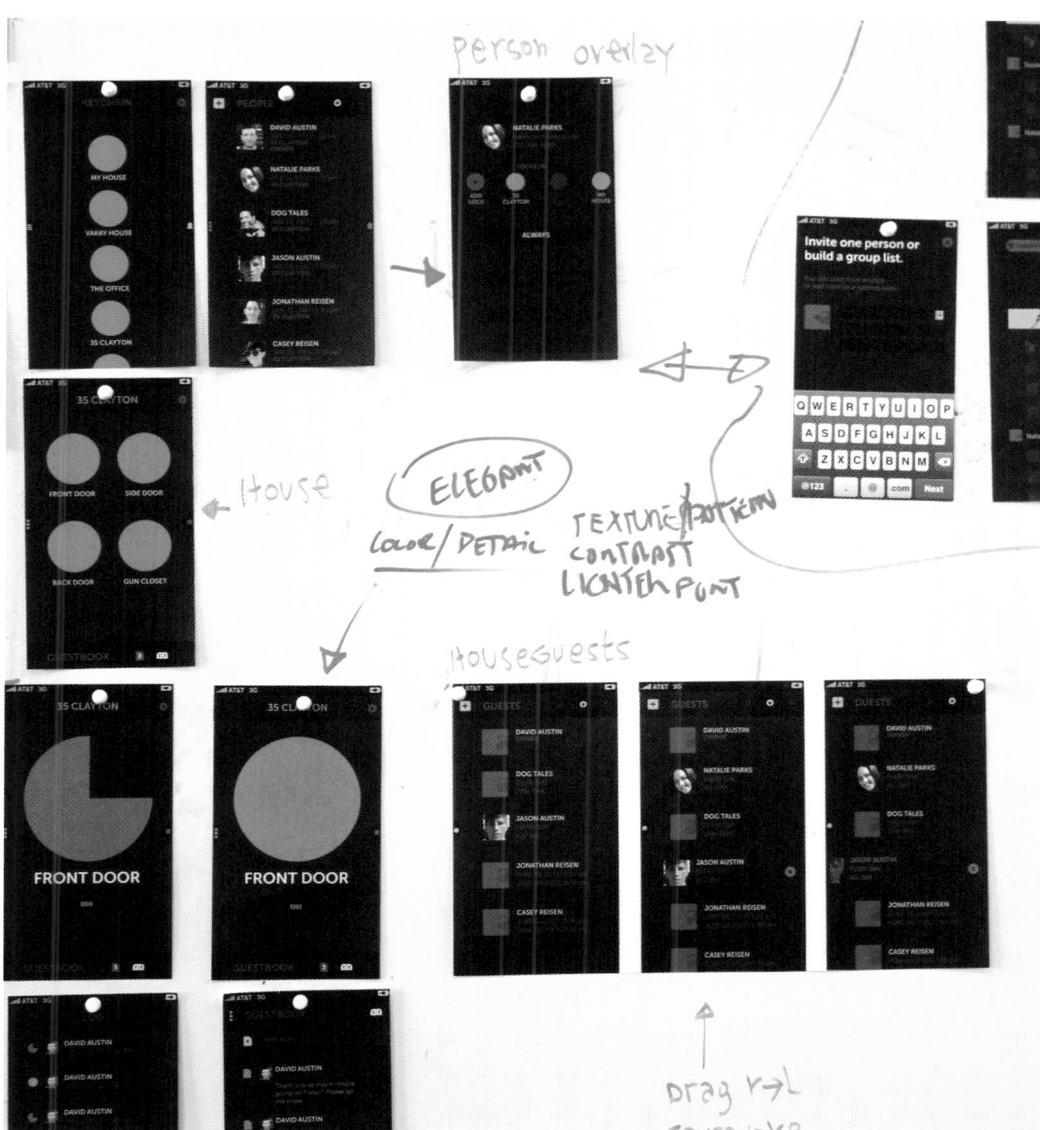

August Smart Lock Concept and Interface Drawings, 2013.
Designed by Yves Béhar (Swiss, b. 1967), fuseproject (USA).
Courtesy of the designer.

idea of a system that connects a physical product with apps and data. The sketch also includes ideas for the product's name and raises questions about potential problems and opportunities (sustainability and stickiness, commoditization of hardware, supply-chain complexity). As the design process moved forward, the interface became as important as the physical device.

The storyboard above shows how users will interact with the product on their smartphone. In the scenario shown here, the homeowner has multiple August locks, including his front and back doors, and on his gun closet. He is giving electronic keys to a circle of guests—from out-of-town visitors to dog walkers—and he can grant each a different level of access.

The design team produced numerous prototypes of the August Smart Lock as well as the colors and patterns employed in the product and app interfaces.

August Smart Lock, 2013. Designed by Yves Béhar (Swiss, b. 1967), fuseproject (USA). Manufactured by August (USA). Metal, glass, electronic components. Courtesy of the designer.

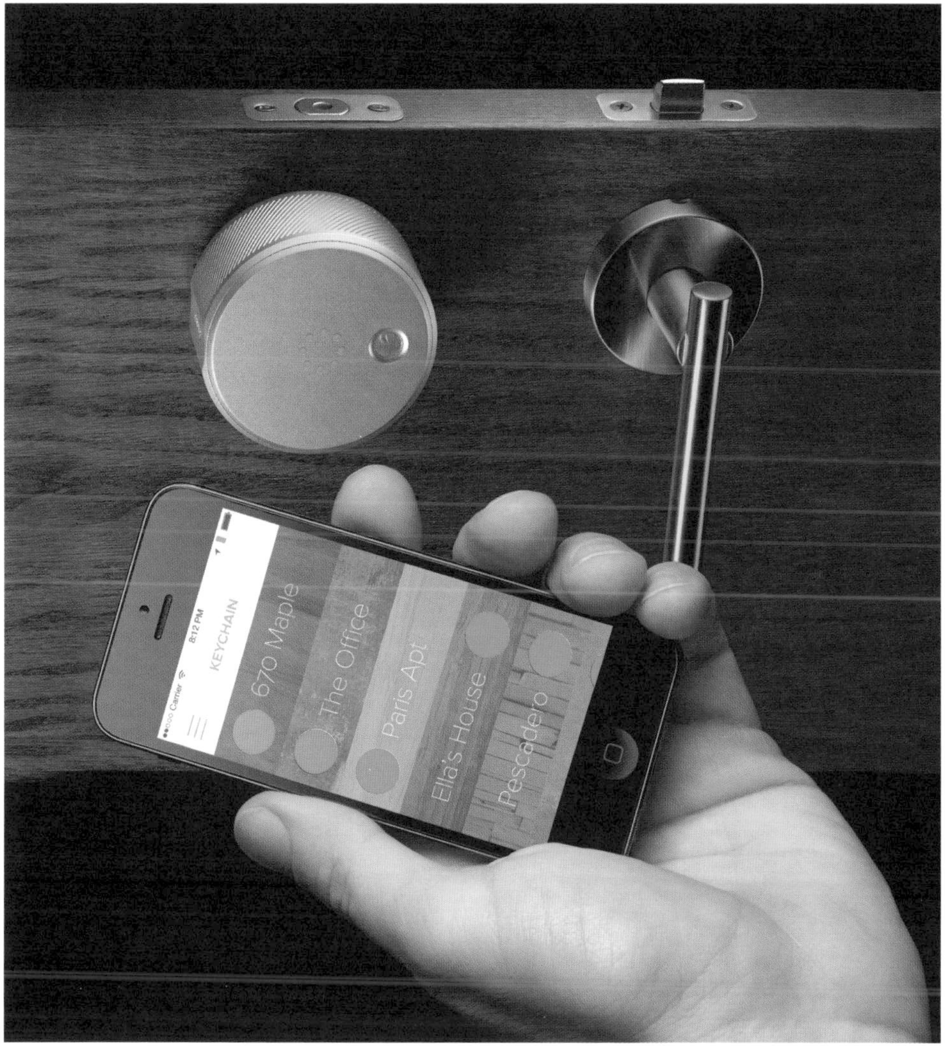

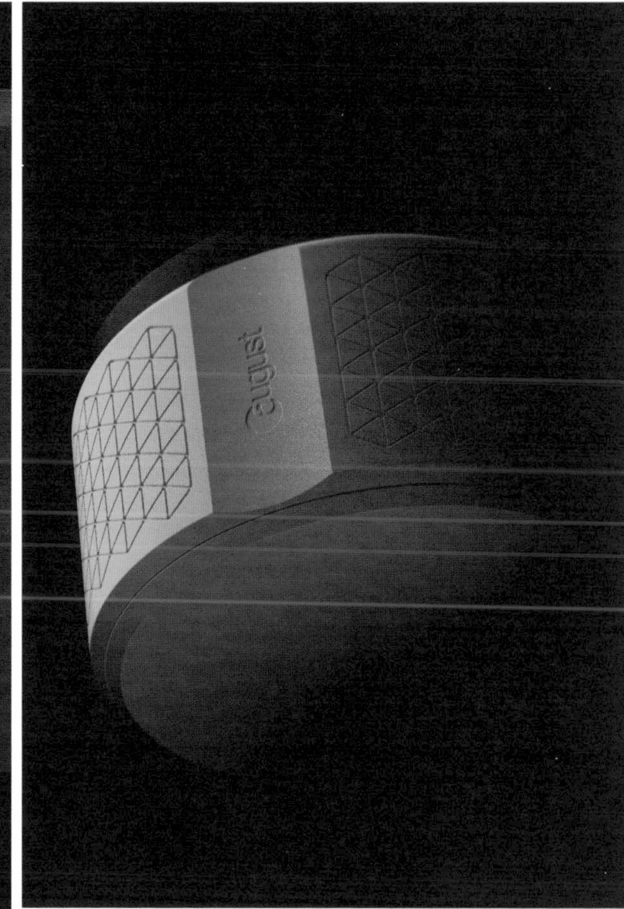

Product-User Relationship over Time

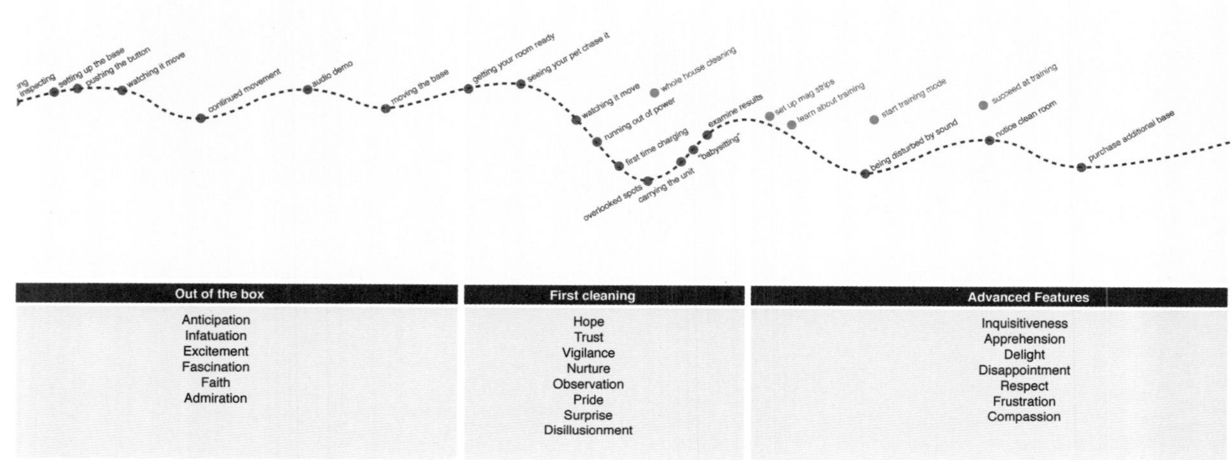

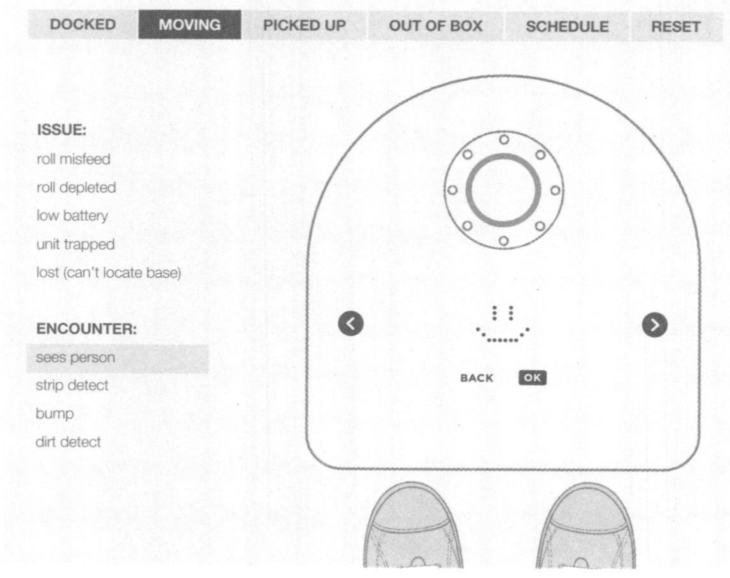

Neato smiles when encountering a person.

When Smart Design set out to create the Neato Robotics Automatic Vacuum Cleaner, the firm began with research, observation, and analysis. How do people interact with existing robotic vacuums, such as the popular Roomba? Carla Diana and Smart's design team visited the homes of Roomba users. The team learned that users express both amazement and disgust at the debris collected by the machine. Users want to activate the machine with their foot instead of bending over, and they want to avoid touching dirt. People often handle their robots gently, like a pet. Additional research revealed that users often give their robots names, seeing them as a bit more than machines. They forgive the device's occasional clumsiness as quirks of individuality. A user's first contact

Neato Robotics Automatic Vacuum Cleaner Interface Research and Prototype, 2013. Designed by Smart Design (USA). Manufactured by Neato (USA). Acrylic, polycarbonate, electrical components (prototype); plastic, electrical components (finished product). Courtesy of the designers.

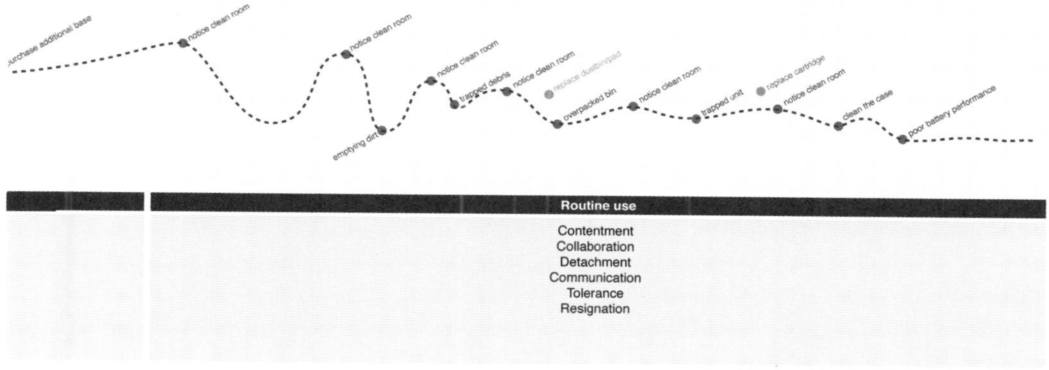

Routine use

Contentment
Collaboration
Detachment
Communication
Tolerance
Resignation

Users will engage with a robotic vacuum cleaner with different parts of their body depending on the distance and situation: hands, feet, eyes, and ears.

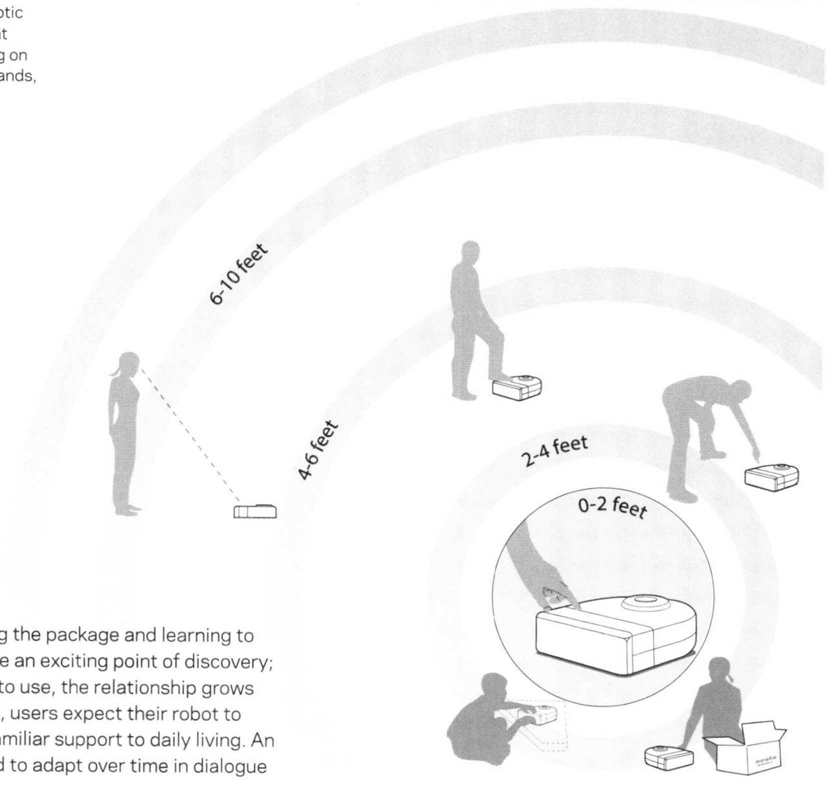

6-10 feet
4-6 feet
2-4 feet
0-2 feet

with the machine (opening the package and learning to operate the device) can be an exciting point of discovery; but as the product is put to use, the relationship grows more distant. Before long, users expect their robot to serve as a dependable, familiar support to daily living. An interface can be designed to adapt over time in dialogue with the user.

People want their robots to communicate clearly. To create the interface for the Neato Vacuum Cleaner, Smart's design team devised a vocabulary of icons, sounds, and text to signal the various states of Neato's operation, ranging from wake-up and sleep tones to utilitarian warnings and alerts. To avoid fatiguing users, the interface employs full tones and melodies sparingly. Neato makes a unique sound when it encounters a person or gets trapped or lost from the base unit; each sound implies a subtle emotion or attitude. Early prototypes for Neato feature large-scale LED graphics that glow through the plastic skin, an innovative display concept that informed the current version of the product and serves as a vision for future designs.

Neato Robotics Automatic Vacuum Cleaner Interface Prototype, 2013. Designed by Smart Design (USA). Acrylic, polycarbonate, electrical components (prototype); plastic, electrical components (finished product). Manufactured by Neato (USA). Courtesy of the designers.

People experience design in relation to their own bodies. The things and spaces we use are extensions of our proportions, perceptions, abilities, and limitations. Designed by Local Projects, this interactive experience invites visitors to see their silhouette in relation to images sampled from Cooper Hewitt's historic collection. Since the Renaissance, designers have conceived of cities, buildings, and even letterforms in relation to idealized human proportions. In the twentieth century, Henry Dreyfuss, Niels Diffrient, and others embraced the diversity of human scale and launched a new approach to "designing for people."

Design for Body Scan, 2014. Interactive media concept, design, and production by Local Projects. Commissioned by Cooper Hewitt, Smithsonian Design Museum. Digital renderings. Courtesy of the designers.

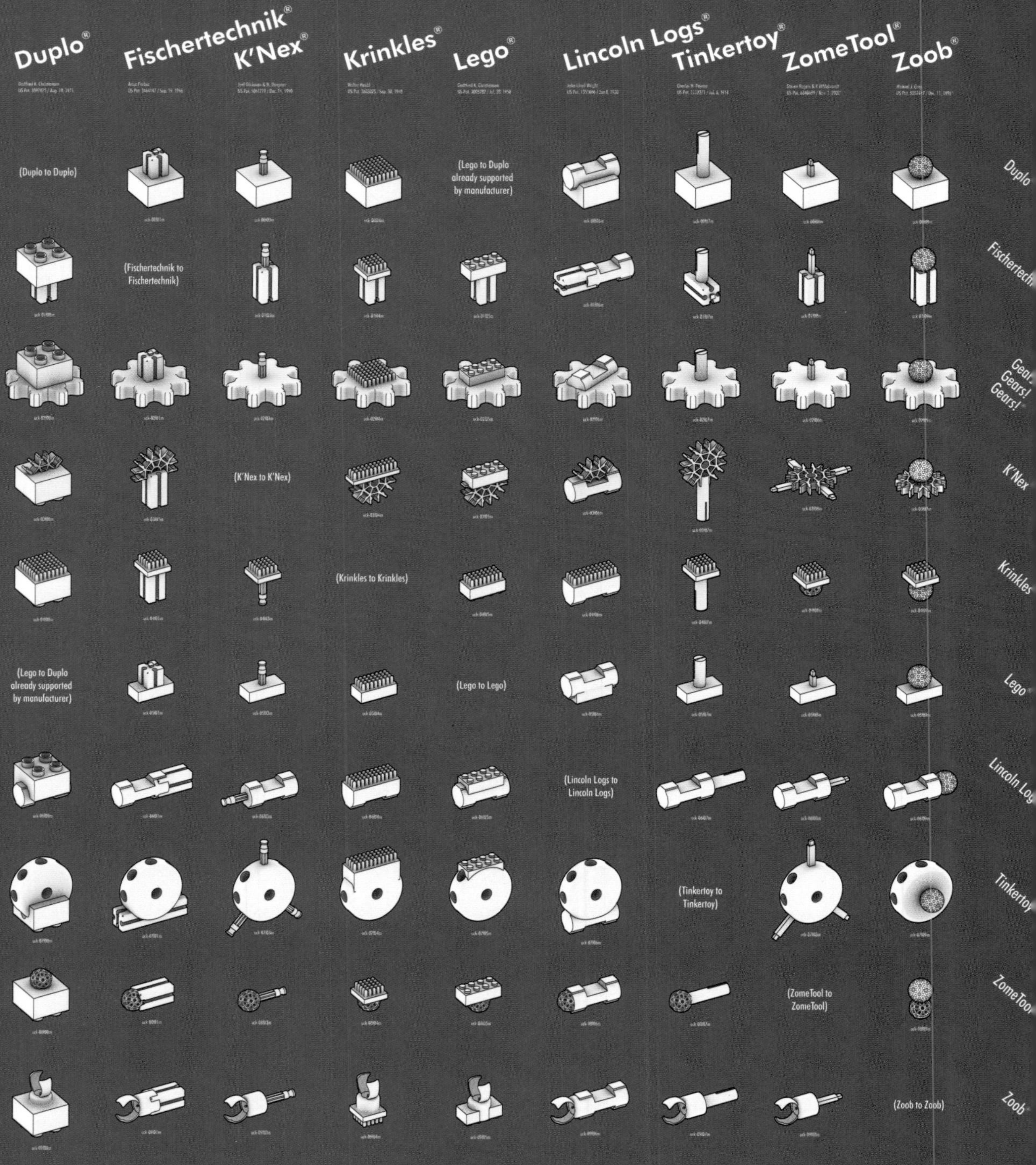

Duplo® Fischertechnik® K'Nex® Krinkles® Lego® Lincoln Logs® Tinkertoy® ZomeTool® Zoob®

(Duplo to Duplo)

(Lego to Duplo already supported by manufacturer)

Duplo

(Fischertechnik to Fischertechnik)

Fischertechnik

Gears! Gears! Gears!

(K'Nex to K'Nex)

K'Nex

(Krinkles to Krinkles)

Krinkles

(Lego to Duplo already supported by manufacturer)

(Lego to Lego)

Lego

(Lincoln Logs to Lincoln Logs)

Lincoln Logs

(Tinkertoy to Tinkertoy)

Tinkertoy

(ZomeTool to ZomeTool)

ZomeTool

(Zoob to Zoob)

Zoob

sy-lab

* Two construction playsets nominally supported by the Kit are still protected (as of March 2012) by active patents: Zoob (patented 1996) and ZomeTool (patented 2002). **For the Zoob and Zome systems, please note that we have delayed the release of adapter models until December 2016 and November 2022, respectively.**

revenge of the user

In a world of complex hi-tech products, some USERS seek to expose the covert workings of manufactured things. OPEN-SOURCE DESIGN builds on the open-source software movement, which invites multiple authors to write and test code. Personal 3D printing technologies are moving design and manufacturing into the hands of users, allowing MAKERS to create (and share) digital files for producing physical objects. HACKING, associated with penetrating the secrets of software, has extended its conquest to the world of physical things. Users are taking apart and reassembling consumer products, treating the world of manufactured goods as a kit of parts to be reworked and rewritten.

Free Universal Construction Kit Poster (detail), 2012. Designed by Golan Levin (American, b. 1972) and Shawn Sims (American, b. 1986). Released by Free Art and Technology (F.A.T.) Lab and Synaptic Lab (USA). Courtesy of the designers.

Confronting questions about intellectual property, open-source culture, and reverse engineering, the Free Universal Construction Kit consists of nearly eighty two-way adapter bricks that enable connections among ten popular children's construction toys. Users can download the files from various sharing sites and print them on a MakerBot or other personal manufacturing device. The Kit demonstrates "reverse engineering as a civic activity: a creative process in which anyone can develop the necessary pieces to bridge the limitations presented by mass-produced commercial artifacts." The designers scanned existing toy components with an optical comparator that is accurate down to one ten-thousandth of an inch (0.0001 inches, or 2.54 microns), allowing them to

Free Universal Construction Kit, 2012. Designed by Golan Levin (American, b. 1972) and Shawn Sims American, b. 1986). Released by Free Art and Technology (F.A.T.) Lab and Synaptic Lab (USA). 3D-printed connectors, various construction toys. Courtesy of the designers.

create precise fits between components. Golan Levin and Shawn Sims conceived the Kit and released it through the Free Art and Technology (F.A.T.) Lab and Synaptic Lab collectives. It was developed with support from the Frank-Ratchye STUDIO for Creative Inquiry at Carnegie Mellon University and is represented, for legal purposes, by Adapterz, LLC.

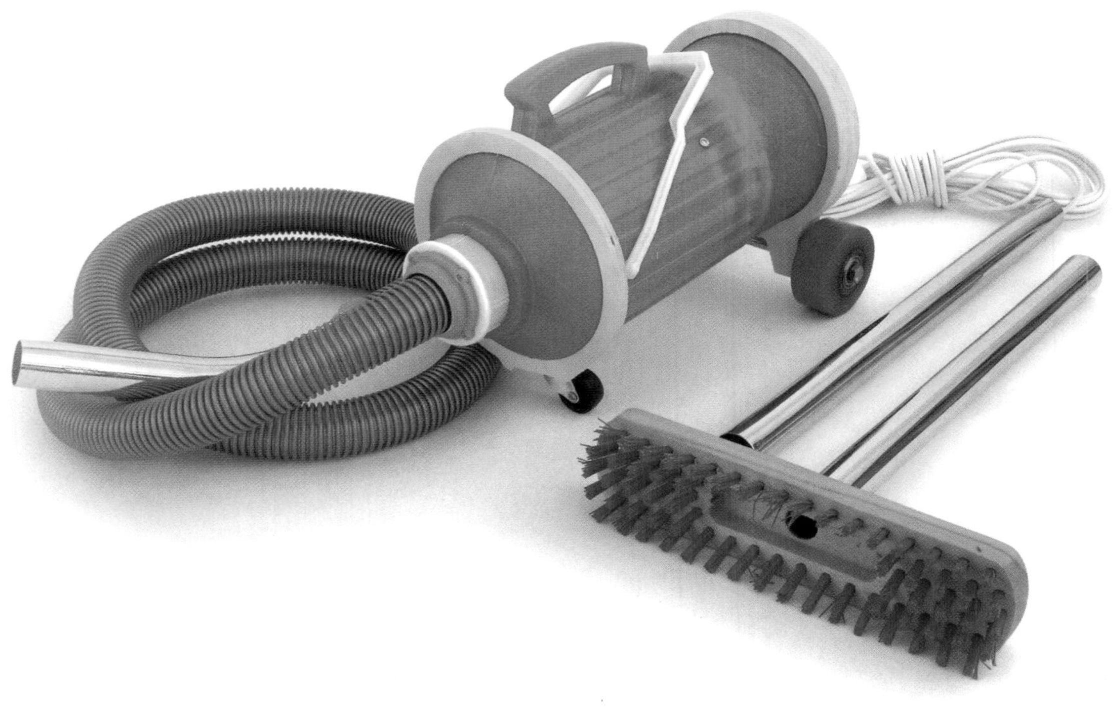

Jesse Howard designs his open-source Transparent Tools from standard wheel assemblies, repurposed motors, 3D-printed parts, and glass and plastic containers so that users can, in principle, make their own. The 3D-printed parts are designed for OpenStructures (OS), a library of universal, modular elements founded by designer Thomas Lommée. OS promotes open-source building and manufacturing; anyone can contribute parts to the system. The canister for Howard's Improvised Vacuum comes from a plastic thermos; the motor was salvaged from a broken vacuum. The instructions for building the vacuum include web addresses and part numbers, inviting users to become makers.

Improvised Vacuum

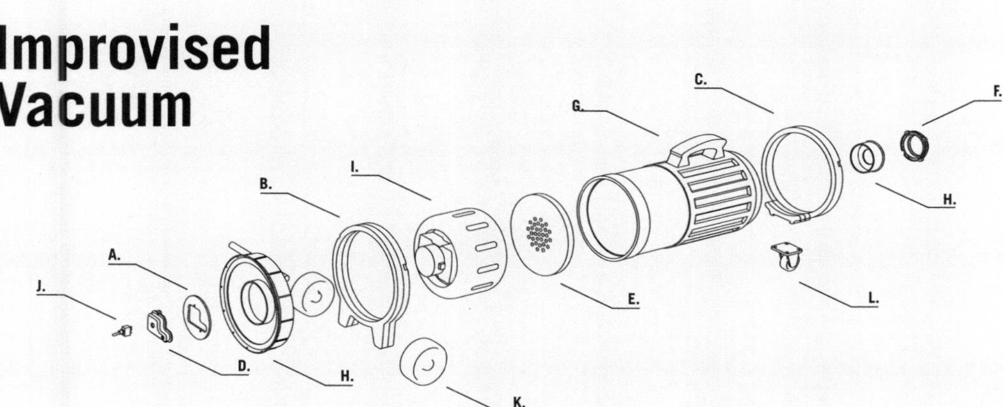

A. Rear Panel - Laser Cut
OpenStrucutres Compatible
thingiverse.com/thing:29923

B. Rear Wheel Support - CNC Milled
OpenStructures Compatible
thingiverse.com/thing:25979

C. Front Wheel Support - CNC Milled
Openstructures Compatible
thingiverse.com/thing:25798

D. Switch Cover - 3D Printed
OpenStructures Compatible
thingiverse.com/thing:25081

E. Chamber Divider - CNC Milled
12mm Multiplex
thingiverse.com/thing:25805

F. Hose Adaptor - 3D Printed
OpenStructures Compatible
thingiverse.com/thing:25802

G. Plastic Thermos Cover
Improvised solution
160mm diameter

H. Plastic Thermos End Caps
Improvised solution

I. AC Motor
Recouperated
from Bosch BSG62023 or similar

J. Toggle Switch
Standard Component
rs-online.com / item# 251-9253

K. Wheels and Axle
Standard Component

L. 35mm Swivel Wheel
Standard Component

Transparent Tool: Improvised Vacuum with Tube and Brush, 2012. Designed and produced by Jesse Howard (American, b. 1978). Plastic, wood, 3D-printed components, electrical components. Courtesy of the designer.

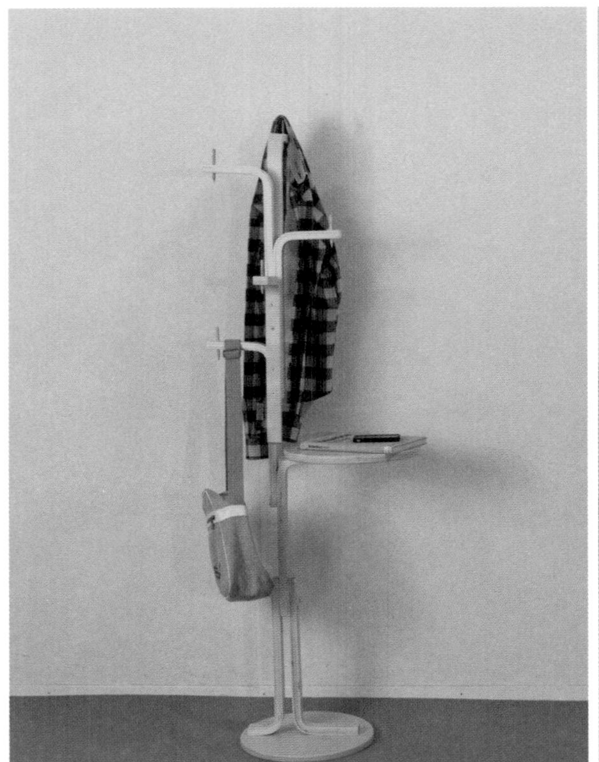

IKEA hackers repurpose existing components into new and surprising objects, approaching the Swedish furniture giant's repertoire of goods as an open catalog of parts and pieces. IKEA's manufacturing strategy already mobilizes the labor of users, exploiting flat-pack design solutions to reduce the cost of assembling, shipping, and storing finished products. Andreas Bhend designed this coat rack with parts from IKEA's Frosta stool. (Frosta is a four-legged version of Alvar Aalto's classic Stool 60, 1933, which has three legs). Bhend publishes his IKEA-based instructions online to encourage other users to implement his hacks and invent their own.

FROSTA Z

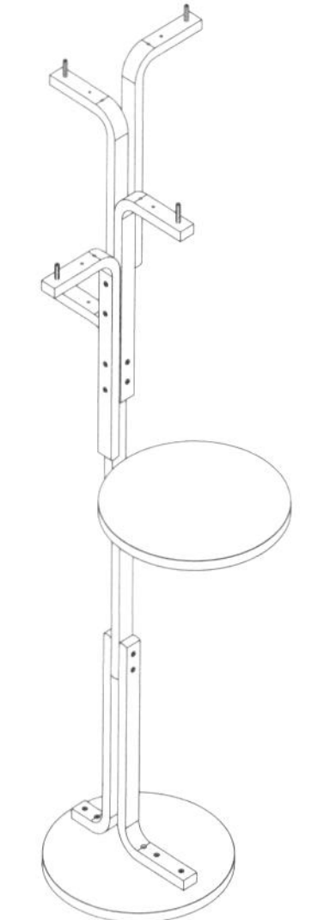

Design and Quality IKEA of Sweden
Redesign by Andreas Bhend

24x 2x 8x 2x 5x

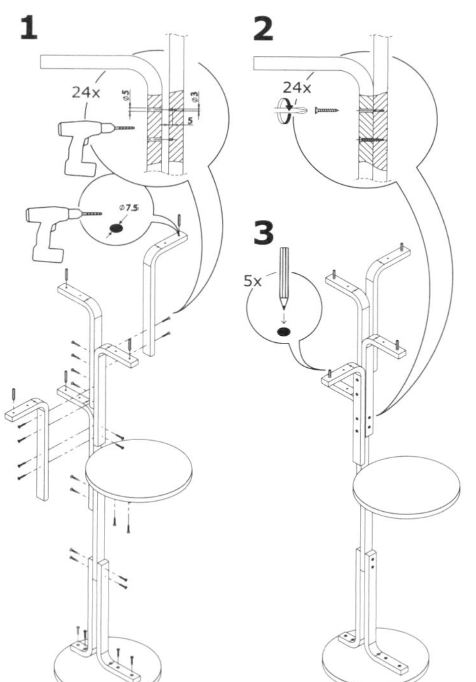

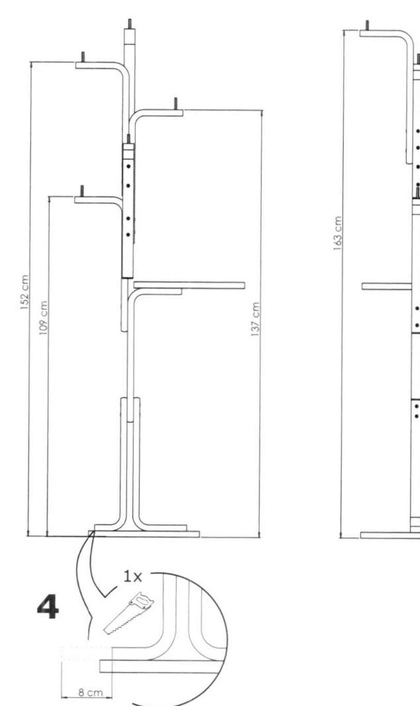

Frosta Z Coat Rack, 2012. Designed and produced by Andreas Bhend (German, b. 1989). Two IKEA Frosta stools (birch plywood, hardware). Courtesy of the designer.

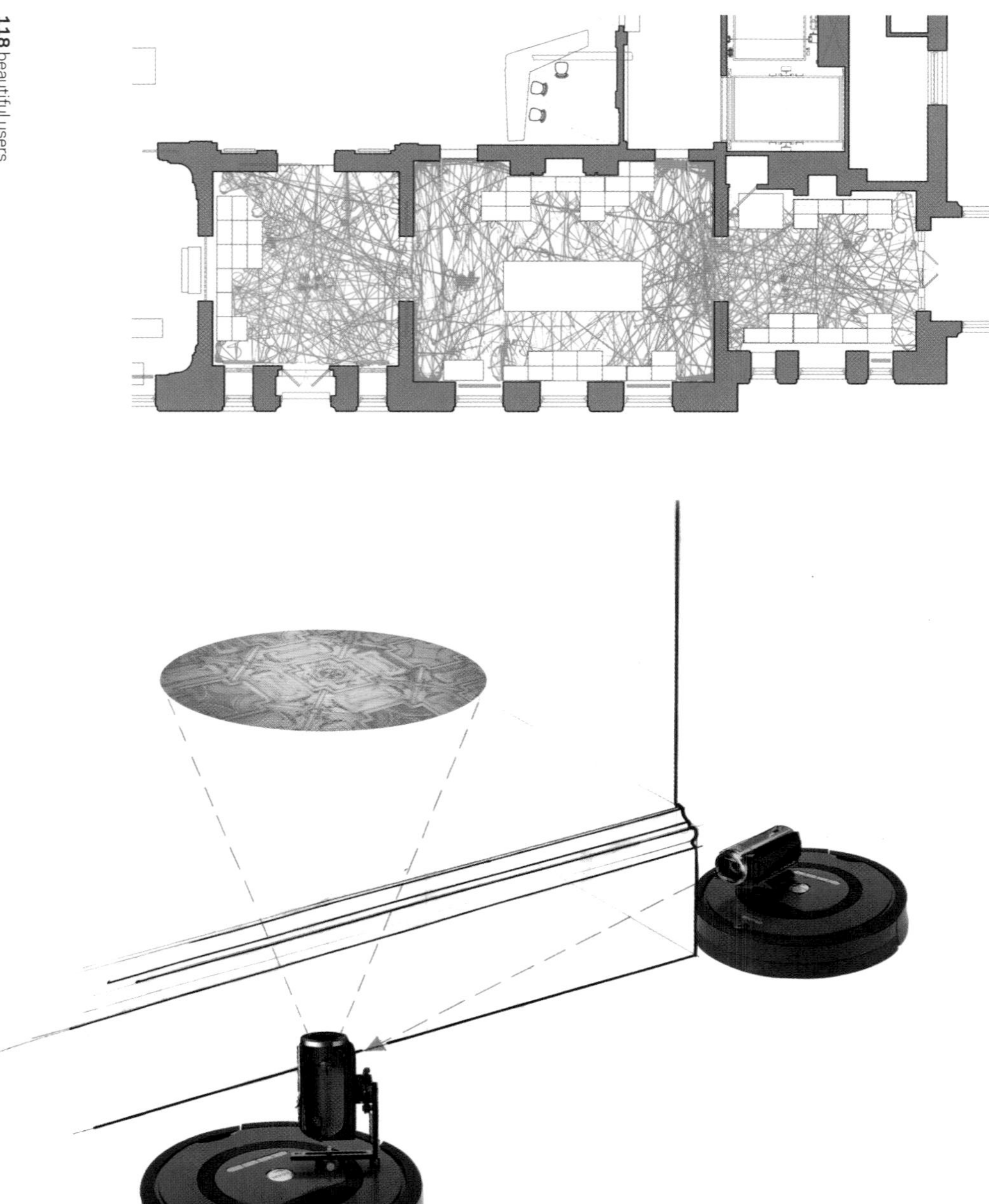

Subverting the Roomba's role as an obliging domestic robot, Diller Scofidio + Renfro have repurposed the popular household gadget to operate as an autonomous surveillance agent. Augmented with video recording capabilities, two Roomba spies patrol the Cooper Hewitt, Smithsonian Design Museum's premises after visitor hours. Video documentation captures chance encounters with other roaming devices and museum staff. Building on Diller Scofidio + Renfro's larger body of work investigating the role of surveillance technologies in architecture, the Roomba Cam provides commentary on our utopian visions of household automation.

Design for Roomba Cam, 2014. Designed by Diller Scofidio + Renfro (USA). Digital renderings. Courtesy of the designers.

Founded in 2011 by Edward Boatman, Sofya Polyakov, and Scott Thomas, the Noun Project is an online platform that uses crowdsourcing to build a pictorial language everyone can understand. Building on the belief that simple graphics enable communication among diverse global communities, thenounproject.com has become a vast dictionary of graphic icons. These are not your grandpa's toilet signs.

With icons ranging from "global warming" and "sustainable energy" to "break dancing" and "Gangnam style," the Noun Project enables anything to be communicated visually. It accepts submissions from users, and its various licensing agreements allow icons to be used for free with proper attribution or, alternatively, without attribution for a small fee. The revenue is then shared with the designer.

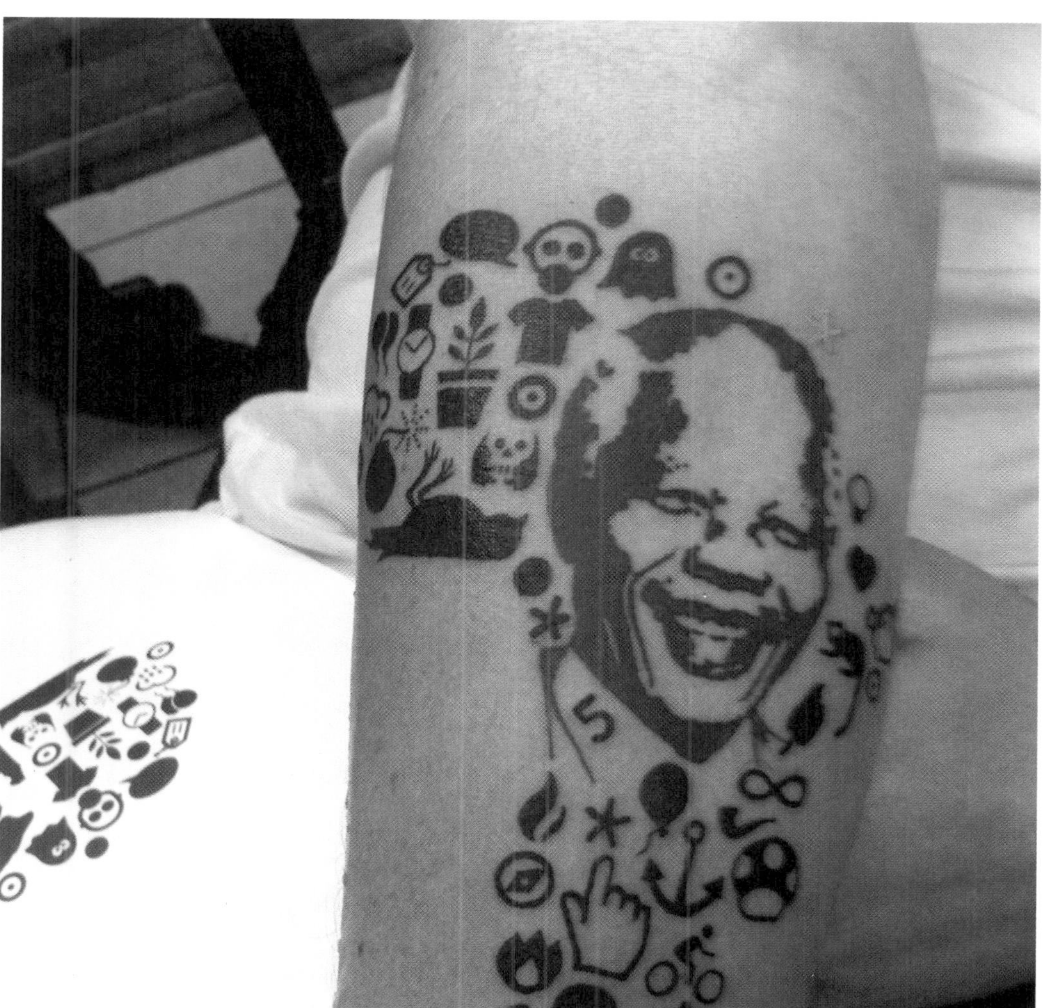

The Noun Project. Founded 2011 (USA). Opposite page: Abduction, by OCHA Visual Information Unit; Protest, Guerrilla Gardening, Hackathon, Latrine, Search-and-Rescue Team, and Sustainable Energy, by Iconathon; Break Dancing, by Marcel LeShell Cornett; Conception and Global Warming, by Luis Prado; Solar Energy, by Trento FuckingCity; Gangnam Style, by Arjun Mahanti. This page, tattoo in Pretoria, South Africa. Courtesy of the Noun Project.

The platform supports creative producers by offering a channel for sharing and profiting from their work. The Noun Project icons are widely used in editorial design, interface design, signage, posters, and information graphics. They build on a long tradition of pictograms created for public education.

MaKey MaKey allows users to connect a simple circuit board with any conductive object—including PlayDoh, metal kitchen utensils, fresh fruit, and graphite pencil drawings. When a human being grounds the current and completes the circuit, these everyday objects take the place of a mouse, arrow keys, or any key on a keyboard. Conceived by two researchers at MIT Media Lab, MaKey MaKey enables people with minimal technical skill to experiment with physical computing and to see the whole world as a construction kit. It allows users to change an object's given function and make it do something else. Working with any software on any computer, MaKey MaKey shows users that technology is a flexible thing that anyone can shape and control.

MaKey MaKey, 2012. Designed by Jay Silver (American, b. 1979) and Eric Rosenbaum (American, b. 1979). Manufactured by JoyLabz (USA). Circuit board, laptop, the everyday world (the design is only complete when combined with a user-supplied physical object and an everyday computer program or webpage). Courtesy of the designers.

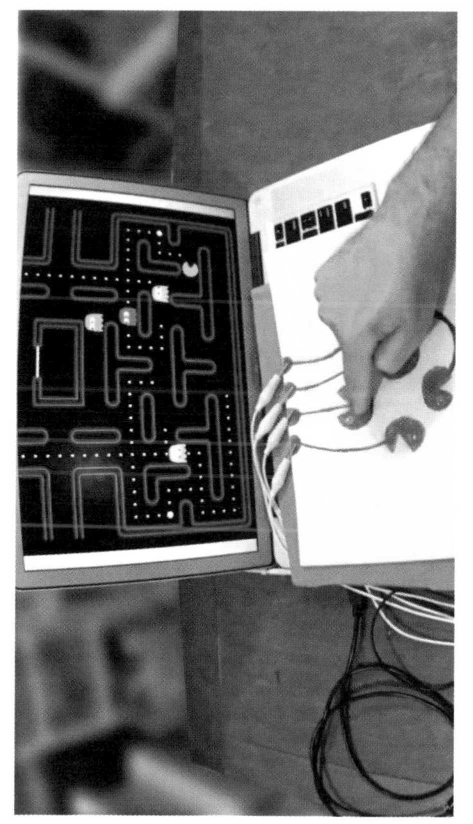

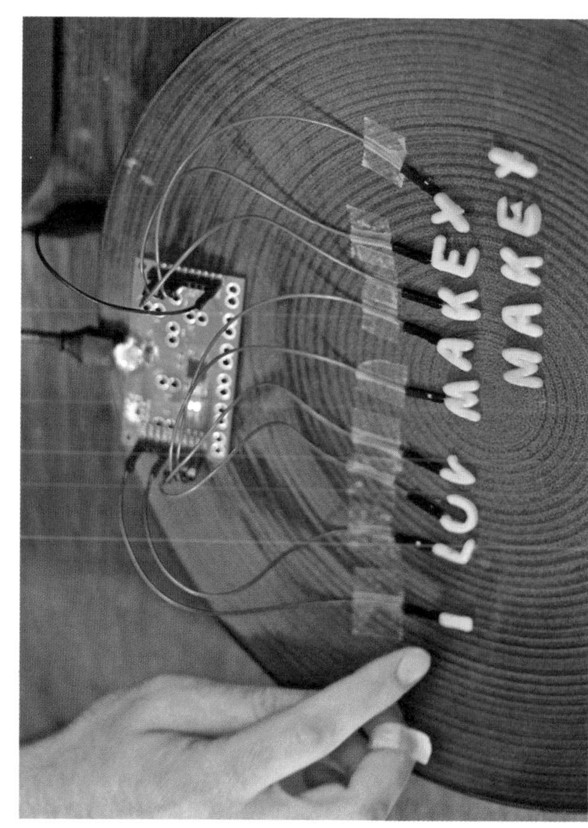

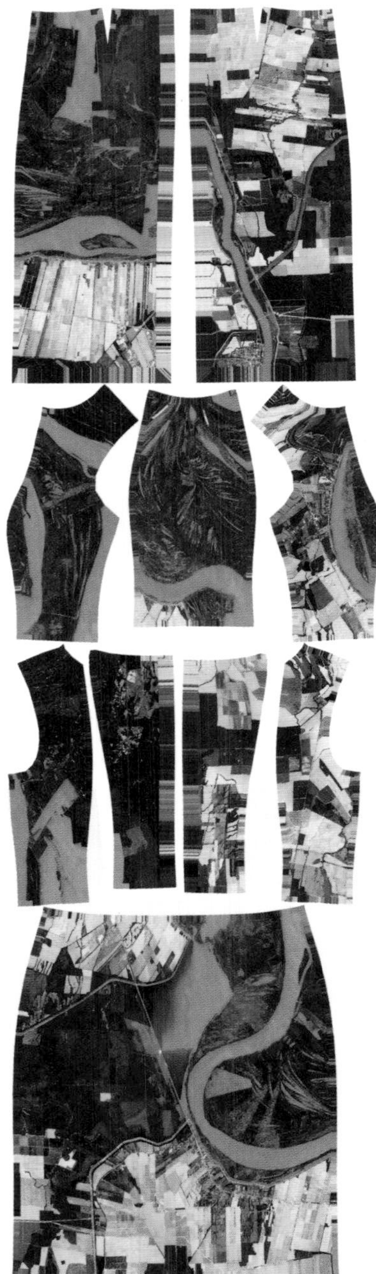

CONSTRVCT Software and Printed Fabric, 2013. Designed by Mary Huang (Chinese, b. 1986) and Jenna Fizel (American, b. 1986), Continuum Fashion (USA). Software, digitally printed cotton jersey. Courtesy of the designers.

CONSTRVCT is a digital platform for making and sharing fashion designs. Mary Huang and Jenna Fizel set out to create a set of 3D tools that users can easily access online. Combining techniques from architecture, animation, and industrial design, the software maps a 3D model of a garment onto fabric to be cut and sewn. The user selects an image or repeating pattern that maps onto the fabric; the resulting print serves as both sewing pattern and printed textile. Digital textile printing is relatively eco-friendly, because most of the dye locks into the fabric and so does not enter into wastewater. To use CONSTRVCT's complete set of e-commerce features, visit continuumfashion.com and create a user account.

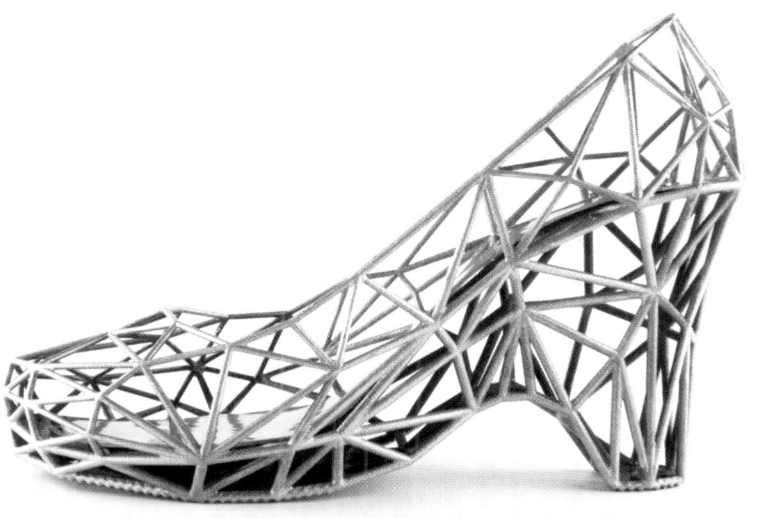

STRVCT Shoes, 2012–13. Designed by Mary Huang (Chinese, b. 1986) and Jenna Fizel (American, b. 1986), Continuum Fashion (USA). 3D-printed nylon with patent-leather insole and synthetic rubber coating. Courtesy of the designers.

The STRVCT collection of fantasy-inspired 3D-printed shoes explores the potential of 3D printing to create designed objects custom-fitted to the user's measurements. 3D-printed nylon can produce forms that are delicate in appearance, light in weight, and remarkably strong. Built from a network of triangulated segments, the transparent pump recalls Cinderella's glass slipper—a magical, materials-defying object that only she could wear. The Daphne series (above) refers to a lovely nymph who, according to Greek mythology, turned into a laurel tree in order to escape the predatory advances of the god Apollo. The shoes' patent-leather inner sole and synthetic rubber coating on the bottom surface make them wearable.

SUBMIT YOUR IDEA >

Sharing your idea on Quirky.com is the first step toward bringing it to life.

HELP US DECIDE >

Go ahead, vote on the ideas you love and help our inventors make their products better.

INFLUENCE & EARN >

You play a role in every decision we make. Clicking buttons on Quirky makes you money.

MAKING IT REAL >

Quirky uses state-of-the-art manufacturing techniques to make high-quality products.

THE WORLD PROSPERS

In the end, the world has access to a great invention, and you have access to more cash.

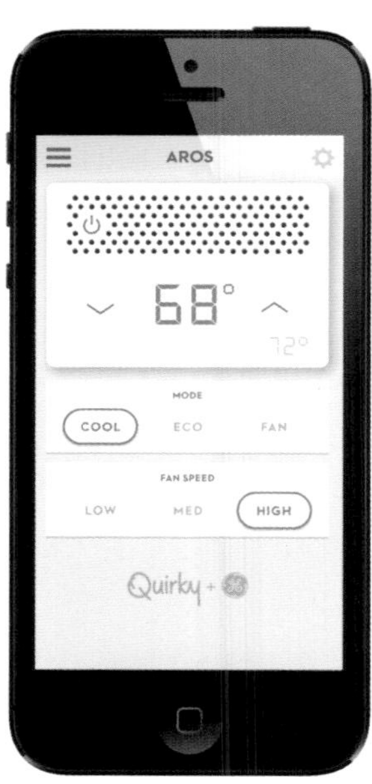

The Aros Window Air Conditioner is an app-enabled appliance developed by Quirky and GE. The concept originated with Dr. Garthen Leslie, a former Department of Energy executive who believed that window air conditioners could be controlled more efficiently. The unit is operated with Wink, a proprietary app that communicates with Quirky's growing family of Wi-Fi-connected gadgets and appliances, including a smart power cord that builds on Quirky's signature line of Pivot Power Flexible Surge Protectors, invented by Jake Zien. Quirky designs and produces odd and innovative products by inviting the public to submit and evaluate ideas. Members of the Quirky community vote on the concepts submitted by inventors. At meetings held online and

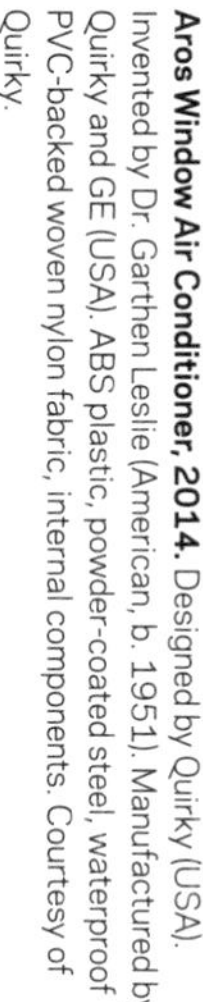

Aros Window Air Conditioner, 2014. Designed by Quirky (USA). Invented by Dr. Garthen Leslie (American, b. 1951). Manufactured by Quirky and GE (USA). ABS plastic, powder-coated steel, waterproof PVC-backed woven nylon fabric, internal components. Courtesy of Quirky.

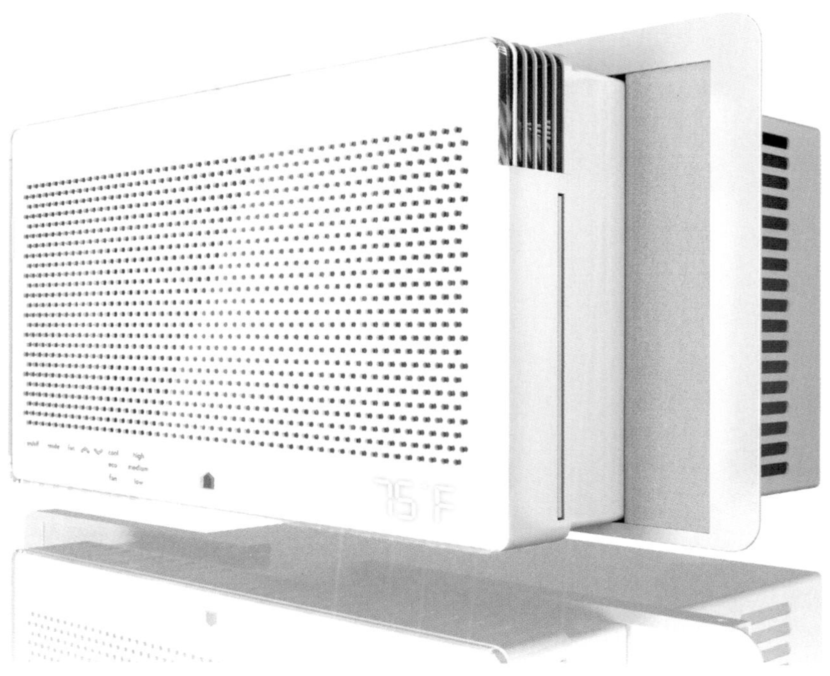

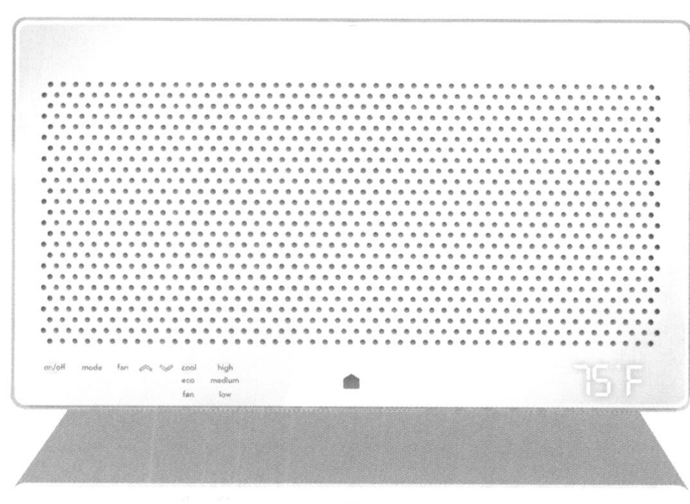

in person in Quirky's New York City office, community members help improve other inventors' ideas. Quirky's designers, engineers, and marketing experts make these crowd-generated ideas real through an intensive cycle of design and prototyping. Every member of the public who contributes to the process receives a royalty when a product is produced. Quirky's process is remarkable not only for its crowdsourcing methodology but also for the speed with which it brings products to market. Each week, the company receives about two thousand ideas and greenlights three or four for further development; each week, around three new Quirky products are ready for sale, through its website and through retailers such as Target, Home Depot, Amazon, and Bed Bath & Beyond.

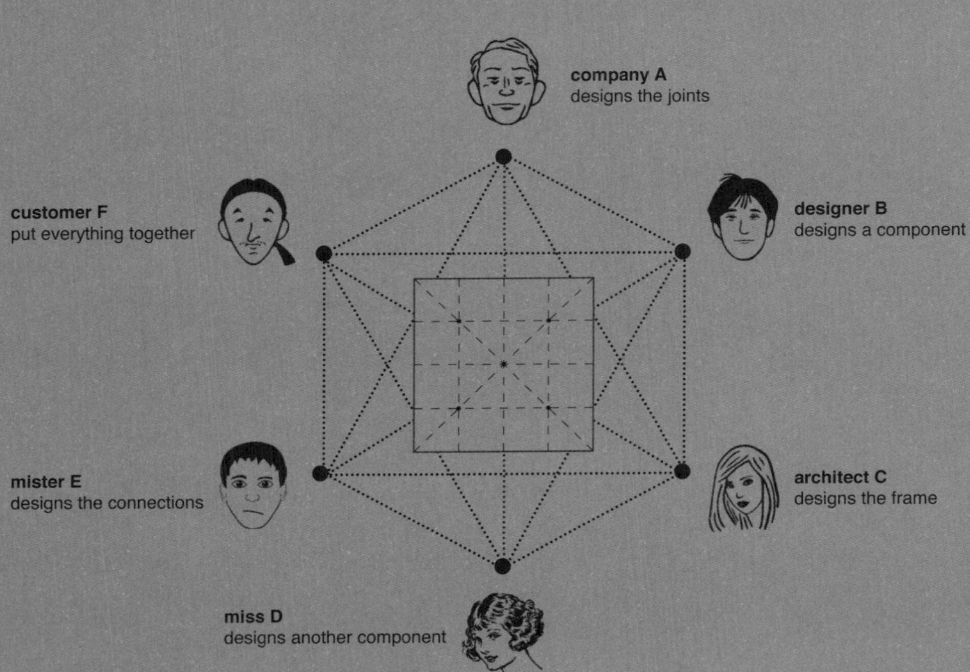
company A
designs the joints
customer F
put everything together
designer B
designs a component
mister E
designs the connections
architect C
designs the frame
miss D
designs another component

Tiffany Lambert

users speak

People spark objects to life. USERS, no longer hidden in plain sight, are increasingly dynamic agents, taking on new roles as contributors and producers themselves. As indicated by the rising interest in self-publishing, 3D printing, and personal manufacturing, users have transformed from passive recipients into proactive makers.

The figure of the user has evolved since the late nineteenth century, when the industrial revolution began bringing design into countless modern households, enabling mass production to abet mass consumption. The social movements prevalent in the 1960s and 1970s sprang up in part to critique the standardization of commodity culture, whereas the 1990s saw rising interest in CUSTOMIZATION and a preoccupation with individual expression, fostering new types of creative agency.

The reforms and uprisings of the past century laid the groundwork for design's current frameworks of public PARTICIPATION, including HACKING, open systems, and networks. Historical markers like these confront the ways we continue to revise and construct the category of the user, who remains a critical component in the endlessly shifting parameters of design.

Regardless of the varying objectives and circumstances that frame contemporary design practices, there is renewed concern today for collaboration and collective action around shared ideas that facilitate design experiences. Focusing on the trajectory of the user in design discourse, the following glossary looks at how people have engaged in the design process and what languages have served to describe this process. It compiles a selection of common terms, each with its own history and meaning, in order to map the critical terrain of design's vocabulary.

Design terminology leaves a time stamp on a continually developing field. The words designers use illuminate the intentions and results of their practice. Exploring the roots of this vocabulary can serve as a starting point or reference tool for users and designers to formulate, challenge, enhance, and compare their respective views and assumptions, prompting new ways to conceive the relationships among objects and humans. Designers—despite the shifting beats of history—can mediate broader cultural and social experiences, going well beyond considerations of aesthetics to explore and transform systems of power, feedback, and communication.

OpenStructures (OS) Diagram, 2009. Designed by Thomas Lommée (Belgian, b. 1979). Courtesy of the designer.

Adhocracy The term was coined in 1970 by Alvin Toffler in his best-selling book *Future Shock*. An adaptable and flexible alternative to bureaucratic organization, ADHOCRACY responds to change quickly by embracing spontaneity and stays open to new ideas in a world of technological upheaval. Applied to design, the word refers to design processes that are open to a broader common, rather than conducted according to the top-down methods typical of star designers. ADHOCRACY embraces people and networks and deletes the signature, challenging established hierarchies between designers and USERS. The exhibition *Adhocracy*, held at the inaugural Istanbul Design Biennial (2012) and subsequently shown at the New Museum in New York (2013), was organized by former *Domus* magazine editor Joseph Grima; the project celebrated "imperfection as evidence of an emerging force of identity, individuality, and nonlinearity in design." By definition, ADHOCRACY is malleable and therefore well suited to confront complex problems of the turbulent environments that design so often seeks to address. The intended outcome is generally rapid innovation.

Affordance Environmental psychologist James J. Gibson coined this term to name features of the environment that present living creatures with opportunities for action. He wrote in 1979, "The verb *to afford* is in the dictionary, but the noun AFFORDANCE is not. I have made it up. I mean by it something that refers to both the animal and the environment in a way that no existing term does" (127). AFFORDANCES occur when creatures transform sense data into conditions for potential action. A rigid horizontal surface AFFORDS support, becoming a ground or floor to walk on. The value of an AFFORDANCE is always relative to the creature perceiving it. A surface capable of supporting a water bug is quite different from a surface that could support an elephant. According to Harry Heft, some AFFORDANCES are learned rather than innate (a telephone can be dialed or a keyboard can be typed). Understanding AFFORDANCES is central to the design of INTERFACES, INTERACTIONS, and EXPERIENCES.

Anthropometry Measuring various attributes of the human body has its roots in statistical science. In 1891, Sir Francis Galton—a cousin of Charles Darwin and the researcher who gave eugenics its name—opened a laboratory in London where "visitors could be measured for height, weight, span, breath power, quickness of blow, seeing, hearing, and colour sense," among other physical attributes. Designers would later adopt ANTHROPOMETRY to better understand the USERS of their objects and better fit them to the human body while increasing the efficiency of the design and production processes. The early study of ANTHROPOMETRY would seed the later fields of ERGONOMICS and HUMAN FACTORS.

Authorship Early views of design AUTHORSHIP cast designers in the mold of independent creators. We rarely acknowledge the many individuals who helped develop the numerous products created by George Nelson's office or the teams that contributed to the collaborative agenda of Ray and Charles Eames. Critiques of AUTHORSHIP include Roland Barthes's 1967 essay "The Death of the Author," which sought to unseat the creator as the sole legislator of a work's significance. Barthes argues that the reader has replaced the author as a site for producing meaning. Adam Richardson's 1993 essay "The Death of the Designer" builds on Barthes's ideas, offering a critique of product semantics, or the ways in which visible features of products communicate meaning to USERS. Today, CROWDSOURCING, CO-DESIGN, and multidisciplinary design teams represent new processes of AUTHORSHIP.

Bricolage, Bricoleur The French word translates as "DO-IT-YOURSELF" in English; its contemporary meaning was introduced in 1927. Earlier definitions hint at creating from scratch, as in "to fix something ingeniously" (1849). In *The Savage Mind* (1962), Claude Lévi-Strauss defines BRICOLAGE as reusing readily available materials to solve new problems. Lévi-Strauss was contrasting the BRICOLEUR with the engineer at a time when designers and architects were looking for alternatives to modernism's focus on function in order to favor freedom and improvisation. Writing about the term in *Candide Journal for Architectural Knowledge* in 2011, critic Irénée Scalbert notes: "Being at once designer, builder, and USER, the BRICOLEUR is central to the process of making things" and is a person who "rebuilds his set of tools and materials by using the debris of previous events, the odds and ends left behind by other ventures." Similar ideas are found in photographer Richard Wentworth's ongoing series *Making Do and Getting By*, which inspired IDEO's Jane Fulton Suri to document provisional, intuitive interventions by everyday people in her influential book *Thoughtless Acts?* (2005).

Co-Creation, Co-Design With strong ties to management and organizational theories, this method of cooperative production counts on designers and marketers to devise solutions based on USER input. Design consulting agencies including Frog Design and Smart Design regularly employ this method of working through problems by combining the expert knowledge of trained designers and researchers with the local knowledge of end USERS. Although the term CO-DESIGN invokes utopian, grassroots ambitions, it has become associated with the fusion of business and design. *Fast Company*'s website Co.Design adopted the term in June 2010 to highlight the intersection of "business + innovation + design."

Consumer Celebrated during the surge of mass production and the birth of the industrial design profession during the 1920s, the term CONSUMER now carries a negative connotation linked to overconsumption and passivity. Cultural critic Raymond Williams traced the historical rise in the use and purchase of goods in the etymology of the word. His book *Keywords: A Vocabulary of Culture and Society* states, "In almost all its early English uses, CONSUME had an unfavourable sense; it meant to destroy, to use up, to waste, to exhaust. It was from the middle eighteenth century that CONSUMER began to emerge in a neutral sense in descriptions of bourgeois political economy, and it was really only in the mid-twentieth century that the word passed from specialized use to popular use."

Crowd Funding, Crowdsourcing Explored in 2006 by Jeff Howe, an editor at *Wired* magazine, CROWDSOURCING invites a large network of volunteers to take part in or complete a task. The underlying principle that innovation comes from unexpected places predates Howe's article, however, as many European governments from the sixteenth century onward offered prizes through an open call for the best solutions to various feats (usually in engineering). Wikipedia, Amazon USER reviews, Ebay, Twitter, and Facebook couldn't exist without the contributions of crowds of people. The notion, which usually involves some mutual benefit, evolved into the related idea of CROWD FUNDING, with websites such as Kickstarter.

Customer The word CUSTOMER has been used since the fifteenth century to describe a person with a regular relationship to a store or supplier, whereas a CONSUMER has a more abstract relationship to a marketplace. CUSTOMER declined in popularity as CONSUMER ascended. In part to combat

CONSUMERS' ennui of passive consumption, the final decades of the twentieth century saw a sharp rise in USER PARTICIPATION, promoted by newly established corporate consultancies such as IDEO. USER input became standard practice in conjunction with the rise of design management, which brought together researchers, psychologists, anthropologists, designers, and USER participants.

Customization In use since 1934, the verb *to customize* means to make something to a particular USER's specifications. Prior to the Industrial Revolution, CUSTOMIZATION was the norm (although it was not named as such). Mass production turned out standardized, low-cost products in high volume, which at the time yielded positive associations with efficiency, hygiene, and modernity. In the 1960s and 1970s, radical designers created modular product systems that could be personalized and adjusted by the end USER. CUSTOMIZATION peaked in the early 2000s with services such as NikeID, which allows people to select various colors and materials for their sneakers. Today, greater access to production tools, such as 3D printers, is taking CUSTOMIZATION to another level, shifting the economies of scale by returning the methods of production to the designer or USER. Although early forms of 3D printing have been used by industry since the late 1980s (also called "additive manufacturing technologies," which build prototypes from layers of material), these techniques were until recently too expensive for individuals to access for personal use.

Democratization Design discourse has begun adopting the term DEMOCRATIZATION to refer to objects or systems that appear to bring people more choices and broader access. Experts on democratic theory, however, agree that a true democracy appoints appropriate decision makers rather than giving equal weight to everyone's singular decisions. Often, when USERS are invited to partake in the design process, the choices available are set by designers and manufacturers. The rhetoric surrounding terms like DEMOCRATIZATION and PARTICIPATION implies that their application inherently benefits the common good. Writing in 1970, Carole Pateman, a British political theorist and feminist, gave this impression: "During the last few years of the 1960s, the word 'PARTICIPATION' became part of the popular vocabulary....It is rather ironical that the idea of PARTICIPATION should have become so popular, for among political theorists and political sociologists the widely accepted theory of democracy (so widely accepted that one might call it the orthodox doctrine) is one in which the concept of participation has only the most minimal role." Supporters of PARTICIPATION note that although the status of the elite practitioner may be eroding, millions of previously unheard voices are rising, their abilities enhanced by new tools and new expertise. Scholars on USERS, PARTICIPATION, and architecture—including Jeremy Till, Markus Miessen, and Kenny Cupers—argue that this friction between optimism and critical questioning forms an overly simplistic dialectic of inclusive/exclusive, democratic/authoritarian, and bottom-up/top-down.

Design Thinking This process of inquiry begins with a period of open-ended problem definition; the goal is to focus on the potential needs and desires of USERS rather than on predetermined outcomes. Often working in interdisciplinary teams, proponents of DESIGN THINKING generate multiple solutions and then create, test, and revise prototypes in an iterative process. Interest in uncovering the methods behind the design process flowered in the 1960s and is commonly traced to architecture schools in England. "If the steps in a designer's processes could be identified, examined, and understood, they could be improved or corrected," writes design historian Peter Downton. The first Conference on Design Methods took place in 1962 in London. The Design Research Society (still active) in England and the Design Methods Group in the U.S. were both founded in 1962. Building on a range of commonly applied design practices, DESIGN THINKING coalesced into a clearly defined methodology—particularly valued as a strategy in corporations and widely taught in design education—with guidance from the founders of IDEO, including Bill Moggridge, Tim Brown, and David and Tom Kelley.

Do-It-Yourself The term DO-IT-YOURSELF, or DIY, refers to self-produced design or construction. DIY has origins in the late 1800s, when "Mr. Fixit" became popular, and later became linked to gardening and home-improvement publications. Stewart Brand's *Whole Earth Catalog* (1968–72), an icon of the 1960s counterculture, celebrated "access to tools," from early computers and electronics to pickaxes, gardening manuals, chainsaws, and tents. Enzo Mari's *Autoprogettazione* (loosely translated as "self-made") project of 1974 embraced the anti-authoritarian spirit of the era's student movements. Mari's pamphlet, still widely available today at used bookshops and online, contains plans and images for nineteen pieces of furniture, easily assembled with simple boards and nails. The DO-IT-YOURSELF instructions were mailed to anyone who paid the postage. When the project was reissued in 2010 by Finnish furniture company Artek, Mari described his original intent: "It's an easy thing to say but we cannot expect everyone to understand complicated production technologies nor to own specialized sets of tools. An idea came to me. If someone actually tried to build, they probably would learn. Design is only design if it communicates knowledge." Today's MAKER movement continues this DIY tradition.

Ergonomics Also referred to as HUMAN ENGINEERING or HUMAN FACTORS, ERGONOMICS aims to tailor the world to better accommodate people. British engineers coined the word during WWII, when they undertook to improve the cockpit environment. While major advances in ERGONOMICS were born out of military research, the concept has its origins in early twentieth-century industrial theory, which focused on forcing people to fit machines instead of designing machines to fit people, seen in the time-and-motion studies and industrial-efficiency techniques of Frederick Winslow Taylor and Frank and Lillian Gilbreth (known as scientific management). In the 1950s and 1960s, ERGONOMICS expanded to everything from books and spaceships to kitchen appliances and office machines. Usability became a selling point. English critic Stephen Bayley wrote in his 1985 publication *Natural Design: The Search for Comfort and Efficiency*, "Educated consumers are not ashamed to complain when they cannot understand or operate new appliances."

Experience Design, Experience Economy Focusing on the USER's sensual, cognitive, and emotional engagement with a product over time, EXPERIENCE DESIGN addresses the associations and behaviors people develop in response to a product or service. Design tasks include building brand recognition. The EXPERIENCE ECONOMY is a business concept described by James H. Gilmore and B. Joseph Pine II in their 1999 book *The Experience Economy*, which argues that "goods and services are no longer enough"; businesses must trigger positive memories and emotions. In digital INTERACTION DESIGN, the atmospheric and emotional qualities of using software and websites can foster meaningful engagement, motivated by the informational needs of USERS.

Hacking With roots in the domain of software security, HACKING has extended to the realm of objects. Using existing products for unintended functions, HACKERS take things apart or add on new components. HACKERS often seek to subvert CONSUMERISM; HACKING often approaches the world of manufactured things as a set of materials and components. Roomba HACKS exploit the sophisticated electronics of the popular robotic vacuum cleaner; IKEA HACKS construct new products from the furniture giant's vast kit of parts. In his influential text *The Practice of Everyday Life* (1984), cultural theorist Michel de Certeau examines the ways people individualize mass culture through reappropriation. By shifting the emphasis from the producer or the object itself onto the USER, de Certeau identifies a crack in the modernist vision of top-down planning.

Human-Centered Design IDEO, a firm that has long advocated for the broad application of DESIGN THINKING to diverse areas of problem solving, has asserted the use of the term HUMAN-CENTERED DESIGN (HCD) in place of USER-CENTERED DESIGN. Looking beyond the USER as a subject configured in relation to products or services, HCD considers people's broader needs, wants, and behaviors, balancing these considerations with the concerns of all stakeholders. HCD identifies problems across the spectrum of human experience and then seeks solutions in innumerable forms, including products, processes, protocols, services, environments, and social institutions.

Human Engineering, Human Factors See ERGONOMICS.

Interaction Design Looking beyond the controls for operating a device to broader actions and relationships, INTERACTION DESIGN includes screen-based experiences (such as websites and apps), interactive products (physical objects with integrated software), and services (engagement between a company and CUSTOMERS involving physical spaces, products, software, and more). The practice of INTERACTION DESIGN draws upon human computer interaction (HCI), computer science, software engineering, cognitive psychology, sociology, and anthropology. Designer Anthony Dunne has noted that a handful of computer scientists and HACKERS began to develop an understanding of interactivity in the early 1990s as "a partnership between people and machines acted out on the computer screen," a partnership made viable in the marketplace by Steve Jobs and the founders of Apple Computer (23).

Interface Design The term INTERFACE appeared in scientific writing in the 1880s to name the surface where two bodies meet; proponents of ERGONOMICS began using the word in reference to human-machine controls in the 1940s. In his 1988 book *The Design of Everyday Things*, cognitive psychologist Donald A. Norman lays out guidelines for USER-CENTERED INTERFACE DESIGN. To fulfill its humane purpose, an INTERFACE should require minimal instruction and explanation, relying as much as possible on intuitive mappings of a USER's action and that action's impact on the system. Feedback should clearly confirm the action, and the INTERFACE should represent the current state of the system. In short, the designer must "make sure that (1) the USER can figure out what to do, and (2) the USER can tell what is going on."

Maker Today's MAKER combines hands-on craftsmanship with TINKERING, invention, and technology-enhanced manufacturing. Richard Sennett asserts in *The Craftsman* that "making is thinking" (ix). With roots in the Arts and Crafts movement, the concept of the MAKER as an emancipated producer resurfaced in the DO-IT-YOURSELF counterculture of the 1960s and in the celebration of personal computing and OPEN-SOURCE code. More recently, Maker Faires have cropped up in the United States, Africa, London, and beyond to gather "tech enthusiasts, crafters, educators, tinkerers, hobbyists, engineers, science clubs, authors, artists, students, and commercial exhibitors." At the heart of MAKER culture is the idea of returning the methods of production to USERS by sharing design knowledge and promoting access to methods of manufacturing.

Open-Source Design The practice of creating products using information that is generally free, available online, and openly modifiable is called OPEN-SOURCE DESIGN. This practice builds on the movement begun by computer programmers around the early 1970s to promote free access to and distribution of software, rejecting centralized control over creative work in favor of transparency. In 1999, an engineer from MIT formed the Open Design Foundation, inspiring many individuals and businesses to follow suit. The OPEN-SOURCE ideology raises questions about intellectual-property rights. How can creators benefit from the outcome of their work or protect the integrity of a concept? Advocates of OPEN-SOURCE DESIGN argue that free access to tools and data enhances the quality of design knowledge overall. This outlook has also led to the formation of sharing economies that thrive on the exchange of tools, knowledge, and services.

Participation, Participatory Design Many designers today actively seek to involve key stakeholders (end USERS, designers, CUSTOMERS, clients, and so on) in the design process. PARTICIPATORY DESIGN has become a blanket term used to describe almost any engagement with USERS. What differs among these engagements is the extent of the participant's involvement, the ethics of that involvement, and the AUTHORSHIP of the work at hand. PARTICIPATORY DESIGN belongs to a larger trajectory that has been called "relational aesthetics," referring to artistic practices that engage audiences in open-ended processes. As John M. Carroll has written, PARTICIPATORY DESIGN practices can be implemented in myriad ways, all "predicated on the concept that the people who will ultimately use a designed artifact are entitled to have a voice in determining how it is designed."

Prosumer Coined in 1980 by futurist Alvin Toffler in his book *The Third Wave*, the word PROSUMER merges several word combinations: *producer* and *consumer, proactive* and *consumer*, and *professional* and *consumer*. Although Toffler did not use the term until 1980, he described the phenomenon of an active, PARTICIPATORY CONSUMER as early as 1970, as did Marshall McLuhan and Barrington Nevitt in their 1972 publication *Take Today: The Executive as Dropout*, which illustrates the "changeover, from matching to making, from acquisition to involvement." As a marketing term, PROSUMER refers to tech gadgets that fall between professional grade and CONSUMER grade. DO-IT-YOURSELF activities often involve consuming specialized supplies and services—most crafters and makers don't function completely off the grid but rely on a range of CONSUMER goods.

Tinkering From the 1590s, the word TINKERING had a negative connotation, suggesting aimless work or keeping busy in a useless way. Today it refers to open-ended and self-motivated experimentation. TINKERING doesn't necessarily pursue an end goal but instead finds value in the process of discovery. Often associated with USERS working independently, TINKERING has strong ties to

DESIGN THINKING and brainstorming sessions used to foster innovation and generate ideas.

Universal Design Accommodating the needs of people with disabilities improves the EXPERIENCE of average USERS as well. UNIVERSAL DESIGN strives to make products, environments, and media accessible to all USERS, including those with physical, sensory, and cognitive differences. From birth through the aging process, disability changes over the course of a lifetime. Pioneering activists in the accessible design movement include Rolf A. Faste, who coauthored the study *Access to the Built Environment* in 1979. The 1990 Americans with Disabilities Act (ADA) establishes rules for accessible design in public places. In practice, it is not possible to meet the needs of all USERS at all times, given the enormous diversity of human ability. However, by considering the needs of diverse USERS, designers greatly expand access to products, places, and information.

User Philosopher and sociologist Henri Lefebvre (among others) has argued that the term USER dehumanizes people, reducing them to functional objects by discounting their agency. Others use the term *citizen* interchangeably with USER to imply the individual's potential instrumentality. First employed in the 1610s to refer to the status, rights, privileges, and responsibilities of a person, *citizen* is prevalent in literature related to USERS, specifically in that of planning and architecture. The Museum of Modern Art's 1944 exhibition *Design for Use* featured works that underlined "the relationship between function, technology, and form as shown in some typical products." László Moholy-Nagy was one of several design minds invited to brainstorm for this exhibition with curator Serge Chermayeff. In notes from the first internal meeting, Moholy-Nagy wrote that the project's goal was to "make the USER realize [the] importance of design." (He went on to found what became the Illinois Institute of Technology in Chicago, the first school in the U.S. to offer a PhD in design.) The USER was becoming an increasingly central concept in the discourse of design.

User-Centered Design A design process organized around the end USER's needs and limitations, USER-CENTERED DESIGN studies the USER as a subject (age, demographic, etc.) in order to inform decisions about product development, often engaging psychologists, anthropologists, and other social scientists. Rather than start the design process with a product concept or new technology in need of an application, USER-CENTERED DESIGN begins by exploring USERS needs and wants. This methodology seeks to improve people's lives and EXPERIENCES while also seeking opportunities to benefit the client.

References

Adhocracy

"Adhocracy" (2013) http://www.newmuseum.org/exhibitions/view/adhocracy.

Encyclopaedia Britannica. Chicago: Encyclopaedia Britannica, 2003.

Fagerberg, Jan, David C. Mowery, and Richard R. Nelson. *The Oxford Handbook of Innovation*. New York: Oxford University Press, 2006. 130.

Grima, Joseph. *Adhokrasi/Adhocracy: 1st Istanbul Design Biennial*. Istanbul: Istanbul Foundation for Culture and Arts, 2012.

Mintzberg, Henry. *The Structuring of Organizations*. Englewood Cliffs, NJ: Prentice-Hall, 1979.

Toffler, Alvin. *Future Shock*. New York: Bantam Books, 1970.

Waterman, Robert H. *Adhocracy: The Power to Change*. Knoxville, TN: Whittle Direct Books, 1990.

Affordance

Gibson, James J. *The Ecological Approach to Visual Perception*. New York: Taylor and Francis, 1979.

Heft, Harry. "Affordances and the Body: An Intentional Analysis of Gibson's Ecological Approach to Visual Perception." *Journal for the Theory of Social Behavior* 19, no. 1 (1989): 1–30.

Anthropometry

Callender, John Hancock. "The Scientific Approach to Design." *The Engineered Dwelling*. Edited by Robert Davison. New York: John B. Pierce Foundation, 1944. 8–11.

Eames, Ray. *A Computer Perspective: Background to the Computer Age*. Cambridge, MA: Harvard University Press, 1990.

Gilbreth, Lillian. *The Home-Maker and Her Job*. New York: D. Appleton, 1927.

Tilley, Alvin R., and Henry Dreyfuss & Associates. *The Measure of Man and Woman, Revised Edition: Human Factors in Design*. New York: John Wiley & Sons, 2002.

Authorship

Barthes, Roland. "The Death of the Author." *Image/Music/Text*. New York: Hill and Wang, 1977. 142–48.

Foucault, Michel. "What Is an Author?" *The Foucault Reader*. Edited by Paul Rabinow. New York: Vintage Books, 2010. 101–20.

Krippendorf, Klauss. *The Semantic Turn: A New Foundation for Design*. Boca Raton, FL: CRC Press, 2006. 1–3.

Richardson, Adam. "The Death of the Designer." *Design Issues* 9, no. 2 (1993): 34–43.

Rudofsky, Bernard. *Architecture Without Architects: A Short Introduction to Non-pedigreed Architecture*. New York: Museum of Modern Art, 1965.

Bricolage, Bricoleur

Fulton Suri, Jane. *Thoughtless Acts? Observations on Intuitive Design*. San Francisco: Chronicle Books, 2005.

Lévi-Strauss, Claude. *The Savage Mind*. Chicago: University of Chicago Press, 1966.

Scalbert, Irénée. "The Architect as Bricoleur." *Candide Journal for Architectural Knowledge* 4 (2011): 69–88.

Simpson, J. A., and E. S. C. Weiner, *Oxford English Dictionary*. Oxford: Oxford University Press, 1989.

Tate Gallery. *Richard Wentworth: 'Making Do and Getting By.'* London: Tate Gallery, 1984.

Co-Creation, Co-Design

Robischon, Noah. "From the Editor" *Co.Design*. (June 21, 2010). http://www.fastcodesign.com/from-the-editor-21062010.

Sanders, Elizabeth B. N. "Postdesign and Participatory Culture" (1999) and "Generative Tools for CoDesigning" (2000). MakeTools. http://www.maketools.com/papers-3.html.

Consumer, Customer

Ayto, John. *Word Origins: The Hidden Histories of English Words from A to Z*. London: A & C Black, 2005.

Packard, Vance. *The Hidden Persuaders*. New York: D. McKay Co., 1957.

Simpson, J. A., and E. S. C. Weiner, *Oxford English Dictionary*. Oxford: Oxford University Press, 1989.

Williams, Raymond. *Keywords: A Vocabulary of Culture and Society*. New York: Oxford University Press, 1976. 68–70.

Crowd Funding, Crowdsourcing

Howe, Jeff. "The Rise of Crowdsourcing." *Wired* 14, no. 6 (2006): 1–4.

Surowiecki, James. *The Wisdom of Crowds*. New York: Anchor, 2005.

Customization

Hounshell, David. *From the American System to Mass Production, 1800–1932*. Baltimore: Johns Hopkins University, 1984.

Lipson, Hod, and Melba Kurman. *Fabricated: The New World of 3D Printing*. Indianapolis: John Wiley & Sons, 2013.

Yelavich, Susan. "Swatch." *Design Studies: A Reader*. Edited by Hazel Clark and David Brody. New York: Berg, 2009. 490–94.

Democratization

Blundell Jones, Peter, Doina Petrescu, and Jeremy Till. "The Negotiation of Hope." *Architecture and Participation*. London: Spon Press, 2005. 25–44.

Pateman, Carole. *Participation and Democratic Theory*. Cambridge: Cambridge University Press, 1970. 1.

Wiener, Philip P. *Dictionary of the History of Ideas: Studies of Selected Pivotal Ideas*. New York: Scribner, 1973–74. 652–67.

Design Thinking

Broadbent, Geoffrey. *Design in Architecture: Architecture and the Human Sciences*. New York: John Wiley & Sons, 1973.

Brown, Tim. *Change by Design: How Design Thinking Transforms Organizations and Inspires Innovation*. New York: Harper Business, 2009.

Downton, Peter. *Design Research*. Melbourne: RMIT Pub, 2003.

Knoblauch, Joy. "Going Soft: Architecture and the Human Sciences in the United States, 1963 to 1974." 98th ACSA Annual Meeting, New Orleans, March 4–7, 2010.

Rowe, Peter G. *Design Thinking*. Cambridge, MA: MIT Press, 1987.

Sachs, Avigail. "Architects, Users, and the Social Sciences in Postwar America." *Use Matters: An Alternative History of Architecture*. Edited by Kenny Cupers. New York: Routledge, 2014. 69–84.

Schorske, Carl. E. "The New Rigorism in the Human Sciences, 1940–1960." *American Academic Culture in Transformation: Fifty Years, Four Disciplines*. Edited by Thomas Bender and Carle E. Schorske. Princeton, NJ: Princeton University Press, 1997. 289–309.

Do-It-Yourself

Hawes, Joseph M., and Elizabeth I. Nybakken. *Family and Society in American History*. Urbana: University of Illinois Press, 2001.

Mari, Enzo. "Enzo Mari for Artek: Homage to Autoprogettazione." http://vimeo.com/39684024.

Turner, Fred. *From Counterculture to Cyberculture: Stewart Brand, The Whole Earth Network, and the Rise of Digital Utopianism*. Chicago: University of Chicago Press, 2006.

Ergonomics

Bayley, Stephen. *Natural Design: The Search for Comfort and Efficiency*. London: Boilerhouse and Victoria & Albert Museum, 1985.

Cohen, H. Harvey, and Wesley E. Woodson. *Principles of Forensic Human Factors/Ergonomics*. Tuscon, AZ: Lawyers & Judges Publishing Co., 2005.

Encyclopaedia Britannica. Chicago: Encyclopaedia Britannica, 2003.

McCormick, Ernest J. *Human Engineering*. New York: McGraw-Hill Book Company, 1957.

Meister, David. *The History of Human Factors and Ergonomics*. Mahwah, NJ: Lawrence Erlbaum Associates, 1999.

Wickens, Christopher D, Justin G. Hollands, Raja Parasuraman, and Simon Banbury. *Engineering Psychology & Human Performance*. Upper Saddle River, NJ: Pearson College Division, 2012.

Experience Design, Experience Economy

Buxton, Bill. *Sketching User Experiences: Getting the Design Right and the Right Design*. San Francisco: Morgan Kaufmann, 2007.

Leung, Linda. *Digital Experience Design: Ideas, Industries, Interaction*. Bristol, U.K.: Intellect, 2008.

Pine, B. Joseph, II, and James H. Gilmore. *The Experience Economy: Work Is Theatre and Every Business a Stage, Goods and Services Are No Longer Enough*. Boston: Harvard Business School Press, 1999.

Hacking

De Certeau, Michel. *The Practice of Everyday Life*. Berkeley: University of California Press, 1984.

Rajagopal, Avinash. *Hacking Design*. New York: Cooper Hewitt, Smithsonian Design Museum, 2013.

Human-Centered Design

IDEO. *Human-Centered Design Toolkit*. Second ed. 2009. http://www.ideo.com/work/human-centered-design-toolkit/.

Rouse, William B. *Explorations of Human-Centered Design*. Hoboken, NJ: John Wiley & Sons, 2007.

Interaction Design

Dunne, Anthony. *Hertzian Tales: Electronic Products, Aesthetic Experience, and Critical Design*. Cambridge, MA: MIT Press, 2005.

Laurel, Brenda. *Computers as Theater*. Second ed. Upper Saddle River, NJ: Addison-Wesley, 2014.

Moggridge, Bill. *Designing Interactions*. Cambridge, MA: MIT Press, 2007.

Murray, Janet H. *Inventing the Medium: Principles of Interaction Design as a Cultural Practice*. Cambridge, MA: MIT Press, 2012.

Turoff, Murray, and Starr Roxanne Hiltz. *The Network Nation: Human Communication via Computer*. Cambridge, MA: MIT Press, 1993.

Interface Design

Harwood, John. *The Interface: IBM and the Transformation of Corporate Design, 1945–1976*. Minneapolis: University of Minnesota Press, 2011.

Norman, Donald A. *The Design of Everyday Things*. New York: Basic Books, 1988.

Maker

Anderson, Chris. *Makers: The New Industrial Revolution*. New York: Crown Business, 2012.

"Maker Faire: A Bit of History." http://makerfaire.com/makerfairehistory/.

Sennett, Richard. *The Craftsman*. New Haven, CT: Yale University Press, 2008.

Open-Source Design

Abel, Bas van, Lucas Evers, Roel Klaassen, and Peter Troxler. *Open Design Now: Why Design Cannot Remain Exclusive*. Amsterdam: BIS Publishers, 2011.

Participation, Participatory Design

Armstrong, Helen, and Zvezdana Stojmirovic. *Participate: Designing with User-Generated Content*. New York: Princeton Architectural Press, 2011.

Bishop, Claire. *Artificial Hells: Participatory Art and the Politics of Spectatorship*. New York: Verso, 2012.

Bourdieu, Pierre. *Outline of a Theory of Practice*. Cambridge: Cambridge University Press, 1977.

Bourriaud, Nicholas. *Relational Aesthetics*. France: Les presses du réel, 1998.

Carroll, John M. "Dimensions of Participation in Simon's Design." *Design Issues* 22, no. 2 (2006): 3–18.

Prosumer

McLuhan, Marshall, and Barrington Nevitt. *Take Today: The Executive as Dropout*. New York: Harcourt Brace Jovanovich, 1972.

Toffler, Alvin. *The Third Wave*. New York: Morrow, 1980.

Tinkering

Ammer, Christine. *The American Heritage Dictionary of Idioms*. Boston: Houghton Mifflin, 1997. 463.

Universal Design

Steinfeld, Edward, Steven Schroeder, James Duncan, Rolf Faste, Deborah Chollett, Marilyn Bishop, Peter Wirth, and Paul Cardell. *Access to the Built Environment: A Review of Literature*. Washington, DC: U.S. Department of Housing and Urban Development, 1979. https://archive.org/details/accesstothebuilt003372mbp.

Lidwell, William, Kritina Holden, and Jill Butler. *Universal Principles of Design*. Gloucester, MA: Rockport Publishers, 2003.

Williamson, Beth. "Getting a Grip: Disability in American Industrial Design in the Late Twentieth Century." *Winterthur Portfolio* 46, no. 4 (Winter 2012): 213–36.

User

Cupers, Kenny. *Use Matters: An Alternative History of Architecture*. London: Routledge, 2013.

Lefebvre, Henri. *The Production of Space*. Oxford: Blackwell, 1991.

Mulcahy, Monica. "Designing the User/ Using the Design." *Social Studies of Science* 31 (2002): 5–37.

Museum of Modern Art Archives, New York. *Design for Use*. Curatorial Exhibition File, Exh. # 258b.

Woolgar, Steve. "Configuring the User: The Case of Usability Trials." *A Sociology of Monsters: Essays on Power, Technology, and Domination*. London: Routledge, 1991.

User-Centered Design

Norman, Donald A. *The Design of Everyday Things*. New York: Basic Books, 1988.

Plowman, Tim. "Ethnography and Critical Design Practice." *Design Research*. Edited by Brenda Laurel. Cambridge, MA: MIT Press, 2003. 30–38.

Ulrich, Karl T., and Steven D. Eppinger. *Product Design and Development*. New York: McGraw-Hill, 2012.

Notes | Essay | **Designing for People**

1. Bill Moggridge, "What Is Design?" Lecture, Cooper Hewitt, Smithsonian Design Museum, 2011.
2. Arthur Pulos, *American Design Ethic: A History of Industrial Design to 1940* (Cambridge, MA: MIT Press, 1983).
3. Russell Flinchum, *Henry Dreyfuss, Industrial Designer: The Man in the Brown Suit* (New York: Cooper-Hewitt, National Design Museum, Smithsonian Institution and Rizzoli, 1997).
4. Flinchum, 102.
5. Margalit Fox, "John E. Karlin, Who Led the Way to All-Digit Dialing, Dies at 94," NYTimes.com, February 8, 2013, http://www.nytimes.com/2013/02/09/business/john-e-karlin-who-led-the-way-to-all-digit-dialing-dies-at-94.html?smid=pl-share.

6. Flinchum, 100.
7. Ellen Lupton, *Mechanical Brides: Women and Machines from Home to Office* (New York: Cooper-Hewitt, National Design Museum and Princeton Architectural Press, 1993).
8. Henry Dreyfuss, *Designing for People* (New York: Viking, 1955).
9. Henry Dreyfuss, *The Measure of Man: Human Factors in Design* (New York: Whitney Library of Design, 1966).
10. Mary McLeod, "'Architecture or Revolution': Taylorism, Technocracy and Social Change," *Art Journal* 43, no. 2 (1983): 132–47.
11. Ernst Neufert, *Bauentwurfslehre* (Berlin: Bauwelt-Verlag, 1938).
12. Nader Vossoughian, "Standardization Reconsidered: Normierung in and after Ernst Neufert's *Bauentwurfslehre* (1936)," *Grey Room* 54 (Winter 2014): 34–55.
13. Toby Lester, *Da Vinci's Ghost: Genius, Obsession, and How Leonardo Created the World in His Image* (New York: Free Press, 2012).
14. Francis de N. Schroeder, *Anatomy for Interior Designers* (New York: Whitney Publications, 1948). Repetto's drawings also appear in J. Gordon Lippincott, *Design for Business* (Chicago: Paul Theobald, 1947).
15. Niels Diffrient with Brian Lutz, *Confessions of a Generalist* (Danbury, CT: Generalist Ink, 2012).
16. Cara McCarty, *Designs for Independent Living* (New York: Museum of Modern Art, 1988), exhibition brochure.
17. Bruce Hannah, *Unlimited by Design*, 1998, exhibition at Cooper-Hewitt, National Design Museum, Smithsonian Institution. http://www.cooperhewitt.org/exhibitions/unlimited-design.
18. Bess Williamson, "Getting a Grip: Disability in American Industrial Design of the Late Twentieth Century," *Winterthur Portfolio* 46, no.4 (2013): 235.
19. John Harwood, *The Interface: IBM and the Transformation of Corporate Design, 1945–1976* (Minneapolis: University of Minnesota Press, 2011).
20. Donald A. Norman, *The Design of Everyday Things* (New York: Basic Books, 1988).
21. Brenda Laurel, *Computers as Theater*, 2nd ed. (Upper Saddle River, NJ: Addison-Wesley, 2014), 2.
22. Bill Moggridge, *Designing Interactions* (Cambridge, MA: MIT Press, 2007).
23. B. Joseph Pine II and James H. Gilmore, *The Experience Economy: Work Is Theatre and Every Business a Stage, Goods and Services Are No Longer Enough* (Boston: Harvard Business School Press, 1999).
24. Harry Heft, "Affordances and the Body: An Intentional Analysis of Gibson's Ecological Approach to Visual Perception," *Journal for the Theory of Social Behavior* 19, no. 1 (1989): 1–30.
25. Avinash Rajagopal, *Hacking Design* (New York: Cooper Hewitt, Smithsonian Design Museum, 2013).
26. Mister Jalopy, "The Maker's Bill of Rights," *Make* 4 (October 28, 2005). http://archive.makezine.com/04/ownyourown/.

index

Page 88, water drop icon by
Edward Boatman, Noun Project

Cooper Hewitt, Smithsonian Design Museum
Board of Trustees

The Measure(s) of Man, 2011. Designed by Thomas Carpentier (French, b. 1986). Degree Project, École Spéciale d'Architecture, Paris. Courtesy of the designer.

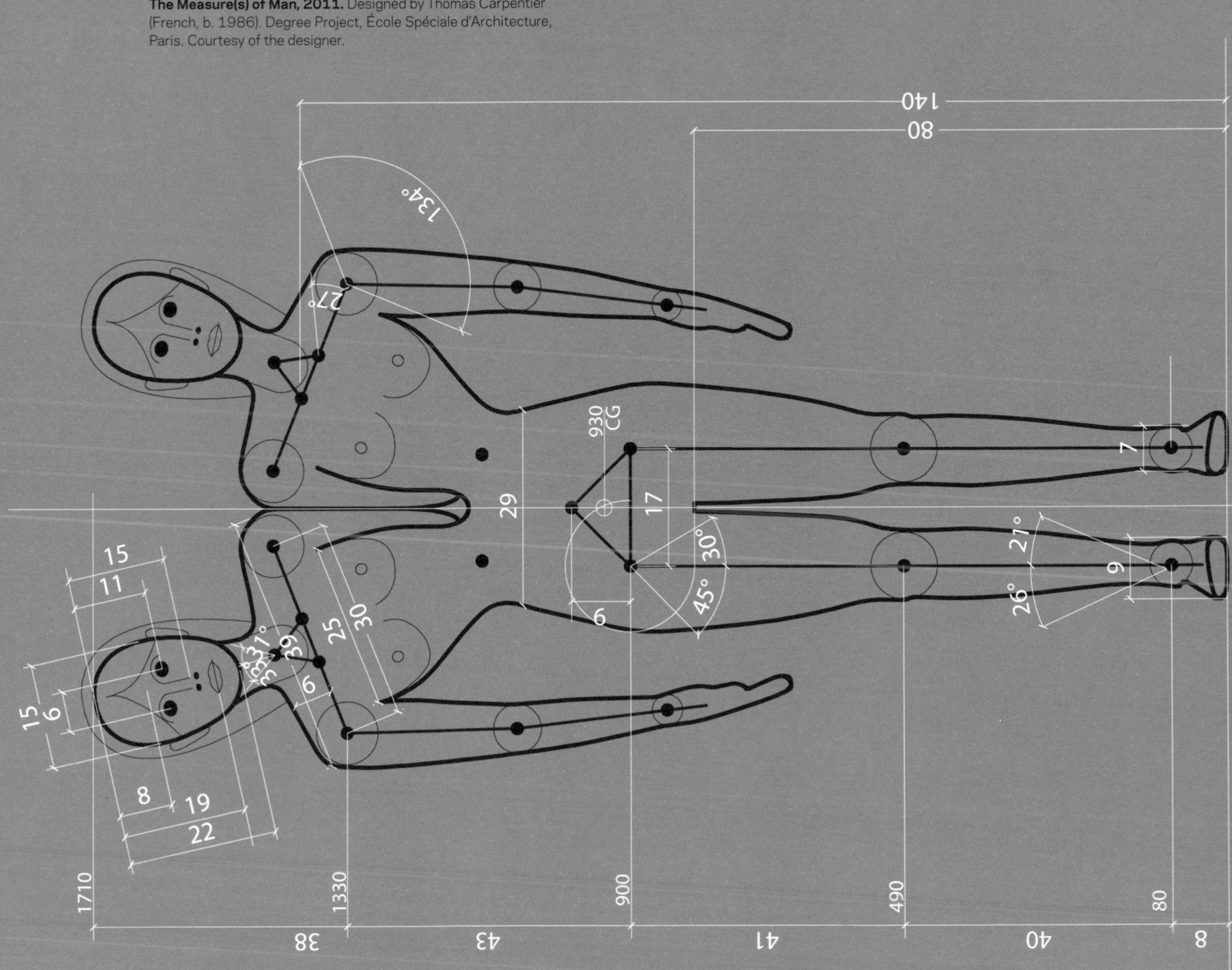

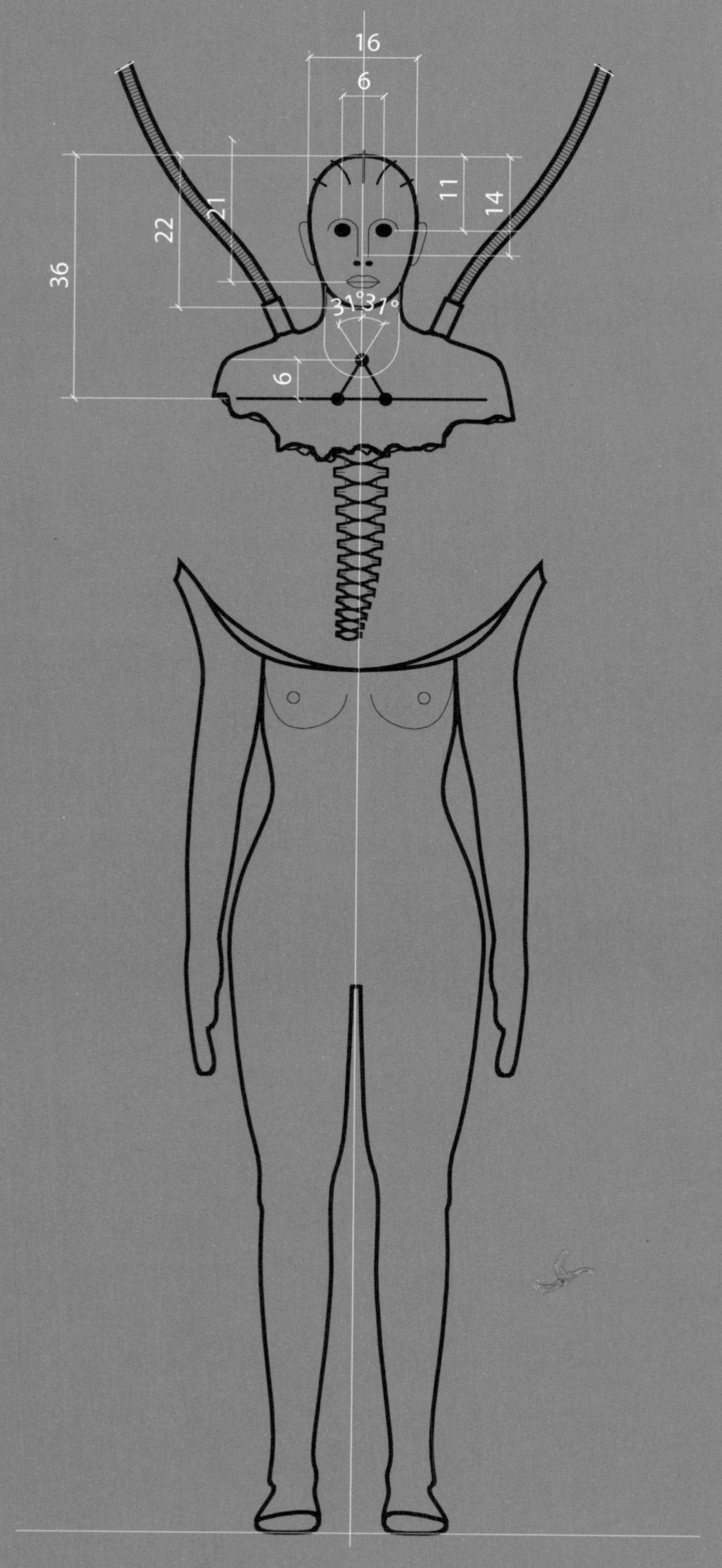
16
6
11
14
22
21
36
31°37°
6